STUDY GUIDE & WORKING PAPERS CHAPTERS 1-12

for

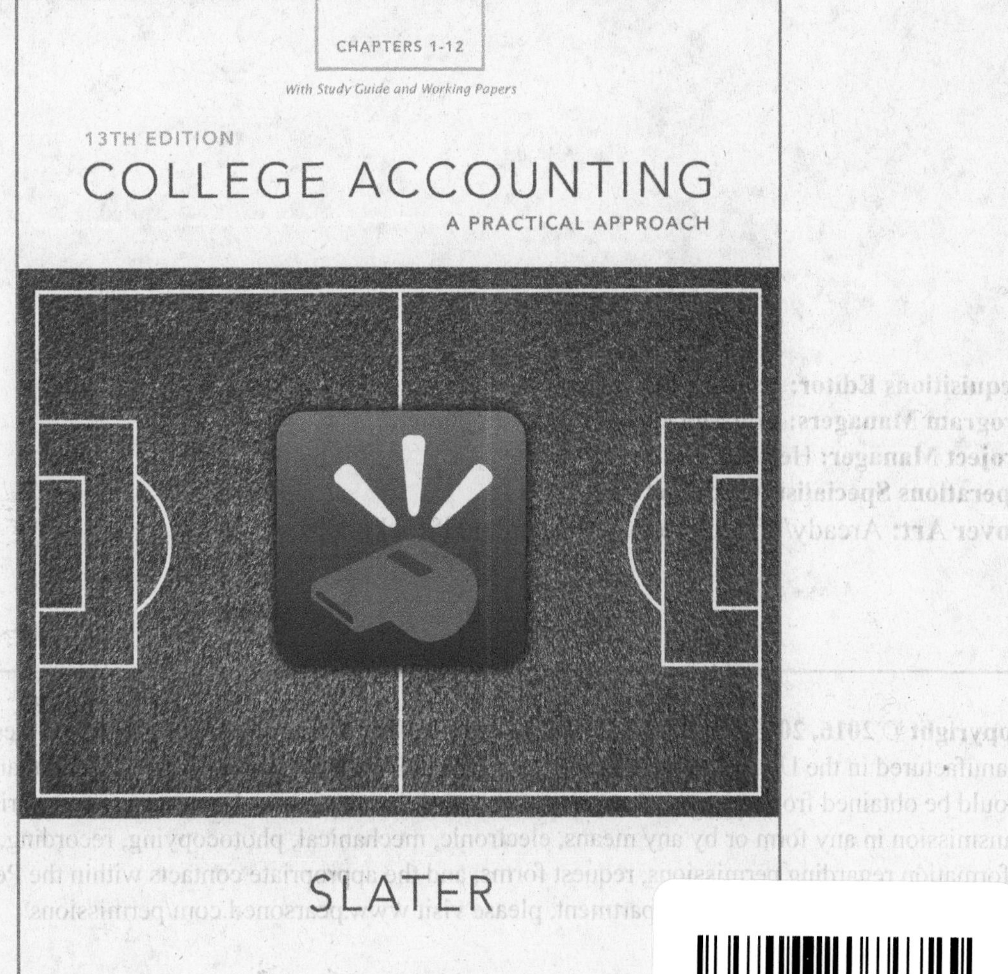

Carolyn Streuly

PEARSON

Boston Columbus Hoboken Indianapolis New York San Francisco
Amsterdam Cape Town Dubai London Madrid Milan Munich Paris Montréal Toronto
Delhi Mexico City São Paulo Sydney Hong Kong Seoul Singapore Taipei Tokyo

Acquisitions Editor: Ellen Geary
Program Managers: Erin McDonagh, Nancy Freihofer
Project Manager: Heather Pagano
Operations Specialist: Carol Melville
Cover Art: Arcady/Shutterstock and Bubaone/iStockphoto

---

4 16

PEARSON

ISBN-10: 0-13-379150-5
ISBN-13: 978-0-13-379150-1

Contents

STUDY GUIDE AND WORKING PAPERS CHAPTERS 1–12

Contents

STUDY GUIDE AND WORKING PAPERS CHAPTERS 1–12

Accounting Concepts and Procedures

Name ____________ Class ____________ Date ____________

FORMS FOR DEMONSTRATION PROBLEM

(1)

MICHAEL BROWN, ATTORNEY AT LAW

ASSETS = LIABILITIES + OWNER'S EQUITY

	Cash	+	Accounts Receivable	+	Office Equipment	=	Accounts Payable	+	M. Brown, Capital	−	M. Brown, Withd.	+	Legal fees	−	Expenses
a.															
Balance															
b.															
Balance															
c.															
Balance															
d.															
Balance															
e.															
Balance															
f.															
Balance															
g.															
Balance															
h.															
Balance															
i.															
Ending Balance		+		+		=		+		−		+		−	
						=									

Name ______________________ Class ______________ Date ______________

DEMONSTRATION PROBLEM (CONTINUED)

(2A)

MICHAEL BROWN, ATTORNEY AT LAW
INCOME STATEMENT
FOR MONTH ENDED JUNE 30, 201X

(2B)

MICHAEL BROWN, ATTORNEY AT LAW
STATEMENT OF OWNER'S EQUITY
FOR MONTH ENDED JUNE 30, 201X

(2C)

MICHAEL BROWN, ATTORNEY AT LAW
BALANCE SHEET
JUNE 30, 201X

ASSETS			LIABILITIES AND OWNER'S EQUITY		

Name ______________________ Class ______________________ Date ______________________

FORMS FOR SET A EXERCISES

1A-1

a. ______________________

b. ______________________

c. ______________________

1A-2

	ASSETS	= LIABILITIES	+	OWNER'S EQUITY
a.				
b.				
c.				

1A-3

RIDEOUT CO. CLEANERS
BALANCE SHEET
NOVEMBER 30, 201X

ASSETS		LIABILITIES AND OWNER'S EQUITY	

Name ______________________ Class ______________ Date ______________

SET A EXERCISES

1A-4

	ASSETS					= LIABILITIES +		OWNER'S EQUITY						
	Cash	+	Accounts Receivable	+	Computer Equipment	=	Accounts Payable	+	B. Black, Capital	−	B. Black, Withd.	+	Revenues	−	Expenses
a.															
b.															
c.															
d.															
e.															
f.															
g.															
Ending Balance															
						=									

Name ______________________ Class ______________ Date ______________

SET A EXERCISES

1A-5

(a)

FREDERICK REALTY
INCOME STATEMENT
FOR MONTH ENDED NOVEMBER 30, 201X

(b)

FREDERICK REALTY
STATEMENT OF OWNER'S EQUITY
FOR MONTH ENDED NOVEMBER 30, 201X

(c)

FREDERICK REALTY
BALANCE SHEET
NOVEMBER 30, 201X

ASSETS			LIABILITIES AND OWNER'S EQUITY	

Name ____________ Class ____________ Date ____________

FORMS FOR SET B EXERCISES

1B-1

a. ____________

b. ____________

c. ____________

1B-2

ASSETS	= LIABILITIES	+	OWNER'S EQUITY
a.			
b.			
c.			

1B-3

ROLAND CO. CLEANERS
BALANCE SHEET
JUNE 30, 201X

ASSETS			LIABILITIES AND OWNER'S EQUITY		

Name ______________________ Class ______________ Date ______________

SET B EXERCISES

1B-4

	ASSETS					= LIABILITIES +		OWNER'S EQUITY						
	Cash	+	Accounts Receivable	+	Computer Equipment	=	Accounts Payable	+	B. Bell, Capital	−	B. Bell, Withd.	+	Revenues	−	Expenses
a.															
b.															
c.															
d.															
e.															
f.															
g.															
Ending Balance															

Name ____________________ Class ____________ Date ____________

SET B EXERCISES

1B-5

(a)

FRENCH REALTY
INCOME STATEMENT
FOR MONTH ENDED SEPTEMBER 30, 201X

(b)

FRENCH REALTY
STATEMENT OF OWNER'S EQUITY
FOR MONTH ENDED SEPTEMBER 30, 201X

(c)

FRENCH REALTY
BALANCE SHEET
SEPTEMBER 30, 201X

ASSETS	LIABILITIES AND OWNER'S EQUITY

Name ____________ Class ____________ Date ____________

FORMS FOR SET A PROBLEMS

PROBLEM 1A-1

MORGAN'S NAIL SPA

	ASSETS			=	LIABILITIES	+	OWNER'S EQUITY
	Cash	+	Store Equipment	=	Accounts Payable	+	M. Amberson, Capital
TRANSACTION a							
NEW BALANCE							
TRANSACTION b							
NEW BALANCE							
TRANSACTION c							
NEW BALANCE							
TRANSACTION d							
ENDING BALANCE							

PROBLEM 1A-2

SHEA'S INTERNET SERVICE
BALANCE SHEET
JUNE 30, 201X

ASSETS			LIABILITIES AND OWNER'S EQUITY		

Name ________________ Class ________________ Date ________________

PROBLEM 1A-3

RICK FONTAN COMPUTER SERVICE

	ASSETS					=	LIABILITIES	+	OWNER'S EQUITY						
	Cash	+	Accounts Receivable	+	Office Equipment	=	Accounts Payable	+	R. Fontan, Capital	−	R. Fontan, Withd.	+	Computer Service Revenue	−	Expenses
a.															
BALANCE															
b.															
BALANCE															
c.															
BALANCE															
d.															
BALANCE															
e.															
BALANCE															
f.															
BALANCE															
g.															
BALANCE															
h.															
ENDING BALANCE															

Name ______________________ Class ______________ Date ______________

PROBLEM 1A-4

(a)

WILLIAMS HOME DECORATING SERVICE
INCOME STATEMENT
FOR MONTH ENDED SEPTEMBER 30, 201X

(b)

WILLIAMS HOME DECORATING SERVICE
STATEMENT OF OWNER'S EQUITY
FOR MONTH ENDED SEPTEMBER 30, 201X

Name ______________________ Class ______________ Date ______________

PROBLEM 1A-4 (CONCLUDED)

(c)

WILLIAMS HOME DECORATING SERVICE
BALANCE SHEET
SEPTEMBER 30, 201X

ASSETS			LIABILITIES AND OWNER'S EQUITY		

Name ______________________ Class ______________ Date ______________

PROBLEM 1A-5

(a)

TANSON'S CATERING SERVICE

	ASSETS			= LIABILITIES +	OWNER'S EQUITY			
	Cash	+ Accounts Receivable	+ Equipment	= Accounts Payable	+ J. Tanson, Capital	− J. Tanson, Withd.	+ Catering Revenue	− Expenses
10/25								
BALANCE								
10/27								
BALANCE								
10/28								
BALANCE								
10/29								
BALANCE								
11/1								
BALANCE								
11/5								
BALANCE								
11/8								
BALANCE								
11/10								
BALANCE								
11/15								
BALANCE								
11/17								
BALANCE								
11/20								
BALANCE								
11/25								
BALANCE								
11/28								
BALANCE								
11/30								
END. BAL.				=				

Name ____________ Class ____________ Date ____________

PROBLEM 1A-5 (CONTINUED)

(b)

TANSON'S CATERING SERVICE
BALANCE SHEET
OCTOBER 31, 201X

ASSETS **LIABILITIES AND OWNER'S EQUITY**

(c)

TANSON'S CATERING SERVICE
INCOME STATEMENT
FOR MONTH ENDED NOVEMBER 30, 201X

Name ____________ Class ____________ Date ____________

PROBLEM 1A-5 (CONCLUDED)

(d)

TANSON'S CATERING SERVICE
STATEMENT OF OWNER'S EQUITY
FOR MONTH ENDED NOVEMBER 30, 201X

(e)

TANSON'S CATERING SERVICE
BALANCE SHEET
NOVEMBER 30, 201X

ASSETS		LIABILITIES AND OWNER'S EQUITY	

Name ______________________ Class ______________ Date ______________

FORMS FOR SET B PROBLEMS

PROBLEM 1B-1

MANDY'S NAIL SPA

	ASSETS			=	LIABILITIES	+	OWNER'S EQUITY
	Cash	+	Store Equipment	=	Accounts Payable	+	M. Anabelle, Capital
TRANSACTION a							
NEW BALANCE							
TRANSACTION b							
NEW BALANCE							
TRANSACTION c							
NEW BALANCE							
TRANSACTION d							
ENDING BALANCE							

PROBLEM 1B-2

SEALY'S INTERNET SERVICE
BALANCE SHEET
NOVEMBER 30, 201X

ASSETS			LIABILITIES AND OWNER'S EQUITY		

Name ______________ Class ______________ Date ______________

PROBLEM 1B-3

RED FUMAN
COMPUTER SERVICE

ASSETS = LIABILITIES + OWNER'S EQUITY

	Cash	+	Accounts Receivable	+	Office Equipment	=	Accounts Payable	+	R. Fuman, Capital	−	R. Fuman, Withd.	+	Computer Service Revenue	−	Expenses
a.															
BALANCE															
b.															
BALANCE															
c.															
BALANCE															
d.															
BALANCE															
e.															
BALANCE															
f.															
BALANCE															
g.															
BALANCE															
h.															
ENDING BALANCE															

Name ______________________ Class ______________ Date ______________

PROBLEM 1B-4

(a)

WU HOME DECORATING SERVICE
INCOME STATEMENT
FOR MONTH ENDED JUNE 30, 201X

(b)

WU HOME DECORATING SERVICE
STATEMENT OF OWNER'S EQUITY
FOR MONTH ENDED JUNE 30, 201X

Name ____________ Class ____________ Date ____________

PROBLEM 1B-4 (CONCLUDED)

(c)

WU HOME DECORATING SERVICE
BALANCE SHEET
JUNE 30, 201X

ASSETS			LIABILITIES AND OWNER'S EQUITY		

Name ______ Class ______ Date ______

PROBLEM 1B-5

(a)

THILDORE'S CATERING SERVICE

	ASSETS					= LIABILITIES	+	OWNER'S EQUITY						
	Cash	+	Accounts Receivable	+	Equipment	= Accounts Payable	+	J. Thildore, Capital	−	J. Thildore, Withd.	+	Catering Revenue	−	Expenses
10/25														
BALANCE														
10/27														
BALANCE														
10/28														
BALANCE														
10/29														
BALANCE														
11/1														
BALANCE														
11/5														
BALANCE														
11/8														
BALANCE														
11/10														
BALANCE														
11/15														
BALANCE														
11/17														
BALANCE														
11/20														
BALANCE														
11/25														
BALANCE														
11/28														
BALANCE														
11/30														
END. BAL.														

______ = ______

PROBLEM 1B-5 (CONTINUED)

(b)

THILDORE'S CATERING SERVICE
BALANCE SHEET
OCTOBER 31, 201X

ASSETS | **LIABILITIES AND OWNER'S EQUITY**

(c)

THILDORE'S CATERING SERVICE
INCOME STATEMENT
FOR MONTH ENDED NOVEMBER 30, 201X

Name ______________________ Class ______________ Date ______________

PROBLEM 1B-5 (CONCLUDED)

(d)

THILDORE'S CATERING SERVICE
STATEMENT OF OWNER'S EQUITY
FOR MONTH ENDED NOVEMBER 30, 201X

(e)

THILDORE'S CATERING SERVICE
BALANCE SHEET
NOVEMBER 30, 201X

ASSETS | **LIABILITIES AND OWNER'S EQUITY**

Name ______________________ Class ______________ Date ______________

ON THE JOB CONTINUING PROBLEM

ASSIGNMENTS 1 AND 2

SMITH COMPUTER CENTER

ASSETS = LIABILITIES + OWNER'S EQUITY

	Cash	+ Supplies	+ Computer Shop Equipment	+ Office Equipment	= Accounts Payable	+ Feldman, Capital	− Feldman, Withdrawals	+ Service Revenue	− Expenses
a									
BALANCE									
b									
BALANCE									
c									
BALANCE									
d									
BALANCE									
e									
BALANCE									
f									
BALANCE									
g									
BALANCE									
h									
BALANCE									
i									
BALANCE									
j									
END BAL.		+	+	+	=	+	−	+	−

=

Name ______________________ Class ______________ Date ______________

ASSIGNMENT 3

SMITH COMPUTER CENTER
INCOME STATEMENT
FOR THE MONTH ENDED JULY 31, 201X

SMITH COMPUTER CENTER
STATEMENT OF OWNER'S EQUITY
FOR MONTH ENDED JULY 31, 201X

SMITH COMPUTER CENTER
BALANCE SHEET
JULY 31, 201X

ASSETS | **LIABILITIES AND OWNER'S EQUITY**

Name ______________________ Class ______________ Date ______________

CHAPTER 1
SUMMARY PRACTICE TEST: ACCOUNTING CONCEPTS AND PROCEDURES

Part I

Fill in the blank(s) to complete the statement.

1. ____________ was passed to prevent corporate fraud.
2. ____________ – Liabilities = Owner's Equity
3. The owner's current investment or equity in the assets of a business is called ____________.
4. A list of assets, liabilities, and owner's equity as of a particular date is reported on a(n) ____________ ____________.
5. ____________ create an outward or potential outward flow of assets.
6. Revenue earned not on account creates an asset entitled ____________.
7. ____________ record personal expenses that are not related to the business. They are a subdivision of owner's equity.
8. The ____________ ____________ reports how well a business performs for a period of time.
9. The ____________ ____________ ____________ ____________ is a report that shows changes in capital.
10. The ending figure for capital from the statement of owner's equity is placed on the ____________ ____________.

Part II

Answer true or false to the following statements.

1. Accounts Receivable is a liability.
2. Liabilities produce revenue.
3. Revenue is an asset.
4. Capital means cash.
5. Bookkeeping is 50% of accounting.
6. The balance sheet lists assets, revenue, and owner's equity.
7. The balance sheet shows where we are now for a specific period of time.
8. Revenue creates an outward flow of assets.
9. Expenses are a subdivision of owner's equity.
10. Withdrawals are the only subdivision of owner's equity.
11. Withdrawals are listed on the income statement.
12. Revenue is a subdivision of owner's equity.
13. Revenues and withdrawals are listed on the income statement.
14. The income statement helps update the statement of owner's equity, and the statement of owner's equity helps update the balance sheet.
15. Withdrawals are listed on the statement of owner's equity.

Name ______________________ Class ______________ Date ______________

Part III

In column B, record the appropriate code(s) that result from recording the transaction in column A.

1. Increase in assets
2. Decrease in assets
3. Increase in liabilities
4. Decrease in liabilities
5. Increase in capital
6. Increase in revenues
7. Increase in expenses
8. Increase in withdrawals

	Column A	Column B
1.	EXAMPLE: Pete Smith invested $5,000 in his business.	1,5
2.	Bought computer equipment on account for $600.	
3.	Paid salaries of $70.	
4.	Bought additional computer equipment for $750 cash.	
5.	Paid rent expense of $90.	
6.	Received $5,000 in cash from revenue earned.	
7.	Paid heat expense of $15.	
8.	Earned revenue of $500 that will not be received until next month.	
9.	Paid amount owed on equipment previously purchased on account.	
10.	Paid for cleaning supplies expense, $15.	
11.	Customers paid $10 of amount previously owed.	
12.	Bought additional equipment of $1,000, half paid in cash and half charged.	
13.	Charged customer $100 for services performed.	
14.	Pete paid home phone bill from the company's cash.	
15.	Advertising expense incurred but not to be paid until next month.	

SOLUTIONS

Part I

1. The Sarbanes-Oxley Act
2. Assets
3. capital
4. balance sheet
5. Expenses
6. Cash
7. Withdrawals
8. income statement
9. statement of owner's equity
10. balance sheet

Name ______________________ Class ______________ Date ______________

Part II

1.	false	**6.**	false	**11.**	false
2.	false	**7.**	false	**12.**	true
3.	false	**8.**	false	**13.**	false
4.	false	**9.**	true	**14.**	true
5.	false	**10.**	false	**15.**	true

Part III

1.	1,5	**6.**	1,6	**11.**	1,2
2.	1,3	**7.**	7,2	**12.**	1,2,3
3.	7,2	**8.**	1,6	**13.**	1,6
4.	1,2	**9.**	4,2	**14.**	8,2
5.	7,2	**10.**	7,2	**15.**	7,3

Debits and Credits: Analyzing and Recording Business Transactions

Name ______________________ Class ______________ Date ______________

FORMS FOR DEMONSTRATION PROBLEM

(1,2,3)

Advertising Expense 511

Gas Expense 512

Salaries Expense 513

Telephone Expense 514

Accounts Payable 211

Mel Free, Capital 311

Mel Free, Withdrawals 312

Delivery Fees Earned 411

Cash 111

Accounts Receivable 112

Office Equipment 121

Delivery Trucks 122

Name ______________ Class ______________ Date ______________

FORMS FOR DEMONSTRATION PROBLEM (CONTINUED)

(4)

MEL'S DELIVERY SERVICE
TRIAL BALANCE
JULY 31, 201X

	Dr.	Cr.

(5a)

MEL'S DELIVERY SERVICE
INCOME STATEMENT
FOR MONTH ENDED JULY 31, 201X

Name ______________________ Class ______________ Date ______________

FORMS FOR DEMONSTRATION PROBLEM (CONCLUDED)

(5b)

MEL'S DELIVERY SERVICE
STATEMENT OF OWNER'S EQUITY
FOR MONTH ENDED JULY 31, 201X

(5c)

MEL'S DELIVERY SERVICE
BALANCE SHEET
JULY 31, 201X

ASSETS			LIABILITIES AND OWNER'S EQUITY		

Name ______________________ Class ______________ Date ______________

FORMS FOR SET A EXERCISES

2A-1

2A-2

1. Accounts Affected	2. Category	3. ↑ ↓	4. Rules	5. T Account Update

2A-3

Account	Category	↑↓	Financial Statement
Computer Supplies			
Legal Fees Earned			
R. Roy, Withdrawals			
Accounts Payable			
Salaries Expense			
Auto			

Name ______________________ Class ______________ Date ______________

SET A EXERCISES

2A-4

Transaction	Dr.	Cr.
A. Paid salaries expense.	8	1
B. Bob paid personal utilities bill from the company checkbook.		
C. Advertising bill received but unpaid.		
D. Received cash from plumbing fees.		
E. Paid supplies expense.		
F. Bob invested in additional equipment for the business.		
G. Billed customers for plumbing services rendered.		
H. Received one-half the balance from transaction G.		
I. Bought equipment on account.		

2A-5

(1)

HUGO'S CLEANERS
INCOME STATEMENT
FOR MONTH ENDED JULY 31, 201X

(2)

HUGO'S CLEANERS
STATEMENT OF OWNER'S EQUITY
FOR MONTH ENDED JULY 31, 201X

Name ____________ Class ____________ Date ____________

SET A EXERCISES

(3)

HUGO'S CLEANERS
BALANCE SHEET
JULY 31, 201X

ASSETS			LIABILITIES AND OWNER'S EQUITY		

Name ____________ Class ____________ Date ____________

FORMS FOR SET B EXERCISES

2B-1

2B-2

1. Accounts Affected	2. Category	3. ↑ ↓	4. Rules	5. T Account Update

2B-3

Account	Category	↑↓	Financial Statement
Office Supplies			
Rental Fees Earned			
A. Troy, Withdrawals			
Accounts Payable			
Wage Expense			
Computer			

Name ______________________ Class ______________ Date ______________

SET B EXERCISES

2B-4

Transaction	Dr.	Cr.
A. Paid salaries expense.		
B. Bill paid personal utilities bill from the company checkbook.		
C. Advertising bill received but unpaid.		
D. Received cash from photography fees.		
E. Paid supplies expense.		
F. Bill invested in additional furniture for the business.		
G. Billed customers for photography services rendered.		
H. Received one-half the balance from transaction G.		
I. Bought furniture on account.		

2B-5

(1)

HELM'S CLEANERS
INCOME STATEMENT
FOR MONTH ENDED MAY 31, 201X

(2)

HELM'S CLEANERS
STATEMENT OF OWNER'S EQUITY
FOR MONTH ENDED MAY 31, 201X

Name ____________________ Class ____________ Date ____________

SET B EXERCISES

(3)

HELM'S CLEANERS
BALANCE SHEET
MAY 31, 201X

ASSETS			LIABILITIES AND OWNER'S EQUITY		

Name ______________________ Class ______________ Date ______________

FORMS FOR SET A PROBLEMS

PROBLEM 2A-1

Accounts Affected	Category	Inc. Dec. ↑ ↓	Rules	T Account Update
A.				
B.				
C.				
D.				
E.				
F.				

Name ______________________ Class ______________ Date ______________

PROBLEM 2A-2

Cash 111

Office Equipment 121

Accounts Payable 211

Brett Pillows, Capital 311

Brett Pillows, Withdrawals 312

Consulting Fees Earned 411

Advertising Expense 511

Rent Expense 512

Name ______________________ Class ____________ Date ____________

PROBLEM 2A-3

(a)

Cash 111

(A)	12,000	(D)	700
(G)	2,500	(E)	250
		(F)	300
		(H)	350
		(I)	300

Accounts Payable 211

(D)	700	(C)	1,300

Cleaning Fees Earned 411

		(B)	9,000

Accounts Receivable 112

(B)	9,000	(G)	2,500

Bill Jolt, Capital 311

		(A)	12,000

Rent Expense 511

(F)	300		

Office Equipment 121

(C)	1,300		
(H)	350		

Bill Jolt, Withdrawals 312

(I)	300		

Utilities Expense 512

(E)	250		

(b)

BILL'S CLEANING SERVICE
TRIAL BALANCE
DECEMBER 31, 201X

	Dr.	Cr.

Name ____________________ Class ____________ Date ____________

PROBLEM 2A-4

(a)

GIRTIE LILLIS, ATTORNEY AT LAW
INCOME STATEMENT
FOR MONTH ENDED MAY 31, 201X

(b)

GIRTIE LILLIS, ATTORNEY AT LAW
STATEMENT OF OWNER'S EQUITY
FOR MONTH ENDED MAY 31, 201X

Name ____________________ Class ____________ Date ____________

PROBLEM 2A-4 (CONCLUDED)

(c)

GIRTIE LILLIS, ATTORNEY AT LAW
BALANCE SHEET
MAY 31, 201X

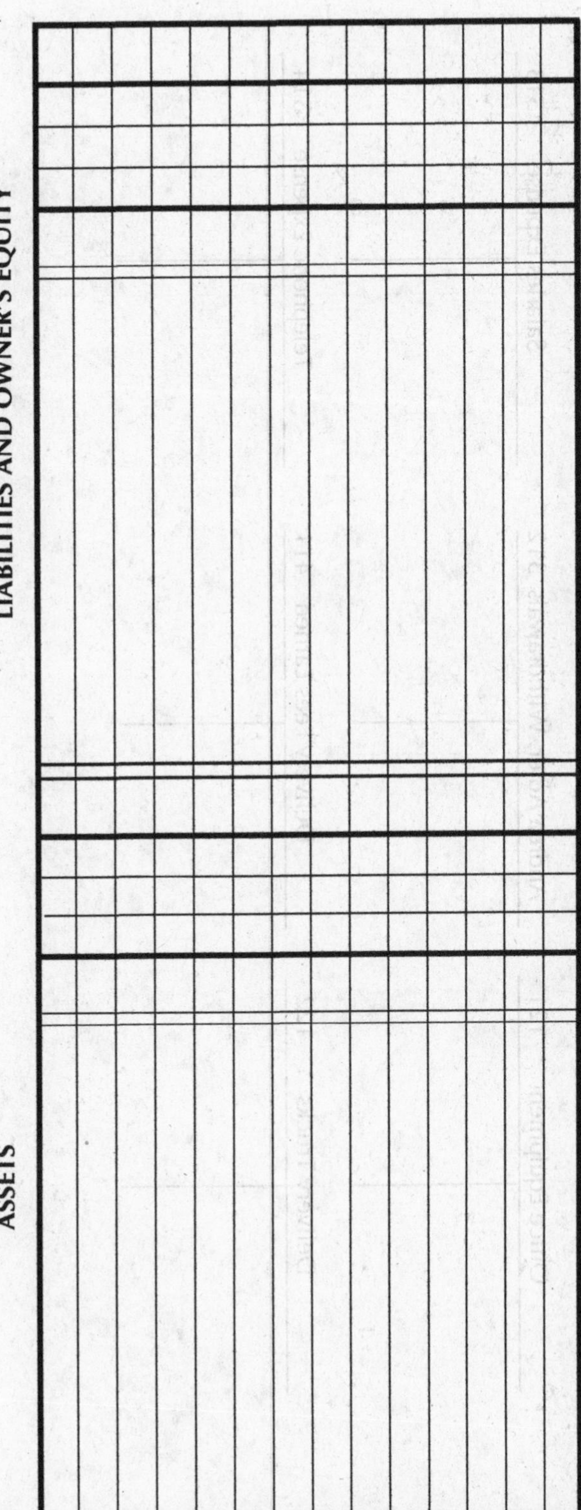

Name ____________________ Class ____________ Date ____________

PROBLEM 2A-5

(1,2)

Cash 111

Accounts Receivable 112

Office Equipment 121

Delivery Trucks 122

Accounts Payable 211

Andrea Adler, Capital 311

Andrea Adler, Withdrawals 312

Delivery Fees Earned 411

Advertising Expense 511

Gas Expense 512

Salaries Expense 513

Telephone Expense 514

Name ______________________ Class ______________ Date ______________

PROBLEM 2A-5 (CONTINUED)

(3)

ADLER'S DELIVERY SERVICE
TRIAL BALANCE
JULY 31, 201X

	Dr.	Cr.

(4a)

ADLER'S DELIVERY SERVICE
INCOME STATEMENT
FOR MONTH ENDED JULY 31, 201X

Name ______________________ Class ______________ Date ______________

PROBLEM 2A-5 (CONCLUDED)

(4b)

ADLER'S DELIVERY SERVICE
STATEMENT OF OWNER'S EQUITY
FOR MONTH ENDED JULY 31, 201X

(4c)

ADLER'S DELIVERY SERVICE
BALANCE SHEET
JULY 31, 201X

ASSETS			LIABILITIES AND OWNER'S EQUITY		

Name ______________________ Class ______________ Date ______________

FORMS FOR SET B PROBLEMS

PROBLEM 2B-1

Accounts Affected	Category	Inc. Dec. ↑ ↓	Rules	T Account Update
A.				
B.				
C.				
D.				
E.				
F.				

Name ____________________ Class ____________ Date ____________

PROBLEM 2B-2

Cash	111

Bill Palu, Withdrawals	312

Office Equipment	121

Consulting Fees Earned	411

Accounts Payable	211

Advertising Expense	511

Bill Palu, Capital	311

Rent Expense	512

Name ______________________ Class ______________ Date ______________

PROBLEM 2B-3

(a)

Cash 111

	Dr.		Cr.
(A)	15,000	(D)	800
(G)	1,000	(E)	200
		(F)	250
		(H)	200
		(I)	1,100

Accounts Payable 211

	Dr.		Cr.
(D)	800	(C)	1,900

Cleaning Fees Earned 411

	Dr.		Cr.
		(B)	15,000

Accounts Receivable 112

	Dr.		Cr.
(B)	15,000	(G)	1,000

Breck Jal, Capital 311

	Dr.		Cr.
		(A)	15,000

Rent Expense 511

	Dr.		Cr.
(F)	250		

Office Equipment 121

	Dr.		Cr.
(C)	1,900		
(H)	200		

Breck Jal, Withdrawals 312

	Dr.		Cr.
(I)	1,100		

Utilities Expense 512

	Dr.		Cr.
(E)	200		

(b)

BRECK'S CLEANING SERVICE
TRIAL BALANCE
MAY 31, 201X

	Dr.	Cr.

Name ____________________ Class ____________ Date ____________

PROBLEM 2B-4

(a)

GRETCHEN LYMAN, ATTORNEY AT LAW
INCOME STATEMENT
FOR MONTH ENDED JANUARY 31, 201X

(b)

GRETCHEN LYMAN, ATTORNEY AT LAW
STATEMENT OF OWNER'S EQUITY
FOR MONTH ENDED JANUARY 31, 201X

Name ____________________ Class ____________________ Date ____________________

PROBLEM 2B-4 (CONCLUDED)

(c)

GRETCHEN LYMAN, ATTORNEY AT LAW
BALANCE SHEET
JANUARY 31, 201X

ASSETS

LIABILITIES AND OWNER'S EQUITY

Name ________________________ Class ________________ Date ________________

PROBLEM 2B-5

(1,2)

Cash 111

Accounts Receivable 112

Office Equipment 121

Delivery Trucks 122

Accounts Payable 211

Andrea Aikman, Capital 311

Andrea Aikman, Withdrawals 312

Delivery Fees Earned 411

Advertising Expense 511

Gas Expense 512

Salaries Expense 513

Telephone Expense 514

PROBLEM 2B-5 (CONTINUED)

(3)

AIKMAN'S DELIVERY SERVICE
TRIAL BALANCE
MAY 31, 201X

	Dr.	Cr.

(4a)

AIKMAN'S DELIVERY SERVICE
INCOME STATEMENT
FOR MONTH ENDED MAY 31, 201X

Name ________________ Class ________________ Date ________________

PROBLEM 2B-5 (CONCLUDED)

(4b)

AIKMAN'S DELIVERY SERVICE
STATEMENT OF OWNER'S EQUITY
FOR MONTH ENDED MAY 31, 201X

(4c)

AIKMAN'S DELIVERY SERVICE
BALANCE SHEET
MAY 31, 201X

ASSETS		LIABILITIES AND OWNER'S EQUITY	

Name ____________________ Class ____________ Date ____________

ON THE JOB CONTINUING PROBLEM

ASSIGNMENTS 1, 2, 3

Account	No.	Debit	Credit
Cash	1000	Bal. 3,425	
Accounts Receivable	1020		
Supplies	1030	Bal. 200	
Computer Shop Equipment	1080	Bal. 1,800	
Office Equipment	1090	Bal. 3,300	
Accounts Payable	2000		275 Bal.
Feldman, Capital	3000		6,000 Bal.
Feldman, Withdrawals	3010	Bal. 175	
Service Revenue	4000		3,200 Bal.
Advertising Expense	5010		
Rent Expense	5020	Bal. 500	
Utilities Expense	5030	Bal. 75	
Phone Expense	5040		
Supplies Expense	5050		
Insurance Expense	5060		
Postage Expense	5070		

Name ______________________ Class ______________ Date ______________

ASSIGNMENT 4

SMITH COMPUTER CENTER
TRIAL BALANCE
AUGUST 31, 201X

	Dr.	Cr.

ASSIGNMENT 5

SMITH COMPUTER CENTER
INCOME STATEMENT
FOR THE TWO MONTHS ENDED AUGUST 31, 201X

Name ______________________ Class ______________ Date ______________

SMITH COMPUTER CENTER
STATEMENT OF OWNER'S EQUITY
FOR THE TWO MONTHS ENDED AUGUST 31, 201X

SMITH COMPUTER CENTER
BALANCE SHEET
AUGUST 31, 201X

ASSETS **LIABILITIES AND OWNER'S EQUITY**

Name ______________________ Class ______________ Date ______________

CHAPTER 2
SUMMARY PRACTICE TEST:
DEBITS AND CREDITS: ANALYZING AND RECORDING BUSINESS TRANSACTIONS

Part I

Fill in the blank(s) to complete the statement.

1. Financial reports do not contain ______________ or ______________.
2. The right side of any T account is called the ______________ ______________.
3. Assets are increased by ______________.
4. The process of balancing an account involves ______________.
5. Transaction analysis charts are an aid in recording ______________ ______________.
6. The ______________ ______________ ______________ indicates the names and numbering system of accounts.
7. A(n) ______________ is a group of accounts.
8. A(n) ______________ ______________ is an informal report that lists accounts and their balances.
9. Withdrawals are increased by ______________.
10. The income statement, statement of owner's equity, and balance sheet may be prepared from a(n) ______________ ______________.
11. Cash, Accounts Receivable, and Equipment are examples of ______________.
12. Increasing expenses ultimately cause owner's equity to ______________.
13. An increase in rent expense is a(n) ______________ by the rules of debits and credits.
14. A debit to one asset and a credit to another asset for the same transaction reflect a(n) ______________ in assets.
15. The category of accounts receivable is a(n) ______________.

Part II

Bea Paul opened a shuttle service company. From the following chart of accounts, indicate in column B (by account number) which account (s) will be debited or credited as related to the transaction in column A.

Name ______________________ Class ______________ Date ______________

Chart of Accounts

ASSETS	LIABILITIES	EXPENSES
10 Cash	50 Accounts Payable	80 Advertising Expense
20 Accounts Receivable		90 Gas Expense
30 Equipment	OWNER'S EQUITY	100 Salaries Expense
40 Shuttle Bus	60 B. Paul, Capital	110 Telephone Expense
	62 B. Paul, Withdrawals	
	REVENUE	
	70 Shuttle Fees Earned	

	COLUMN A	COLUMN B DEBIT(S)	CREDIT(S)
1.	EXAMPLE: Bea Paul invested $40,000 in the shuttle service.	10	60
2.	Purchased a shuttle bus on account for $25,000.		
3.	Bought equipment on account for $3,000.		
4.	Advertising bill received, but not paid until next month, $60.		
5.	Bea paid home telephone bill from company checkbook, $20.		
6.	Collected $100 in cash from daily shuttle fees earned.		
7.	Customer charged a shuttle ride of $20.		
8.	Received partial payment for Transaction #7 of $10.		
9.	Paid business telephone bill, $32.		
10.	Purchased additional equipment for cash, $550.		
11.	Paid shuttle driver salaries of $150.		
12.	Drove customer on account to local train station for $6.		
13.	Received $5 from customer who hired a shuttle for ride across town.		
14.	Collected from past charged revenue, $15.		
15.	Bought office equipment on account for $110.		

Part III

Answer true or false to the following statements.

1. There are no debit and credit columns found on the three financial statements.
2. A trial balance could balance but be wrong.
3. Withdrawals are listed on the credit column of the trial balance.
4. Double entry bookkeeping results in a system where the sum of all the debits is equal to the sum of all the credits.
5. The ledger is numbered like a textbook.

Name ______________________ Class ______________ Date ______________

6. Withdrawals are always increased by credits.
7. An expense could create a liability.
8. A shift in assets means the total of assets must change.
9. The rules of debit and credit are constantly changing.
10. The transaction analysis chart is a teaching device.
11. The chart of accounts makes locating and identifying accounts easier.
12. The left side of any account is a credit.
13. A debit means all accounts are decreasing.
14. Financial statements are prepared from a trial balance.
15. The statement of owner's equity is prepared before the income statement.
16. Liabilities increase by credits.
17. Footings aid in balancing accounts.
18. Withdrawals are listed on the income statement.
19. The balance sheet contains the old figure for capital.
20. Think of a credit as always meaning something good.

SOLUTIONS

Part I

1. debits/credits
2. credit side
3. debits
4. footings
5. journal entries
6. chart of accounts
7. ledger (general)
8. trial balance
9. debits
10. trial balance
11. assets
12. decrease
13. debit
14. shift
15. asset

Part II

	Debit	Credit		Debit	Credit		Debit	Credit
1.	10	60	6.	10	70	11.	100	10
2.	40	50	7.	20	70	12.	20	70
3.	30	50	8.	10	20	13.	10	70
4.	80	50	9.	110	10	14.	10	20
5.	62	10	10.	30	10	15.	30	50

Part III

1. true
2. true
3. false
4. true
5. false
6. false
7. true
8. false
9. false
10. true
11. true
12. false
13. false
14. true
15. false
16. true
17. true
18. false
19. false
20. false

Study Guide and Working Papers

Beginning the Accounting Cycle

Name ______________________ Class ______________ Date ______________

FORMS FOR DEMONSTRATION PROBLEM
(1)

ABBY'S EMPLOYMENT AGENCY
GENERAL JOURNAL

PAGE 1

Date		Account Titles and Description	PR	Dr.	Cr.

Name ______________________ Class ______________ Date ______________

FORMS FOR DEMONSTRATION PROBLEM (CONTINUED)
(2, 3)

GENERAL LEDGER OF ABBY'S EMPLOYMENT AGENCY

CASH — **ACCOUNT NO. 111**

Date	Explanation	Post Ref.	Debit	Credit	Balance	
					Debit	Credit

ACCOUNTS RECEIVABLE — **ACCOUNT NO. 112**

Date	Explanation	Post Ref.	Debit	Credit	Balance	
					Debit	Credit

SUPPLIES — **ACCOUNT NO. 131**

Date	Explanation	Post Ref.	Debit	Credit	Balance	
					Debit	Credit

EQUIPMENT — **ACCOUNT NO. 141**

Date	Explanation	Post Ref.	Debit	Credit	Balance	
					Debit	Credit

Name ____________________ Class ____________________ Date ____________________

FORMS FOR DEMONSTRATION PROBLEM (CONTINUED)

ACCOUNTS PAYABLE — **ACCOUNT NO. 211**

Date		Explanation	Post Ref.	Debit	Credit	Balance	
						Debit	Credit

A. TODD, CAPITAL — **ACCOUNT NO. 311**

Date		Explanation	Post Ref.	Debit	Credit	Balance	
						Debit	Credit

A. TODD, WITHDRAWALS — **ACCOUNT NO. 321**

Date		Explanation	Post Ref.	Debit	Credit	Balance	
						Debit	Credit

EMPLOYMENT FEES EARNED — **ACCOUNT NO. 411**

Date		Explanation	Post Ref.	Debit	Credit	Balance	
						Debit	Credit

Name ______________________ Class ______________ Date ______________

FORMS FOR DEMONSTRATION PROBLEM (CONTINUED)

WAGE EXPENSE **ACCOUNT NO. 511**

Date	Explanation	Post Ref.	Debit	Credit	Balance Debit	Balance Credit

TELEPHONE EXPENSE **ACCOUNT NO. 521**

Date	Explanation	Post Ref.	Debit	Credit	Balance Debit	Balance Credit

ADVERTISING EXPENSE **ACCOUNT NO. 531**

Date	Explanation	Post Ref.	Debit	Credit	Balance Debit	Balance Credit

Name ____________________ Class ____________________ Date ____________________

FORMS FOR DEMONSTRATION PROBLEM (CONCLUDED)
(4)

ABBY'S EMPLOYMENT AGENCY
TRIAL BALANCE
MARCH 31, 201X

	Dr.	Cr.

Name ______________________ Class ______________ Date ______________

FORMS FOR SET A EXERCISES

3A-1

Date	Account Titles and Description	PR	Dr.	Cr.

Name ______________ Class ______________ Date ______________

SET A EXERCISES

3A-2

Date	Account Titles and Description	PR	Dr.	Cr.

Name ____________________ Class ____________ Date ____________

SET A EXERCISES

3A-3

Date 201X		Account Titles and Description	PR	Dr.	Cr.
Feb.	6	Cash		12 000 00	
		A. Kramer, Capital			12 000 00
		Cash investment			
	14	Equipment		8 000 00	
		Cash			5 000 00
		Accounts Payable			3 000 00
		Purchase of equipment			

CASH — **ACCOUNT NO. 111**

Date		Explanation	Post Ref.	Debit	Credit	Balance Debit	Balance Credit

EQUIPMENT — **ACCOUNT NO. 121**

Date		Explanation	Post Ref.	Debit	Credit	Balance Debit	Balance Credit

ACCOUNTS PAYABLE — **ACCOUNT NO. 211**

Date		Explanation	Post Ref.	Debit	Credit	Balance Debit	Balance Credit

A. KRAMER, CAPITAL — **ACCOUNT NO. 311**

Date		Explanation	Post Ref.	Debit	Credit	Balance Debit	Balance Credit

Name ______________________ Class ______________ Date ______________

SET A EXERCISES

3A-4

(a)

PAGE 1

Date		Account Titles and Description	PR	Dr.	Cr.

(b)

CASH **ACCOUNT NO. 111**

Date		Explanation	Post Ref.	Debit	Credit	Balance	
						Debit	Credit

ACCOUNTS RECEIVABLE **ACCOUNT NO. 112**

Date		Explanation	Post Ref.	Debit	Credit	Balance	
						Debit	Credit

Name ______________________ Class ______________ Date ______________

SET A EXERCISES

EQUIPMENT — **ACCOUNT NO. 121**

Date		Explanation	Post Ref.	Debit	Credit	Balance Debit	Balance Credit

ACCOUNTS PAYABLE — **ACCOUNT NO. 211**

Date		Explanation	Post Ref.	Debit	Credit	Balance Debit	Balance Credit

J. LUCAS, CAPITAL — **ACCOUNT NO. 311**

Date		Explanation	Post Ref.	Debit	Credit	Balance Debit	Balance Credit

J. LUCAS, WITHDRAWALS — **ACCOUNT NO. 312**

Date		Explanation	Post Ref.	Debit	Credit	Balance Debit	Balance Credit

FEES EARNED — **ACCOUNT NO. 411**

Date		Explanation	Post Ref.	Debit	Credit	Balance Debit	Balance Credit

SALARIES EXPENSE — **ACCOUNT NO. 511**

Date		Explanation	Post Ref.	Debit	Credit	Balance Debit	Balance Credit

Name ____________________ Class ____________________ Date ____________________

SET A EXERCISES

(c)

LUCAS COMPANY
TRIAL BALANCE
MAY 31, 201X

	Dr.	Cr.

3A-5

SALT LAKE CO.
TRIAL BALANCE
OCTOBER 31, 201X

	Dr.	Cr.

3A-6

Date 201X	Account Titles and Description	PR	Dr.	Cr.
Feb. 6	Office Equipment		800 00	
	Accounts Payable			800 00
	Purchase of office equip. on account			

Name ____________________ Class ____________ Date ____________

FORMS FOR SET B EXERCISES

3B-1

Date	Account Titles and Description	PR	Dr.	Cr.

Name ______________________ Class ______________ Date ______________

SET B EXERCISES

3B-2

Date		Account Titles and Description	PR	Dr.	Cr.

Name ______________________ Class ______________ Date ______________

SET B EXERCISES

3B-3

Date 201X		Account Titles and Description	PR	Dr.	Cr.
Nov.	6	Cash		52 000 00	
		A. Kingston, Capital			52 000 00
		Cash investment			
	14	Equipment		3 000 00	
		Cash			1 000 00
		Accounts Payable			2 000 00
		Purchase of equipment			

CASH ACCOUNT NO. 111

Date		Explanation	Post Ref.	Debit	Credit	Balance Debit	Balance Credit

EQUIPMENT ACCOUNT NO. 121

Date		Explanation	Post Ref.	Debit	Credit	Balance Debit	Balance Credit

ACCOUNTS PAYABLE ACCOUNT NO. 211

Date		Explanation	Post Ref.	Debit	Credit	Balance Debit	Balance Credit

A. KINGSTON, CAPITAL ACCOUNT NO. 311

Date		Explanation	Post Ref.	Debit	Credit	Balance Debit	Balance Credit

Name ______________ Class ______________ Date ______________

SET B EXERCISES

3B-4

(a)

PAGE 1

Date		Account Titles and Description	PR	Dr.	Cr.

(b)

CASH **ACCOUNT NO. 111**

Date		Explanation	Post Ref.	Debit	Credit	Balance	
						Debit	Credit

ACCOUNTS RECEIVABLE **ACCOUNT NO. 112**

Date		Explanation	Post Ref.	Debit	Credit	Balance	
						Debit	Credit

Name ______________________ Class ______________ Date ______________

SET B EXERCISES

EQUIPMENT — **ACCOUNT NO. 121**

Date	Explanation	Post Ref.	Debit	Credit	Balance Debit	Balance Credit

ACCOUNTS PAYABLE — **ACCOUNT NO. 211**

Date	Explanation	Post Ref.	Debit	Credit	Balance Debit	Balance Credit

J. LOWE, CAPITAL — **ACCOUNT NO. 311**

Date	Explanation	Post Ref.	Debit	Credit	Balance Debit	Balance Credit

J. LOWE, WITHDRAWALS — **ACCOUNT NO. 312**

Date	Explanation	Post Ref.	Debit	Credit	Balance Debit	Balance Credit

FEES EARNED — **ACCOUNT NO. 411**

Date	Explanation	Post Ref.	Debit	Credit	Balance Debit	Balance Credit

SALARIES EXPENSE — **ACCOUNT NO. 511**

Date	Explanation	Post Ref.	Debit	Credit	Balance Debit	Balance Credit

Name ____________ Class ____________ Date ____________

SET B EXERCISES

(c)

LOWE COMPANY
TRIAL BALANCE
DECEMBER 31, 201X

	Dr.	Cr.

3B-5

SUNG CO.
TRIAL BALANCE
AUGUST 31, 201X

	Dr.	Cr.

3B-6

Date 201X	Account Titles and Description	PR	Dr.	Cr.
Feb. 6	Office Equipment		9 00	
	Accounts Payable			9 00
	Purchase of office equip. on account			

Name ____________ Class ____________ Date ____________

FORMS FOR SET A PROBLEMS

PROBLEM 3A-1

JASON'S CLEANING SERVICE
GENERAL JOURNAL

PAGE 1

Date		Account Titles and Description	PR	Dr.	Cr.

Name ____________ Class ____________ Date ____________

PROBLEM 3A-1 (CONCLUDED)

JASON'S CLEANING SERVICE
GENERAL JOURNAL

PAGE 2

Date		Account Titles and Description	PR	Dr.	Cr.

Name ____________ Class ____________ Date ____________

PROBLEM 3A-2

(a, b)

BRENDA'S ART STUDIO
GENERAL JOURNAL

PAGE 1

Date		Account Titles and Description	PR	Dr.	Cr.

Name ____________________ Class ____________ Date ____________

PROBLEM 3A-2 (CONTINUED)

GENERAL LEDGER OF BRENDA'S ART STUDIO

CASH — ACCOUNT NO. 111

Date	Explanation	Post Ref.	Debit	Credit	Balance Debit	Balance Credit

ACCOUNTS RECEIVABLE — ACCOUNT NO. 112

Date	Explanation	Post Ref.	Debit	Credit	Balance Debit	Balance Credit

PREPAID RENT — ACCOUNT NO. 114

Date	Explanation	Post Ref.	Debit	Credit	Balance Debit	Balance Credit

ART SUPPLIES — ACCOUNT NO. 121

Date	Explanation	Post Ref.	Debit	Credit	Balance Debit	Balance Credit

Name ______________________ Class ______________ Date ______________

PROBLEM 3A-2 (CONTINUED)

EQUIPMENT **ACCOUNT NO. 131**

Date		Explanation	Post Ref.	Debit	Credit	Balance Debit	Balance Credit

ACCOUNTS PAYABLE **ACCOUNT NO. 211**

Date		Explanation	Post Ref.	Debit	Credit	Balance Debit	Balance Credit

B. RENNICKE, CAPITAL **ACCOUNT NO. 311**

Date		Explanation	Post Ref.	Debit	Credit	Balance Debit	Balance Credit

B. RENNICKE, WITHDRAWALS **ACCOUNT NO. 312**

Date		Explanation	Post Ref.	Debit	Credit	Balance Debit	Balance Credit

PROBLEM 3A-2 (CONTINUED)

ART FEES EARNED ACCOUNT NO. 411

Date	Explanation	Post Ref.	Debit	Credit	Balance	
					Debit	Credit

ELECTRICAL EXPENSE ACCOUNT NO. 511

Date	Explanation	Post Ref.	Debit	Credit	Balance	
					Debit	Credit

SALARIES EXPENSE ACCOUNT NO. 521

Date	Explanation	Post Ref.	Debit	Credit	Balance	
					Debit	Credit

TELEPHONE EXPENSE ACCOUNT NO. 531

Date	Explanation	Post Ref.	Debit	Credit	Balance	
					Debit	Credit

PROBLEM 3A-2 (CONCLUDED)

(c)

BRENDA'S ART STUDIO
TRIAL BALANCE
JUNE 30, 201X

	Dr.	Cr.

Name ____________ Class ____________ Date ____________

PROBLEM 3A-3
(a, b)

A. ONE'S PLACEMENT AGENCY
GENERAL JOURNAL

PAGE 1

Date		Account Titles and Description	PR	Dr.	Cr.

Name ________________ Class ________________ Date ________________

PROBLEM 3A-3 (CONTINUED)

GENERAL LEDGER OF A. ONE'S PLACEMENT AGENCY

CASH **ACCOUNT NO. 111**

Date	Explanation	Post Ref.	Debit	Credit	Balance Debit	Balance Credit

ACCOUNTS RECEIVABLE **ACCOUNT NO. 112**

Date	Explanation	Post Ref.	Debit	Credit	Balance Debit	Balance Credit

SUPPLIES **ACCOUNT NO. 131**

Date	Explanation	Post Ref.	Debit	Credit	Balance Debit	Balance Credit

EQUIPMENT **ACCOUNT NO. 141**

Date	Explanation	Post Ref.	Debit	Credit	Balance Debit	Balance Credit

Name ______________________ Class ______________ Date ______________

PROBLEM 3A-3 (CONTINUED)

ACCOUNTS PAYABLE ACCOUNT NO. 211

Date		Explanation	Post Ref.	Debit	Credit	Balance	
						Debit	Credit

A. ONE, CAPITAL ACCOUNT NO. 311

Date		Explanation	Post Ref.	Debit	Credit	Balance	
						Debit	Credit

A. ONE, WITHDRAWALS ACCOUNT NO. 312

Date		Explanation	Post Ref.	Debit	Credit	Balance	
						Debit	Credit

PLACEMENT FEES EARNED ACCOUNT NO. 411

Date		Explanation	Post Ref.	Debit	Credit	Balance	
						Debit	Credit

Name ____________________ Class ____________ Date ____________

PROBLEM 3A-3 (CONTINUED)

WAGE EXPENSE **ACCOUNT NO. 511**

Date	Explanation	Post Ref.	Debit	Credit	Balance	
					Debit	Credit

TELEPHONE EXPENSE **ACCOUNT NO. 521**

Date	Explanation	Post Ref.	Debit	Credit	Balance	
					Debit	Credit

ADVERTISING EXPENSE **ACCOUNT NO. 531**

Date	Explanation	Post Ref.	Debit	Credit	Balance	
					Debit	Credit

Name ______________________ Class ______________ Date ______________

PROBLEM 3A-3 (CONCLUDED)

(c)

A. ONE'S PLACEMENT AGENCY
TRIAL BALANCE
JUNE 30, 201X

	Dr.	Cr.

Name ____________________ Class ____________________ Date ____________________

FORMS FOR SET B PROBLEMS

PROBLEM 3B-1

JIMMY'S CLEANING SERVICE
GENERAL JOURNAL

PAGE 1

Date		Account Titles and Description	PR	Dr.	Cr.

Name ______________________ Class ______________ Date ______________

PROBLEM 3B-1 (CONCLUDED)

JIMMY'S CLEANING SERVICE
GENERAL JOURNAL

PAGE 2

Date	Account Titles and Description	PR	Dr.	Cr.

Name ______________________ Class ______________ Date ______________

PROBLEM 3B-2
(a, b)

BETH'S ART STUDIO
GENERAL JOURNAL

PAGE 1

Date	Account Titles and Description	PR	Dr.	Cr.

Name ____________________ Class ____________________ Date ____________________

PROBLEM 3B-2 (CONTINUED)

GENERAL LEDGER OF BETH'S ART STUDIO

CASH ACCOUNT NO. 111

Date	Explanation	Post Ref.	Debit	Credit	Balance Debit	Balance Credit

ABLE ACCOUNT NO. 112

Date	Expla		bit	Credit	Balance Debit	Balance Credit

PREPAID RE ACCOUNT NO. 114

Date	Explanation	Post Ref.		Credit	Balance Debit	Balance Credit

ART SUPPLIES ACCOUNT NO. 121

Date	Explanation	Post Ref.	Debit	redit	Balance Debit	Balance Credit

PROBLEM 3B-2 (CONTINUED)

EQUIPMENT **ACCOUNT NO. 131**

Date	Explanation	Post Ref.	Debit	Credit	Balance Debit	Balance Credit

ACCOUNTS PAYABLE **ACCOUNT NO. 211**

Date	Explanation	Post Ref.	Debit	Credit	Balance Debit	Balance Credit

BETH ORTH, CAPITAL **ACCOUNT NO. 311**

Date	Explanation	Post Ref.	Debit	Credit	Balance Debit	Balance Credit

BETH ORTH, WITHDRAWALS **ACCOUNT NO. 312**

Date	Explanation	Post Ref.	Debit	Credit	Balance Debit	Balance Credit

Name ____________ Class ____________ Date ____________

PROBLEM 3B-2 (CONTINUED)

ART FEES EARNED **ACCOUNT NO. 411**

Date		Explanation	Post Ref.	Debit	Credit	Balance	
						Debit	Credit

ELECTRICAL EXPENSE **ACCOUNT NO. 511**

Date		Explanation	Post Ref.	Debit	Credit	Balance	
						Debit	Credit

SALARIES EXPENSE **ACCOUNT NO. 521**

Date		Explanation	Post Ref.	Debit	Credit	Balance	
						Debit	Credit

TELEPHONE EXPENSE **ACCOUNT NO. 531**

Date		Explanation	Post Ref.	Debit	Credit	Balance	
						Debit	Credit

PROBLEM 3B-2 (CONCLUDED)

(c)

BETH'S ART STUDIO
TRIAL BALANCE
APRIL 30, 201X

	Dr.	Cr.

Name ______________________ Class ____________ Date ______________

PROBLEM 3B-3

(a, b)

A. FRENCH'S PLACEMENT AGENCY
GENERAL JOURNAL

PAGE 1

Date	Account Titles and Description	PR	Dr.	Cr.

Name ____________________ Class ____________ Date ____________

PROBLEM 3B-3 (CONTINUED)

GENERAL LEDGER OF A. FRENCH'S PLACEMENT AGENCY

CASH — **ACCOUNT NO. 111**

Date	Explanation	Post Ref.	Debit	Credit	Balance	
					Debit	Credit

ACCOUNTS RECEIVABLE — **ACCOUNT NO. 112**

Date	Explanation	Post Ref.	Debit	Credit	Balance	
					Debit	Credit

SUPPLIES — **ACCOUNT NO. 131**

Date	Explanation	Post Ref.	Debit	Credit	Balance	
					Debit	Credit

EQUIPMENT — **ACCOUNT NO. 141**

Date	Explanation	Post Ref.	Debit	Credit	Balance	
					Debit	Credit

Name ____________________ Class ____________________ Date ____________________

PROBLEM 3B-3 (CONTINUED)

ACCOUNTS PAYABLE **ACCOUNT NO. 211**

Date		Explanation	Post Ref.	Debit	Credit	Balance Debit	Balance Credit

A. FRENCH, CAPITAL **ACCOUNT NO. 311**

Date		Explanation	Post Ref.	Debit	Credit	Balance Debit	Balance Credit

A. FRENCH, WITHDRAWALS **ACCOUNT NO. 312**

Date		Explanation	Post Ref.	Debit	Credit	Balance Debit	Balance Credit

PLACEMENT FEES EARNED **ACCOUNT NO. 411**

Date		Explanation	Post Ref.	Debit	Credit	Balance Debit	Balance Credit

Name ______________________ Class ______________ Date ______________

PROBLEM 3B-3 (CONTINUED)

WAGE EXPENSE **ACCOUNT NO. 511**

Date		Explanation	Post Ref.	Debit	Credit	Balance	
						Debit	Credit

TELEPHONE EXPENSE **ACCOUNT NO. 521**

Date		Explanation	Post Ref.	Debit	Credit	Balance	
						Debit	Credit

ADVERTISING EXPENSE **ACCOUNT NO. 531**

Date		Explanation	Post Ref.	Debit	Credit	Balance	
						Debit	Credit

Name ____________________ Class ____________________ Date ____________________

PROBLEM 3B-3 (CONCLUDED)

(c)

A. FRENCH'S PLACEMENT AGENCY
TRIAL BALANCE
APRIL 30, 201X

	Dr.	Cr.

Name ____________________ Class ____________ Date ____________

ON THE JOB CONTINUING PROBLEM

ASSIGNMENT 1

SMITH COMPUTER CENTER
GENERAL JOURNAL

PAGE 1

Date	Account Titles and Description	PR	Dr.	Cr.

Name ____________ Class ____________ Date ____________

SMITH COMPUTER CENTER
GENERAL JOURNAL

PAGE 1 (Cont.)

Date		Account Titles and Description	PR	Dr.	Cr.

Name ______________________ Class ______________ Date ______________

ASSIGNMENT 2

CASH **ACCOUNT NO. 1000**

Date		Explanation	Post Ref.	Debit	Credit	Balance Debit	Balance Credit
9/1	1X	Balance forward	✓			3 0 8 0 00	

Name ______________________ Class ____________ Date ____________

ACCOUNTS RECEIVABLE ACCOUNT NO. 1020

Date		Explanation	Post Ref.	Debit	Credit	Balance Debit	Balance Credit
9/1	1X	Balance forward	✓			1 7 0 0 00	

PREPAID RENT ACCOUNT NO. 1025

Date		Explanation	Post Ref.	Debit	Credit	Balance Debit	Balance Credit

SUPPLIES ACCOUNT NO. 1030

Date		Explanation	Post Ref.	Debit	Credit	Balance Debit	Balance Credit
9/1		Balance forward	✓			5 0 0 00	

COMPUTER SHOP EQUIPMENT ACCOUNT NO. 1080

Date		Explanation	Post Ref.	Debit	Credit	Balance Debit	Balance Credit
9/1	1X	Balance forward	✓			1 8 0 0 00	

Name ______________________ Class ______________ Date ______________

OFFICE EQUIPMENT ACCOUNT NO. 1090

Date		Explanation	Post Ref.	Debit	Credit	Balance Debit	Balance Credit
9/1	1X	Balance forward	✓			3,300.00	

ACCOUNTS PAYABLE ACCOUNT NO. 2000

Date		Explanation	Post Ref.	Debit	Credit	Balance Debit	Balance Credit
9/1	1X	Balance forward	✓				430.00

FELDMAN, CAPITAL ACCOUNT NO. 3000

Date		Explanation	Post Ref.	Debit	Credit	Balance Debit	Balance Credit
9/1	1X	Balance forward	✓				6,000.00

FELDMAN, WITHDRAWALS ACCOUNT NO. 3010

Date		Explanation	Post Ref.	Debit	Credit	Balance Debit	Balance Credit
9/1	1X	Balance forward	✓			175.00	

Name ______________________ Class ______________ Date ______________

SERVICE REVENUE **ACCOUNT NO. 4000**

Date		Explanation	Post Ref.	Debit	Credit	Balance Debit	Balance Credit
9/1	1X	Balance forward	✓				6 2 0 0 00

ADVERTISING EXPENSE **ACCOUNT NO. 5010**

Date		Explanation	Post Ref.	Debit	Credit	Balance Debit	Balance Credit
9/1	1X	Balance forward	✓			9 0 0 00	

RENT EXPENSE **ACCOUNT NO. 5020**

Date		Explanation	Post Ref.	Debit	Credit	Balance Debit	Balance Credit
9/1	1X	Balance forward	✓			5 0 0 00	

Name ______________________ Class ______________ Date ______________

UTILITIES EXPENSE ACCOUNT NO. 5030

Date		Explanation	Post Ref.	Debit	Credit	Balance Debit	Balance Credit
9/1	1X	Balance forward	✓			75 00	

PHONE EXPENSE ACCOUNT NO. 5040

Date		Explanation	Post Ref.	Debit	Credit	Balance Debit	Balance Credit
9/1	1X	Balance forward	✓			80 00	

SUPPLIES EXPENSE ACCOUNT NO. 5050

Date		Explanation	Post Ref.	Debit	Credit	Balance Debit	Balance Credit

Name ______________________ Class ______________ Date ______________

INSURANCE EXPENSE **ACCOUNT NO. 5060**

Date		Explanation	Post Ref.	Debit	Credit	Balance Debit	Balance Credit
9/1	1X	Balance forward	✓			450 00	

POSTAGE EXPENSE **ACCOUNT NO. 5070**

Date		Explanation	Post Ref.	Debit	Credit	Balance Debit	Balance Credit
9/1	1X	Balance forward	✓			70 00	

Name ______________________ Class ______________ Date ______________

ASSIGNMENT 3

SMITH COMPUTER CENTER
TRIAL BALANCE
SEPTEMBER 30, 201X

	Dr.	Cr.

Name ______________________ Class ______________ Date ______________

ASSIGNMENT 4

SMITH COMPUTER CENTER
INCOME STATEMENT
FOR THE QUARTER ENDED 9/30/1X

SMITH COMPUTER CENTER
STATEMENT OF OWNER'S EQUITY
FOR THE QUARTER ENDED 9/30/1X

Name ______________________ Class ______________ Date ______________

SMITH COMPUTER CENTER
BALANCE SHEET
9/30/1X

ASSETS	LIABILITIES AND OWNER'S EQUITY

Name ______________________ Class ______________ Date ______________

CHAPTER 3
SUMMARY PRACTICE TEST: BEGINNING THE ACCOUNTING CYCLE

Part I

Fill in the blank(s) to complete the statement.

1. A fiscal year runs for ____________ months.
2. ____________ ____________ are prepared for parts of a fiscal year (monthly, quarterly, etc.).
3. The ____________ ____________ ____________ eliminates the need for footings.
4. The positive balance of each account is referred to as its ____________ ____________.
5. The process of recording transactions in a journal is called ____________.
6. Entries are journalized in ____________ ____________.
7. A ledger is often called a(n) ____________ ____________ ____________ ____________.
8. The ____________ portion of a journal entry is indented and placed below the ____________ portion.
9. A journal entry requiring three or more accounts is called a(n) ____________ ____________ ____________.
10. Accounts receivable is a(n) ____________ on the balance sheet.
11. When supplies are used up or consumed they become a(n) ____________.
12. The book of original entry usually refers to a(n) ____________.
13. The process of transferring information from a journal to a ledger is called ____________.
14. ____________ ____________ deals with the process of updating the PR of the journal from the account number of the ledger to indicate to which account in the ledger information has been posted.
15. Recording $995.00 as $99.50 is an example of a(n) ____________.

Name ______________________ Class ______________ Date ______________

Part II

Match the term in column A to the definition, example, or phrase in column B. Be sure to use a letter only once.

COLUMN A		COLUMN B
g	**1.** EXAMPLE: Book of original entry	a. 243 — 2430
______	**2.** Non-Business Expense	b. Transferring information from a general journal to a ledger
______	**3.** Slide	c. Chronological order
______	**4.** Transposition	d. Increased by a credit
______	**5.** Posting	e. Withdrawal
______	**6.** General Journal	f. Compound journal entry
______	**7.** Cross-reference	g. General journal
______	**8.** Journalizing	h. Rearrangement of digits of a number by accident
______	**9.** Balance Sheet prepared monthly	i. Updating PR column of journal from ledger account
______	**10.** A fiscal year	j. Trial balance
		k. Place to record transactions
		l. Accounting cycle
		m. Accounting period
		n. Interim statements

Part III

Answer true or false to the following statements.

1. A slide results in a rearrangement of digits in a number by error.

2. The totals of a trial balance may possibly not balance due to transpositions.

3. Withdrawals has a normal balance of a credit.

4. The running balance of an account can be kept in a four-column account.

5. The journal links debits and credits in alphabetical order.

6. The ledger accumulates information from the journal.

7. The post reference column of a ledger records the account number of that account.

8. An accounting cycle must be from January 1 to December 31.

9. The ledger is the book of original entry.

10. The income statement is prepared for a specific accounting period.

11. Interim statements are prepared for an entire fiscal year.

12. A calendar year could be a fiscal year.

13. 390 written by mistake as 3,900 is an example of a slide.

Name ______________________ Class ______________ Date ______________

14. If the totals of a trial balance balance, the individual balance of items must be correct.

15. The equality of debits and credits on a trial balance does not guarantee that transactions have been properly recorded.

16. The trial balance is prepared from the journal.

17. Cross-referencing means never updating the post reference column of the journal.

18. Journals and ledgers are always in the same book.

19. The normal balance of each account is located on the same side that increases the acccount.

20. To increase the Capital account, we credit the Capital account.

SOLUTIONS

Part I

1. 12
2. Interim statements
3. four-column account
4. normal balance
5. journalizing
6. chronological order
7. book of final entry
8. credit, debit
9. compound journal entry
10. asset
11. expense
12. journal
13. posting
14. Cross-reference
15. slide

Part II

1. g
2. e
3. a
4. h
5. b
6. k
7. i
8. c
9. n
10. m

Part III

1. false
2. true
3. false
4. true
5. false
6. true
7. false
8. false
9. false
10. true
11. false
12. true
13. true
14. false
15. true
16. false
17. false
18. false
19. true
20. true

Study Guide and Working Papers

The Accounting Cycle Continued

Name ______________________ Class ______________ Date ______________

FORMS FOR DEMONSTRATION PROBLEM

(1) Worksheet
Use one of the blank fold-out worksheets that accompanied your textbook.

(2)

FROST COMPANY
INCOME STATEMENT
FOR MONTH ENDED DECEMBER 31, 201X

FROST COMPANY
STATEMENT OF OWNER'S EQUITY
FOR MONTH ENDED DECEMBER 31, 201X

Name ______________________ Class ______________ Date ______________

DEMONSTRATION PROBLEM (CONCLUDED)

FROST COMPANY
BALANCE SHEET
DECEMBER 31, 201X

ASSETS

LIABILITIES AND OWNER'S EQUITY

Name ____________ Class ____________ Date ____________

FORMS FOR SET A EXERCISES

4A-1

Account	Category	Normal Balance	Financial Statement(s) Found on
Accumulated Depreciation, Office Equipment			
Prepaid Rent			
Office Equipment			
Depreciation Expense, Office Equipment			
B. Reel, Capital			
B. Reel, Withdrawals			
Wages Payable			

4A-2

	Accounts Affected	Category	↑ ↓	Rules	Amount
a.					
b.					

4A-3

	Accounts	Dr.	Cr.
a.			
b.			

4A-4

Use one of the blank fold-out worksheets that accompanied your textbook.

Name ______________________ Class ______________ Date ______________

SET A EXERCISES

4A-5

(a)

J. REVERE
INCOME STATEMENT
FOR MONTH ENDED JANUARY 31, 201X

(b)

J. REVERE
STATEMENT OF OWNER'S EQUITY
FOR MONTH ENDED JANUARY 31, 201X

Name ______________________ Class ______________ Date ______________

SET A EXERCISES

(c)

J. REVERE
BALANCE SHEET
JANUARY 31, 201X

ASSETS	LIABILITIES AND OWNER'S EQUITY

Name ______________________ Class ______________ Date ______________

FORMS FOR SET B EXERCISES

4B-1

Account	Category	Normal Balance	Financial Statement(s) Found on
Accounts Payable			
Prepaid Insurance			
Computer Equipment			
Depreciation Expense, Computer Equipment			
B. Free, Capital			
B. Free, Withdrawals			
Salaries Payable			
Accumulated Depreciation, Computer Equipment			

4B-2

	Accounts Affected	Category	↑ ↓	Rules	Amount
a.					
b.					

4B-3

	Accounts	Dr.	Cr.
a.			
b.			

4B-4

Use one of the blank fold-out worksheets that accompanied your textbook.

Name ______________________ Class ______________ Date ______________

SET B EXERCISES

4B-5

(a)

J. TUTLE
INCOME STATEMENT
FOR MONTH ENDED MARCH 31, 201X

(b)

J. TUTLE
STATEMENT OF OWNER'S EQUITY
FOR MONTH ENDED MARCH 31, 201X

Name ______________________ Class ______________ Date ______________

SET B EXERCISES
(c)

J. TUTLE
BALANCE SHEET
MARCH 31, 201X

ASSETS			LIABILITIES AND OWNER'S EQUITY		

Name ____________________ Class ____________________ Date ____________________

FORMS FOR SET A PROBLEMS

PROBLEM 4A-1

Use one of the blank fold-out worksheets that accompanied your textbook.

PROBLEM 4A-2

Use one of the blank fold-out worksheets that accompanied your textbook.

PROBLEM 4A-3

(1) Use one of the blank fold-out worksheets that accompanied your textbook.

(2)

KENT'S MOVING CO.
INCOME STATEMENT
FOR MONTH ENDED DECEMBER 31, 201X

KENT'S MOVING CO.
STATEMENT OF OWNER'S EQUITY
FOR MONTH ENDED DECEMBER 31, 201X

Name ______________________ Class ______________ Date ______________

PROBLEM 4A-3 (CONCLUDED)

KENT'S MOVING CO.
BALANCE SHEET
DECEMBER 31, 201X

ASSETS		LIABILITIES AND OWNER'S EQUITY	

Name ____________________ Class ____________ Date ____________

PROBLEM 4A-4

(1) Use one of the blank fold-out worksheets that accompanied your textbook.

(2)

DAMON'S REPAIR SERVICE
INCOME STATEMENT
FOR MONTH ENDED APRIL 30, 201X

DAMON'S REPAIR SERVICE
STATEMENT OF OWNER'S EQUITY
FOR MONTH ENDED APRIL 30, 201X

Name ______________________ Class ______________ Date ______________

PROBLEM 4A-4 (CONCLUDED)

DAMON'S REPAIR SERVICE
BALANCE SHEET
APRIL 30, 201X

LIABILITIES AND OWNER'S EQUITY

ASSETS

Name ______________________ Class ______________ Date ______________

FORMS FOR SET B PROBLEMS

PROBLEM 4B-1

Use one of the blank fold-out worksheets that accompanied your textbook.

PROBLEM 4B-2

Use one of the blank fold-out worksheets that accompanied your textbook.

PROBLEM 4B-3

(1) Use one of the blank fold-out worksheets that accompanied your textbook.

(2)

KYLE'S MOVING CO.
INCOME STATEMENT
FOR MONTH ENDED OCTOBER 31, 201X

KYLE'S MOVING CO.
STATEMENT OF OWNER'S EQUITY
FOR MONTH ENDED OCTOBER, 201X

Name ______________________ Class ______________ Date ______________

PROBLEM 4B-3 (CONCLUDED)

KYLE'S MOVING CO.
BALANCE SHEET
OCTOBER 31, 201X

ASSETS			LIABILITIES AND OWNER'S EQUITY		

Name ______________________ Class ______________ Date ______________

PROBLEM 4B-4

(1) Use one of the blank fold-out worksheets that accompanied your textbook.

(2)

DON'S REPAIR SERVICE
INCOME STATEMENT
FOR MONTH ENDED SEPTEMBER 30, 201X

DON'S REPAIR SERVICE
STATEMENT OF OWNER'S EQUITY
FOR MONTH ENDED SEPTEMBER 30, 201X

Name ____________________ Class ____________ Date ____________

PROBLEM 4B-4 (CONCLUDED)

DON'S REPAIR SERVICE
BALANCE SHEET
SEPTEMBER 30, 201X

ASSETS

LIABILITIES AND OWNER'S EQUITY

Name ______________________ Class ______________________ Date ______________________

ON THE JOB CONTINUING PROBLEM

ASSIGNMENT

Use the blank fold-out worksheet for Chapter 4 that accompanied your textbook. Complete the worksheet using the trial balance below.

SMITH COMPUTER CENTER
TRIAL BALANCE
SEPTEMBER 30, 201X

	Dr.	Cr.
Cash	2,120.00	
Accounts Receivable	2,700.00	
Prepaid Rent	1,500.00	
Supplies	500.00	
Computer Shop Equipment	3,900.00	
Office Equipment	3,300.00	
Accounts Payable		1,700.00
Feldman, Capital		6,000.00
Feldman, Withdrawals	175.00	
Service Revenue		10,220.00
Advertising Expense	900.00	
Rent Expense	500.00	
Utilities Expense	160.00	
Phone Expense	115.00	
Insurance Expense	450.00	
Postage Expense	70.00	
Totals	16,390.00	16,390.00

Name ______________________ Class ______________ Date ______________

ON THE JOB CONTINUING PROBLEM

SMITH COMPUTER CENTER
INCOME STATEMENT
FOR THE THREE MONTHS ENDED SEPTEMBER 30, 201X

SMITH COMPUTER CENTER
STATEMENT OF OWNER'S EQUITY
FOR THE THREE MONTHS ENDED SEPTEMBER 30, 201X

Name ______________________ Class ______________ Date ______________

SMITH COMPUTER CENTER
BALANCE SHEET
SEPTEMBER 30, 201X

ASSETS		LIABILITIES AND OWNER'S EQUITY	

Name ______________________ Class ______________ Date ______________

CHAPTER 4
SUMMARY PRACTICE TEST: THE ACCOUNTING CYCLE CONTINUED

Part I

Fill in the blank(s) to complete the statement.

1. ______________ is an estimate.
2. A(n) ______________ will decrease accumulated depreciation.
3. ______________ affect both the income statement and balance sheet.
4. The adjustment for supplies reflects the amount of supplies ______________.
5. Supplies Expense is found on the income statement. Supplies are found on the ______________ ______________.
6. ______________ ______________ reflects the cost of equipment at time of purchase.
7. Depreciation Expense is found on the ______________.
8. ______________ ______________ is a contra asset that has a credit balance.
9. Accumulated Depreciation, a contra asset, is found on the ______________ ______________.
10. Historical or original cost of an auto less ______________ ______________ reflects the unused amount of the auto on the accounting books.
11. Withdrawals are found in the ______________ column of the balance sheet section of the worksheet.
12. Salaries Payable is a liability that will appear in the ______________ ______________ ______________ of the worksheet.
13. The figure for net income on the worksheet is carried over to the ______________ column of the balance sheet.
14. A worksheet is a(n) ______________ report.
15. ______________ ______________ are prepared after the completion of the worksheet.

Part II

Complete the following statements by circling the letter of the appropriate answer.

Name ______________________ Class ______________ Date ______________

1. The adjustment for depreciation results in Accumulated Depreciation

a. decreasing.
b. staying the same.
c. increasing.

2. The historical or original cost of an asset on the worksheet

a. never changes.
b. sometimes changes.
c. continually changes.

3. Net income on the worksheet is carried over to the

a. trial balance.
b. adjusted trial balance.
c. balance sheet column.

4. Accumulated Depreciation is found on

a. a worksheet.
b. an income statement.
c. both a worksheet and an income statement.

5. Accumulated Depreciation, a contra asset, is increased by a

a. debit.
b. credit.
c. both a and b.

6. A worksheet is usually completed

a. one column at a time.
b. two columns at a time.
c. three columns at a time.

7. Withdrawals on the worksheet are found in the

a. debit column of the income statement.
b. debit column of the balance sheet.
c. both a and b.

8. The worksheet specifically shows the

a. beginning figure for owner's capital.
b. ending figure for owner's capital.
c. average figure for owner's capital.

9. The balance sheet will report Depreciation Expense and Accumulated Depreciation.

a. always
b. sometimes
c. never

10. The adjustment for depreciation affects

a. the income statement.
b. the balance sheet.
c. both a and b.

11. The adjustment for supplies requires one to know

a. beginning supplies plus supplies purchased.
b. supplies on hand.
c. both a and b.

Name ______________________________ Class ________________ Date ________________

12. The purpose of adjustments is to

a. adjust accounts on the balance sheet.
b. adjust accounts on the income statement.
c. both a. and b.

13. The book value of equipment equals cost less

a. expenses.
b. accumulated depreciation.
c. neither a nor b.

14. The ____________ is an informal report.

a. income statement
b. balance sheet
c. worksheet

Part III

Answer true or false to the following statements.

1. The normal balance of accumulated depreciation is a credit.
2. Liabilities are only income statement accounts.
3. The total of the adjustments columns on the worksheet may balance but be incorrect.
4. Prepaid rent is found on the income statement.
5. Rent expense is found on the income statement.
6. Debits and credits are found on financial statements.
7. Historical cost relates only to automobiles.
8. Accumulated Depreciation is found on the income statement.
9. As Accumulated Depreciation increases, the historical cost changes.
10. The adjustment for depreciation directly affects cash.
11. An expense is only recorded when it is paid.
12. The ending figure for owner's capital is found in the trial balance columns of the worksheet.
13. Withdrawals have the same balance as Accumulated Depreciation.
14. Salaries Payable is an asset on the income statement.
15. Net loss would never be shown on a worksheet.
16. The net income on the worksheet is the same amount on the income statement.
17. Worksheets must use dollar signs.
18. The worksheet eliminates the need to prepare financial statements.
19. Cost less accumulated depreciation equals book value.
20. Accrued salaries payable are an asset on the balance sheet.

Name ______________________ Class ______________ Date ______________

SOLUTIONS

Part I

1.	Depreciation Expense	**9.**	balance sheet
2.	sale of a plant asset	**10.**	accumulated depreciation
3.	Adjustments	**11.**	debit
4.	used up	**12.**	balance sheet credit column
5.	balance sheet	**13.**	credit
6.	Historical (original) cost	**14.**	informal
7.	income statement	**15.**	Financial statements
8.	Accumulated Depreciation		

Part II

1.	c	**6.**	b	**11.**	c
2.	a	**7.**	b	**12.**	c
3.	c	**8.**	a	**13.**	b
4.	a	**9.**	c	**14.**	c
5.	b	**10.**	c		

Part III

1.	true	**6.**	false	**11.**	false	**16.**	true
2.	false	**7.**	false	**12.**	false	**17.**	false
3.	true	**8.**	false	**13.**	false	**18.**	false
4.	false	**9.**	false	**14.**	false	**19.**	true
5.	true	**10.**	false	**15.**	false	**20.**	false

Study Guide and Working Papers

The Accounting Cycle Completed

Name ______________________ Class ______________ Date ______________

FORMS FOR DEMONSTRATION PROBLEM

(1)

ROLO COMPANY
GENERAL JOURNAL

PAGE 1

Date	Account Titles and Description	PR	Dr.	Cr.

Name ______________________ Class ______________ Date ______________

FORMS FOR DEMONSTRATION PROBLEM (CONTINUED)

ROLO COMPANY
GENERAL JOURNAL

PAGE 2

Date	Account Titles and Description	PR	Dr.	Cr.

Name ______________________ Class ______________ Date ______________

FORMS FOR DEMONSTRATION PROBLEM (CONTINUED)

CASH **ACCOUNT NO. 111**

Date	Explanation	Post Ref.	Debit	Credit	Balance Debit	Balance Credit

ACCOUNTS RECEIVABLE **ACCOUNT NO. 112**

Date	Explanation	Post Ref.	Debit	Credit	Balance Debit	Balance Credit

PREPAID RENT **ACCOUNT NO. 114**

Date	Explanation	Post Ref.	Debit	Credit	Balance Debit	Balance Credit

OFFICE SUPPLIES **ACCOUNT NO. 115**

Date	Explanation	Post Ref.	Debit	Credit	Balance Debit	Balance Credit

Name ______________________ Class ______________ Date ______________

FORMS FOR DEMONSTRATION PROBLEM (CONTINUED)

OFFICE EQUIPMENT **ACCOUNT NO. 121**

Date	Explanation	Post Ref.	Debit	Credit	Balance Debit	Balance Credit

ACCUMULATED DEPRECIATION, OFFICE EQUIPMENT **ACCOUNT NO. 122**

Date	Explanation	Post Ref.	Debit	Credit	Balance Debit	Balance Credit

ACCOUNTS PAYABLE **ACCOUNT NO. 211**

Date	Explanation	Post Ref.	Debit	Credit	Balance Debit	Balance Credit

Name ____________ Class ____________ Date ____________

FORMS FOR DEMONSTRATION PROBLEM (CONTINUED)

SALARIES PAYABLE **ACCOUNT NO. 212**

Date	Explanation	Post Ref.	Debit	Credit	Balance	
					Debit	Credit

R. KERN, CAPITAL **ACCOUNT NO. 311**

Date	Explanation	Post Ref.	Debit	Credit	Balance	
					Debit	Credit

R. KERN, WITHDRAWALS **ACCOUNT NO. 312**

Date	Explanation	Post Ref.	Debit	Credit	Balance	
					Debit	Credit

INCOME SUMMARY **ACCOUNT NO. 313**

Date	Explanation	Post Ref.	Debit	Credit	Balance	
					Debit	Credit

FEES EARNED **ACCOUNT NO. 411**

Date	Explanation	Post Ref.	Debit	Credit	Balance	
					Debit	Credit

Name ______________ Class ______________ Date ______________

FORMS FOR DEMONSTRATION PROBLEM (CONTINUED)

SALARIES EXPENSE **ACCOUNT NO. 511**

Date		Explanation	Post Ref.	Debit	Credit	Balance	
						Debit	Credit

ADVERTISING EXPENSE **ACCOUNT NO. 512**

Date		Explanation	Post Ref.	Debit	Credit	Balance	
						Debit	Credit

RENT EXPENSE **ACCOUNT NO. 513**

Date		Explanation	Post Ref.	Debit	Credit	Balance	
						Debit	Credit

OFFICE SUPPLIES EXPENSE **ACCOUNT NO. 514**

Date		Explanation	Post Ref.	Debit	Credit	Balance	
						Debit	Credit

DEPRECIATION EXPENSE, OFFICE EQUIPMENT **ACCOUNT NO. 515**

Date		Explanation	Post Ref.	Debit	Credit	Balance	
						Debit	Credit

Name ______________________ Class ______________ Date ______________

FORMS FOR DEMONSTRATION PROBLEM (CONTINUED)

(2) Use one of the blank fold-out worksheets that accompanied your textbook.

(3)

ROLO COMPANY
INCOME STATEMENT
FOR MONTH ENDED JANUARY 31, 201X

ROLO COMPANY
STATEMENT OF OWNER'S EQUITY
FOR MONTH ENDED JANUARY 31, 201X

Name ____________ Class ____________ Date ____________

FORMS FOR DEMONSTRATION PROBLEM (CONTINUED)

ROLO COMPANY
BALANCE SHEET
JANUARY 31, 201X

ASSETS				LIABILITIES AND OWNER'S EQUITY			

Name ______________________ Class ______________ Date ______________

FORMS FOR DEMONSTRATION PROBLEM (CONCLUDED)

(4)

ROLO COMPANY
POST-CLOSING TRIAL BALANCE
JANUARY 31, 201X

	Dr.	Cr.

Name ______________________ Class ______________ Date ______________

FORMS FOR SET A EXERCISES

5A-1

Date		Account Titles and Description	PR	Dr.	Cr.

5A-2

	TEMPORARY	PERMANENT	WILL BE CLOSED
1. Income Summary			
2. Jan Ralls, Capital			
3. Rent Expense			
4. Jan Ralls, Withdrawals			
5. Fees Earned			
6. Accounts Payable			
7. Cash			

Name ______________________ Class ______________ Date ______________

SET A EXERCISES

5A-3

Date		Account Titles and Description	PR	Dr.	Cr.

Name ______________________ Class ______________ Date ______________

SET A EXERCISES

5A-4

Date	Account Titles and Description	PR	Dr.	Cr.

5A-5

WURLEY CO.
POST-CLOSING TRIAL BALANCE
MARCH 31, 201X

	Dr.	Cr.

Name ______________________ Class ______________ Date ______________

FORMS FOR SET B EXERCISES

5B-1

Date	Account Titles and Description	PR	Dr.	Cr.

5B-2

	TEMPORARY	PERMANENT	WILL BE CLOSED
1. Income Summary			
2. Jen Rich, Capital			
3. Salary Expense			
4. Jen Rich, Withdrawals			
5. Fees Earned			
6. Accounts Payable			
7. Cash			

Name ____________________ Class ____________ Date ____________

SET B EXERCISES

5B-3

Date		Account Titles and Description	PR	Dr.	Cr.

Name ______________________ Class ______________ Date ______________

SET B EXERCISES

5B-4

Date		Account Titles and Description	PR	Dr.	Cr.

5B-5

WASHINGTON CO.
POST-CLOSING TRIAL BALANCE
DECEMBER 31, 201X

	Dr.	Cr.

Name ______________________ Class ______________ Date ______________

FORMS FOR SET A PROBLEMS

PROBLEM 5A-1

(1) Use one of the blank fold-out worksheets that accompanied your textbook.

(2)

DREW'S DANCE STUDIO
GENERAL JOURNAL

PAGE 3

Date	Account Titles and Description	PR	Dr.	Cr.

Name ______________ Class ______________ Date ______________

PROBLEM 5A-2

(1)

PARKHOUSE'S CLEANING SERVICE
GENERAL JOURNAL

PAGE 2

Date	Account Titles and Description	PR	Dr.	Cr.

Name ______________________ Class ______________ Date ______________

PROBLEM 5A-2 (CONTINUED)

CASH **ACCOUNT NO. 112**

Date	Explanation	Post Ref.	Debit	Credit	Balance Debit	Balance Credit

PREPAID INSURANCE **ACCOUNT NO. 114**

Date	Explanation	Post Ref.	Debit	Credit	Balance Debit	Balance Credit

CLEANING SUPPLIES **ACCOUNT NO. 115**

Date	Explanation	Post Ref.	Debit	Credit	Balance Debit	Balance Credit

AUTO **ACCOUNT NO. 121**

Date	Explanation	Post Ref.	Debit	Credit	Balance Debit	Balance Credit

ACCUMULATED DEPRECIATION, AUTO **ACCOUNT NO. 122**

Date	Explanation	Post Ref.	Debit	Credit	Balance Debit	Balance Credit

Name ______________________ Class ______________ Date ______________

PROBLEM 5A-2 (CONTINUED)

ACCOUNTS PAYABLE **ACCOUNT NO. 212**

Date	Explanation	Post Ref.	Debit	Credit	Balance Debit	Balance Credit

SALARIES PAYABLE **ACCOUNT NO. 213**

Date	Explanation	Post Ref.	Debit	Credit	Balance Debit	Balance Credit

B. PARKHOUSE, CAPITAL **ACCOUNT NO. 312**

Date	Explanation	Post Ref.	Debit	Credit	Balance Debit	Balance Credit

B. PARKHOUSE, WITHDRAWALS **ACCOUNT NO. 313**

Date	Explanation	Post Ref.	Debit	Credit	Balance Debit	Balance Credit

INCOME SUMMARY **ACCOUNT NO. 314**

Date	Explanation	Post Ref.	Debit	Credit	Balance Debit	Balance Credit

Name ______________________ Class ______________ Date ______________

PROBLEM 5A-2 (CONTINUED)

CLEANING FEES **ACCOUNT NO. 412**

Date		Explanation	Post Ref.	Debit	Credit	Balance Debit	Balance Credit

SALARIES EXPENSE **ACCOUNT NO. 513**

Date		Explanation	Post Ref.	Debit	Credit	Balance Debit	Balance Credit

TELEPHONE EXPENSE **ACCOUNT NO. 514**

Date		Explanation	Post Ref.	Debit	Credit	Balance Debit	Balance Credit

ADVERTISING EXPENSE **ACCOUNT NO. 515**

Date		Explanation	Post Ref.	Debit	Credit	Balance Debit	Balance Credit

GAS EXPENSE **ACCOUNT NO. 516**

Date		Explanation	Post Ref.	Debit	Credit	Balance Debit	Balance Credit

Name ______________________ Class ______________ Date ______________

PROBLEM 5A-2 (CONTINUED)

INSURANCE EXPENSE **ACCOUNT NO. 517**

Date	Explanation	Post Ref.	Debit	Credit	Balance	
					Debit	Credit

CLEANING SUPPLIES EXPENSE **ACCOUNT NO. 518**

Date	Explanation	Post Ref.	Debit	Credit	Balance	
					Debit	Credit

DEPRECIATION EXPENSE, AUTO **ACCOUNT NO. 519**

Date	Explanation	Post Ref.	Debit	Credit	Balance	
					Debit	Credit

Name ______________________ Class ______________ Date ______________

PROBLEM 5A-2 (CONCLUDED)

(2)

PARKHOUSE'S CLEANING SERVICE
POST-CLOSING TRIAL BALANCE
DECEMBER 31, 201X

	Dr.	Cr.

PROBLEM 5A-3

Use one of the blank fold-out worksheets that accompanied your textbook.

Name ________________ Class ________________ Date ________________

PROBLEM 5A-3 (CONTINUED)

PAT'S PLOWING
GENERAL JOURNAL

PAGE 1

Date		Account Titles and Description	PR	Dr.	Cr.

PROBLEM 5A-3 (CONTINUED)

PAT'S PLOWING
GENERAL JOURNAL

PAGE 2

Date		Account Titles and Description	PR	Dr.	Cr.

Name ______________________ Class ______________ Date ______________

PROBLEM 5A-3 (CONTINUED)

PAT'S PLOWING
GENERAL JOURNAL

PAGE 3

Date	Account Titles and Description	PR	Dr.	Cr.

Name ____________________ Class ____________________ Date ____________________

PROBLEM 5A-3 (CONTINUED)

CASH **ACCOUNT NO. 111**

Date		Explanation	Post Ref.	Debit	Credit	Balance Debit	Balance Credit

ACCOUNTS RECEIVABLE **ACCOUNT NO. 112**

Date		Explanation	Post Ref.	Debit	Credit	Balance Debit	Balance Credit

PREPAID RENT **ACCOUNT NO. 114**

Date		Explanation	Post Ref.	Debit	Credit	Balance Debit	Balance Credit

SNOW SUPPLIES **ACCOUNT NO. 115**

Date		Explanation	Post Ref.	Debit	Credit	Balance Debit	Balance Credit

Name ____________________ Class ____________ Date ____________

PROBLEM 5A-3 (CONTINUED)

OFFICE EQUIPMENT **ACCOUNT NO. 121**

Date	Explanation	Post Ref.	Debit	Credit	Balance Debit	Balance Credit

ACCUMULATED DEPRECIATION, OFFICE EQUIPMENT **ACCOUNT NO. 122**

Date	Explanation	Post Ref.	Debit	Credit	Balance Debit	Balance Credit

SNOW EQUIPMENT **ACCOUNT NO. 123**

Date	Explanation	Post Ref.	Debit	Credit	Balance Debit	Balance Credit

ACCUMULATED DEPRECIATION, SNOW EQUIPMENT **ACCOUNT NO. 124**

Date	Explanation	Post Ref.	Debit	Credit	Balance Debit	Balance Credit

ACCOUNTS PAYABLE **ACCOUNT NO. 211**

Date	Explanation	Post Ref.	Debit	Credit	Balance Debit	Balance Credit

Name ______________________ Class ______________ Date ______________

PROBLEM 5A-3 (CONTINUED)

SALARIES PAYABLE **ACCOUNT NO. 212**

Date	Explanation	Post Ref.	Debit	Credit	Balance Debit	Balance Credit

P. MUNRO, CAPITAL **ACCOUNT NO. 311**

Date	Explanation	Post Ref.	Debit	Credit	Balance Debit	Balance Credit

P. MUNRO, WITHDRAWALS **ACCOUNT NO. 312**

Date	Explanation	Post Ref.	Debit	Credit	Balance Debit	Balance Credit

INCOME SUMMARY **ACCOUNT NO. 313**

Date	Explanation	Post Ref.	Debit	Credit	Balance Debit	Balance Credit

PLOWING FEES **ACCOUNT NO. 411**

Date	Explanation	Post Ref.	Debit	Credit	Balance Debit	Balance Credit

Name ____________ Class ____________ Date ____________

PROBLEM 5A-3 (CONTINUED)

SALARIES EXPENSE **ACCOUNT NO. 511**

Date	Explanation	Post Ref.	Debit	Credit	Balance	
					Debit	Credit

ADVERTISING EXPENSE **ACCOUNT NO. 512**

Date	Explanation	Post Ref.	Debit	Credit	Balance	
					Debit	Credit

TELEPHONE EXPENSE **ACCOUNT NO. 513**

Date	Explanation	Post Ref.	Debit	Credit	Balance	
					Debit	Credit

RENT EXPENSE **ACCOUNT NO. 514**

Date	Explanation	Post Ref.	Debit	Credit	Balance	
					Debit	Credit

SNOW SUPPLIES EXPENSE **ACCOUNT NO. 515**

Date	Explanation	Post Ref.	Debit	Credit	Balance	
					Debit	Credit

Name ______________ Class ______________ Date ______________

PROBLEM 5A-3 (CONTINUED)

DEPRECIATION EXPENSE, OFFICE EQUIPMENT **ACCOUNT NO. 516**

Date		Explanation	Post Ref.	Debit	Credit	Balance	
						Debit	Credit

DEPRECIATION EXPENSE, SNOW EQUIPMENT **ACCOUNT NO. 517**

Date		Explanation	Post Ref.	Debit	Credit	Balance	
						Debit	Credit

Name ________________ Class ________________ Date ________________

PROBLEM 5A-3 (CONTINUED)

PAT'S PLOWING
INCOME STATEMENT
FOR MONTH ENDED JANUARY 31, 201X

PAT'S PLOWING
STATEMENT OF OWNER'S EQUITY
FOR MONTH ENDED JANUARY 31, 201X

Name ______________________ Class ______________ Date ______________

PROBLEM 5A-3 (CONTINUED)

PAT'S PLOWING
BALANCE SHEET
JANUARY 31, 201X

ASSETS		LIABILITIES AND OWNER'S EQUITY	

Name ______________________ Class ______________ Date ______________

PROBLEM 5A-3 (CONCLUDED)

PAT'S PLOWING
POST-CLOSING TRIAL BALANCE
JANUARY 31, 201X

	Dr.	Cr.

Name ______________ Class ______________ Date ______________

FORMS FOR SET B PROBLEMS

PROBLEM 5B-1

(1) Use one of the blank fold-out worksheets that accompanied your textbook.

(2)

DEB'S DANCE STUDIO
GENERAL JOURNAL

PAGE 3

Date		Account Titles and Description	PR	Dr.	Cr.

Name ______________________ Class ______________ Date ______________

PROBLEM 5B-2

(1)

POTTER'S CLEANING SERVICE
GENERAL JOURNAL

PAGE 2

Date	Account Titles and Description	PR	Dr.	Cr.

Name ______________________ Class ______________ Date ______________

PROBLEM 5B-2 (CONTINUED)

CASH **ACCOUNT NO. 112**

Date	Explanation	Post Ref.	Debit	Credit	Balance	
					Debit	Credit

PREPAID INSURANCE **ACCOUNT NO. 114**

Date	Explanation	Post Ref.	Debit	Credit	Balance	
					Debit	Credit

CLEANING SUPPLIES **ACCOUNT NO. 115**

Date	Explanation	Post Ref.	Debit	Credit	Balance	
					Debit	Credit

AUTO **ACCOUNT NO. 121**

Date	Explanation	Post Ref.	Debit	Credit	Balance	
					Debit	Credit

ACCUMULATED DEPRECIATION, AUTO **ACCOUNT NO. 122**

Date	Explanation	Post Ref.	Debit	Credit	Balance	
					Debit	Credit

Name ______________ Class ______________ Date ______________

PROBLEM 5B-2 (CONTINUED)

ACCOUNTS PAYABLE **ACCOUNT NO. 212**

Date		Explanation	Post Ref.	Debit	Credit	Balance	
						Debit	Credit

SALARIES PAYABLE **ACCOUNT NO. 213**

Date		Explanation	Post Ref.	Debit	Credit	Balance	
						Debit	Credit

B. POTTER, CAPITAL **ACCOUNT NO. 312**

Date		Explanation	Post Ref.	Debit	Credit	Balance	
						Debit	Credit

B. POTTER, WITHDRAWALS **ACCOUNT NO. 313**

Date		Explanation	Post Ref.	Debit	Credit	Balance	
						Debit	Credit

INCOME SUMMARY **ACCOUNT NO. 314**

Date		Explanation	Post Ref.	Debit	Credit	Balance	
						Debit	Credit

Name ________________ Class ________________ Date ________________

PROBLEM 5B-2 (CONTINUED)

CLEANING FEES **ACCOUNT NO. 412**

Date		Explanation	Post Ref.	Debit	Credit	Balance Debit	Balance Credit

SALARIES EXPENSE **ACCOUNT NO. 513**

Date		Explanation	Post Ref.	Debit	Credit	Balance Debit	Balance Credit

TELEPHONE EXPENSE **ACCOUNT NO. 514**

Date		Explanation	Post Ref.	Debit	Credit	Balance Debit	Balance Credit

ADVERTISING EXPENSE **ACCOUNT NO. 515**

Date		Explanation	Post Ref.	Debit	Credit	Balance Debit	Balance Credit

GAS EXPENSE **ACCOUNT NO. 516**

Date		Explanation	Post Ref.	Debit	Credit	Balance Debit	Balance Credit

Name ______________________ Class ______________ Date ______________

PROBLEM 5B-2 (CONTINUED)

INSURANCE EXPENSE — **ACCOUNT NO. 517**

Date	Explanation	Post Ref.	Debit	Credit	Balance	
					Debit	Credit

CLEANING SUPPLIES EXPENSE — **ACCOUNT NO. 518**

Date	Explanation	Post Ref.	Debit	Credit	Balance	
					Debit	Credit

DEPRECIATION EXPENSE, AUTO — **ACCOUNT NO. 519**

Date	Explanation	Post Ref.	Debit	Credit	Balance	
					Debit	Credit

Name ______________________ Class ______________ Date ______________

PROBLEM 5B-2 (CONCLUDED)

(2)

POTTER'S CLEANING SERVICE
POST-CLOSING TRIAL BALANCE
JULY 31, 201X

	Dr.	Cr.

PROBLEM 5B-3

Use one of the blank fold-out worksheets that accompanied your textbook.

Name ______________________ Class ____________ Date ______________

PROBLEM 5B-3 (CONTINUED)

PALMER'S PLOWING
GENERAL JOURNAL

PAGE 1

Date		Account Titles and Description	PR	Dr.	Cr.

Name ____________ Class ____________ Date ____________

PROBLEM 5B-3 (CONTINUED)

PALMER'S PLOWING
GENERAL JOURNAL

PAGE 2

Date	Account Titles and Description	PR	Dr.	Cr.

Name ____________________ Class ____________________ Date ____________________

PROBLEM 5B-3 (CONTINUED)

PALMER'S PLOWING
GENERAL JOURNAL

PAGE 3

Date		Account Titles and Description	PR	Dr.	Cr.

Name ____________ Class ____________ Date ____________

PROBLEM 5B-3 (CONTINUED)

CASH **ACCOUNT NO. 111**

Date		Explanation	Post Ref.	Debit	Credit	Balance	
						Debit	Credit

ACCOUNTS RECEIVABLE **ACCOUNT NO. 112**

Date		Explanation	Post Ref.	Debit	Credit	Balance	
						Debit	Credit

PREPAID RENT **ACCOUNT NO. 114**

Date		Explanation	Post Ref.	Debit	Credit	Balance	
						Debit	Credit

SNOW SUPPLIES **ACCOUNT NO. 115**

Date		Explanation	Post Ref.	Debit	Credit	Balance	
						Debit	Credit

Name ______________________ Class ______________ Date ______________

PROBLEM 5B-3 (CONTINUED)

OFFICE EQUIPMENT ACCOUNT NO. 121

Date	Explanation	Post Ref.	Debit	Credit	Balance Debit	Balance Credit

ACCUMULATED DEPRECIATION, OFFICE EQUIPMENT ACCOUNT NO. 122

Date	Explanation	Post Ref.	Debit	Credit	Balance Debit	Balance Credit

SNOW EQUIPMENT ACCOUNT NO. 123

Date	Explanation	Post Ref.	Debit	Credit	Balance Debit	Balance Credit

ACCUMULATED DEPRECIATION, SNOW EQUIPMENT ACCOUNT NO. 124

Date	Explanation	Post Ref.	Debit	Credit	Balance Debit	Balance Credit

ACCOUNTS PAYABLE ACCOUNT NO. 211

Date	Explanation	Post Ref.	Debit	Credit	Balance Debit	Balance Credit

Name ______________________ Class ______________ Date ______________

PROBLEM 5B-3 (CONTINUED)

SALARIES PAYABLE **ACCOUNT NO. 212**

Date		Explanation	Post Ref.	Debit	Credit	Balance	
						Debit	Credit

P. MAO, CAPITAL **ACCOUNT NO. 311**

Date		Explanation	Post Ref.	Debit	Credit	Balance	
						Debit	Credit

P. MAO, WITHDRAWALS **ACCOUNT NO. 312**

Date		Explanation	Post Ref.	Debit	Credit	Balance	
						Debit	Credit

INCOME SUMMARY **ACCOUNT NO. 313**

Date		Explanation	Post Ref.	Debit	Credit	Balance	
						Debit	Credit

PLOWING FEES **ACCOUNT NO. 411**

Date		Explanation	Post Ref.	Debit	Credit	Balance	
						Debit	Credit

Name ____________________ Class ____________ Date ____________

PROBLEM 5B-3 (CONTINUED)

SALARIES EXPENSE **ACCOUNT NO. 511**

Date	Explanation	Post Ref.	Debit	Credit	Balance Debit	Balance Credit

ADVERTISING EXPENSE **ACCOUNT NO. 512**

Date	Explanation	Post Ref.	Debit	Credit	Balance Debit	Balance Credit

TELEPHONE EXPENSE **ACCOUNT NO. 513**

Date	Explanation	Post Ref.	Debit	Credit	Balance Debit	Balance Credit

RENT EXPENSE **ACCOUNT NO. 514**

Date	Explanation	Post Ref.	Debit	Credit	Balance Debit	Balance Credit

SNOW SUPPLIES EXPENSE **ACCOUNT NO. 515**

Date	Explanation	Post Ref.	Debit	Credit	Balance Debit	Balance Credit

Name ______________________ Class ______________ Date ______________

PROBLEM 5B-3 (CONTINUED)

DEPRECIATION EXPENSE, OFFICE EQUIPMENT **ACCOUNT NO. 516**

Date		Explanation	Post Ref.	Debit	Credit	Balance	
						Debit	Credit

DEPRECIATION EXPENSE, SNOW EQUIPMENT **ACCOUNT NO. 517**

Date		Explanation	Post Ref.	Debit	Credit	Balance	
						Debit	Credit

PROBLEM 5B-3 (CONTINUED)

PALMER'S PLOWING
INCOME STATEMENT
FOR MONTH ENDED JANUARY 31, 201X

PALMER'S PLOWING
STATEMENT OF OWNER'S EQUITY
FOR MONTH ENDED JANUARY 31, 201X

Name ______________________ Class ______________ Date ______________

PROBLEM 5B-3 (CONTINUED)

PALMER'S PLOWING
BALANCE SHEET
JANUARY 31, 201X

ASSETS

LIABILITIES AND OWNER'S EQUITY

Name ____________________ Class ____________________ Date ____________________

PROBLEM 5B-3 (CONCLUDED)

PALMER'S PLOWING
POST-CLOSING TRIAL BALANCE
JANUARY 31, 201X

	Dr.	Cr.

Name ______________________ Class ______________ Date ______________

ON THE JOB CONTINUING PROBLEM

ASSIGNMENTS 1, 3

SMITH COMPUTER CENTER
GENERAL JOURNAL

PAGE 2

Date		Account Titles and Description	PR	Dr.	Cr.

Name ______________ Class ______________ Date ______________

ASSIGNMENTS 2, 4

CASH **ACCOUNT NO. 1000**

Date		Explanation	Post Ref.	Debit	Credit	Balance Debit	Balance Credit
9/30	1X	Balance forward	✓			2 1 2 0 00	

ACCOUNTS RECEIVABLE **ACCOUNT NO. 1020**

Date		Explanation	Post Ref.	Debit	Credit	Balance Debit	Balance Credit
9/30	1X	Balance forward	✓			2 7 0 0 00	

PREPAID RENT **ACCOUNT NO. 1025**

Date		Explanation	Post Ref.	Debit	Credit	Balance Debit	Balance Credit
9/30	1X	Balance forward	✓			1 5 0 0 00	

SUPPLIES **ACCOUNT NO. 1030**

Date		Explanation	Post Ref.	Debit	Credit	Balance Debit	Balance Credit
9/30	1X	Balance forward	✓			5 0 0 00	

Name ______________ Class ______________ Date ______________

COMPUTER SHOP EQUIPMENT **ACCOUNT NO. 1080**

Date		Explanation	Post Ref.	Debit	Credit	Balance Debit	Balance Credit
9/30	1X	Balance forward	✓			3 9 0 0 00	

ACCUMULATED DEPRECIATION, COMPUTER SHOP EQUIPMENT **ACCOUNT NO. 1081**

Date		Explanation	Post Ref.	Debit	Credit	Balance Debit	Balance Credit

OFFICE EQUIPMENT **ACCOUNT NO. 1090**

Date		Explanation	Post Ref.	Debit	Credit	Balance Debit	Balance Credit
9/30	1X	Balance forward	✓			3 3 0 0 00	

ACCUMULATED DEPRECIATION, OFFICE EQUIPMENT **ACCOUNT NO. 1091**

Date		Explanation	Post Ref.	Debit	Credit	Balance Debit	Balance Credit

Name ________________ Class ________________ Date ________________

ACCOUNTS PAYABLE **ACCOUNT NO. 2000**

Date		Explanation	Post Ref.	Debit	Credit	Balance Debit	Balance Credit
9/30	1X	Balance forward	✓				1 7 0 00

T. FELDMAN, CAPITAL **ACCOUNT NO. 3000**

Date		Explanation	Post Ref.	Debit	Credit	Balance Debit	Balance Credit
9/30	1X	Balance forward	✓				6 0 0 0 00

T. FELDMAN, WITHDRAWALS **ACCOUNT NO. 3010**

Date		Explanation	Post Ref.	Debit	Credit	Balance Debit	Balance Credit
9/30	1X	Balance forward	✓			1 7 5 00	

Name ______________________ Class ______________ Date ______________

INCOME SUMMARY ACCOUNT NO. 3020

Date		Explanation	Post Ref.	Debit	Credit	Balance Debit	Balance Credit

SERVICE REVENUE ACCOUNT NO. 4000

Date		Explanation	Post Ref.	Debit	Credit	Balance Debit	Balance Credit
9/30	1X	Balance forward	✓				10 2 2 0 00

ADVERTISING EXPENSE ACCOUNT NO. 5010

Date		Explanation	Post Ref.	Debit	Credit	Balance Debit	Balance Credit
9/30	1X	Balance forward	✓			9 0 0 00	

RENT EXPENSE ACCOUNT NO. 5020

Date		Explanation	Post Ref.	Debit	Credit	Balance Debit	Balance Credit
9/30	1X	Balance forward	✓			5 0 0 00	

Name ______________________ Class ______________ Date ______________

UTILITIES EXPENSE **ACCOUNT NO. 5030**

Date		Explanation	Post Ref.	Debit	Credit	Balance Debit	Balance Credit
9/30	1X	Balance forward	✓			160 00	

PHONE EXPENSE **ACCOUNT NO. 5040**

Date		Explanation	Post Ref.	Debit	Credit	Balance Debit	Balance Credit
9/30	1X	Balance forward	✓			115 00	

SUPPLIES EXPENSE **ACCOUNT NO. 5050**

Date		Explanation	Post Ref.	Debit	Credit	Balance Debit	Balance Credit

INSURANCE EXPENSE **ACCOUNT NO. 5060**

Date		Explanation	Post Ref.	Debit	Credit	Balance Debit	Balance Credit
9/30	1X	Balance forward	✓			450 00	

Name ______________________ Class ______________ Date ______________

POSTAGE EXPENSE **ACCOUNT NO. 5070**

Date		Explanation	Post Ref.	Debit	Credit	Balance Debit	Balance Credit
9/30	1X	Balance forward	✓			7 0 00	

DEPRECIATION EXPENSE, C.S. EQUIPMENT **ACCOUNT NO. 5080**

Date		Explanation	Post Ref.	Debit	Credit	Balance Debit	Balance Credit

DEPRECIATION EXPENSE, OFFICE EQUIPMENT **ACCOUNT NO. 5090**

Date		Explanation	Post Ref.	Debit	Credit	Balance Debit	Balance Credit

Name ____________________ Class ____________ Date ____________

ASSIGNMENT 5

SMITH COMPUTER CENTER
POST-CLOSING TRIAL BALANCE
SEPTEMBER 30, 201X

	Dr.	Cr.

Name ______________________ Class ______________ Date ______________

MINI PRACTICE SET
SOUSA REALTY

(1)

SOUSA REALTY
GENERAL JOURNAL

PAGE 1

Date	Account Titles and Description	PR	Dr.	Cr.

Name ______________________ Class ______________ Date ______________

MINI PRACTICE SET
SOUSA REALTY

SOUSA REALTY
GENERAL JOURNAL

PAGE 2

Date		Account Titles and Description	PR	Dr.	Cr.

Name ______________ Class ______________ Date ______________

MINI PRACTICE SET
SOUSA REALTY

SOUSA REALTY
GENERAL JOURNAL

PAGE 3

Date	Account Titles and Description	PR	Dr.	Cr.

Name ______________________ Class ______________ Date ______________

MINI PRACTICE SET
SOUSA REALTY

SOUSA REALTY
GENERAL JOURNAL

PAGE 4

Date	Account Titles and Description	PR	Dr.	Cr.

Name ______________________ Class ______________ Date ______________

MINI PRACTICE SET
SOUSA REALTY

SOUSA REALTY
GENERAL JOURNAL

PAGE 5

Date		Account Titles and Description	PR	Dr.	Cr.

Name ______________________ Class ______________ Date ______________

MINI PRACTICE SET
SOUSA REALTY

SOUSA REALTY
GENERAL JOURNAL

PAGE 6

Date		Account Titles and Description	PR	Dr.	Cr.

Name ____________________ Class ____________ Date ____________

MINI PRACTICE SET
SOUSA REALTY

CASH **ACCOUNT NO. 111**

Date	Explanation	Post Ref.	Debit	Credit	Balance	
					Debit	Credit

Name ______________________ Class ______________ Date ______________

MINI PRACTICE SET
SOUSA REALTY

ACCOUNTS RECEIVABLE — ACCOUNT NO. 112

Date	Explanation	Post Ref.	Debit	Credit	Balance	
					Debit	Credit

PREPAID RENT — ACCOUNT NO. 114

Date	Explanation	Post Ref.	Debit	Credit	Balance	
					Debit	Credit

OFFICE SUPPLIES — ACCOUNT NO. 115

Date	Explanation	Post Ref.	Debit	Credit	Balance	
					Debit	Credit

OFFICE EQUIPMENT — ACCOUNT NO. 121

Date	Explanation	Post Ref.	Debit	Credit	Balance	
					Debit	Credit

Name ____________ Class ____________ Date ____________

MINI PRACTICE SET: SOUSA REALTY

ACCUMULATED DEPRECIATION, OFFICE EQUIPMENT — ACCOUNT NO. 122

Date	Explanation	Post Ref.	Debit	Credit	Balance Debit	Balance Credit

AUTOMOBILE — ACCOUNT NO. 123

Date	Explanation	Post Ref.	Debit	Credit	Balance Debit	Balance Credit

ACCUMULATED DEPRECIATION, AUTOMOBILE — ACCOUNT NO. 124

Date	Explanation	Post Ref.	Debit	Credit	Balance Debit	Balance Credit

ACCOUNTS PAYABLE — ACCOUNT NO. 211

Date	Explanation	Post Ref.	Debit	Credit	Balance Debit	Balance Credit

SALARIES PAYABLE — ACCOUNT NO. 212

Date	Explanation	Post Ref.	Debit	Credit	Balance Debit	Balance Credit

Name ______________________ Class ____________ Date ____________

MINI PRACTICE SET
SOUSA REALTY

JAMES SOUSA, CAPITAL **ACCOUNT NO. 311**

Date	Explanation	Post Ref.	Debit	Credit	Balance	
					Debit	Credit

JAMES SOUSA, WITHDRAWALS **ACCOUNT NO. 312**

Date	Explanation	Post Ref.	Debit	Credit	Balance	
					Debit	Credit

INCOME SUMMARY **ACCOUNT NO. 313**

Date	Explanation	Post Ref.	Debit	Credit	Balance	
					Debit	Credit

Name ____________________ Class ____________________ Date ____________________

MINI PRACTICE SET
SOUSA REALTY

COMMISSIONS EARNED **ACCOUNT NO. 411**

Date	Explanation	Post Ref.	Debit	Credit	Balance	
					Debit	Credit

RENT EXPENSE **ACCOUNT NO. 511**

Date	Explanation	Post Ref.	Debit	Credit	Balance	
					Debit	Credit

SALARIES EXPENSE **ACCOUNT NO. 512**

Date	Explanation	Post Ref.	Debit	Credit	Balance	
					Debit	Credit

Name ______________________ Class ______________ Date ______________

MINI PRACTICE SET
SOUSA REALTY

GAS EXPENSE — ACCOUNT NO. 513

Date		Explanation	Post Ref.	Debit	Credit	Balance Debit	Balance Credit

REPAIRS EXPENSE — ACCOUNT NO. 514

Date		Explanation	Post Ref.	Debit	Credit	Balance Debit	Balance Credit

TELEPHONE EXPENSE — ACCOUNT NO. 515

Date		Explanation	Post Ref.	Debit	Credit	Balance Debit	Balance Credit

ADVERTISING EXPENSE — ACCOUNT NO. 516

Date		Explanation	Post Ref.	Debit	Credit	Balance Debit	Balance Credit

Name ______________________ Class ______________________ Date ______________________

MINI PRACTICE SET
SOUSA REALTY

OFFICE SUPPLIES EXPENSE **ACCOUNT NO. 517**

Date	Explanation	Post Ref.	Debit	Credit	Balance Debit	Balance Credit

DEPRECIATION EXPENSE, OFFICE EQUIPMENT **ACCOUNT NO. 518**

Date	Explanation	Post Ref.	Debit	Credit	Balance Debit	Balance Credit

DEPRECIATION EXPENSE, AUTOMOBILE **ACCOUNT NO. 519**

Date	Explanation	Post Ref.	Debit	Credit	Balance Debit	Balance Credit

MISCELLANEOUS EXPENSE **ACCOUNT NO. 524**

Date	Explanation	Post Ref.	Debit	Credit	Balance Debit	Balance Credit

Name ______________________ Class ______________ Date ______________

MINI PRACTICE SET
SOUSA REALTY

(2) Use one of the blank fold-out worksheets that accompanied your textbook.

(3)

SOUSA REALTY
INCOME STATEMENT
FOR MONTH ENDED SEPTEMBER 30, 201X

Name ______________________ Class ______________ Date ______________

MINI PRACTICE SET
SOUSA REALTY

SOUSA REALTY
STATEMENT OF OWNER'S EQUITY
FOR MONTH ENDED SEPTEMBER 30, 201X

Name ______________________ Class ____________ Date ____________

MINI PRACTICE SET
SOUSA REALTY

SOUSA REALTY
BALANCE SHEET
SEPTEMBER 30, 201X

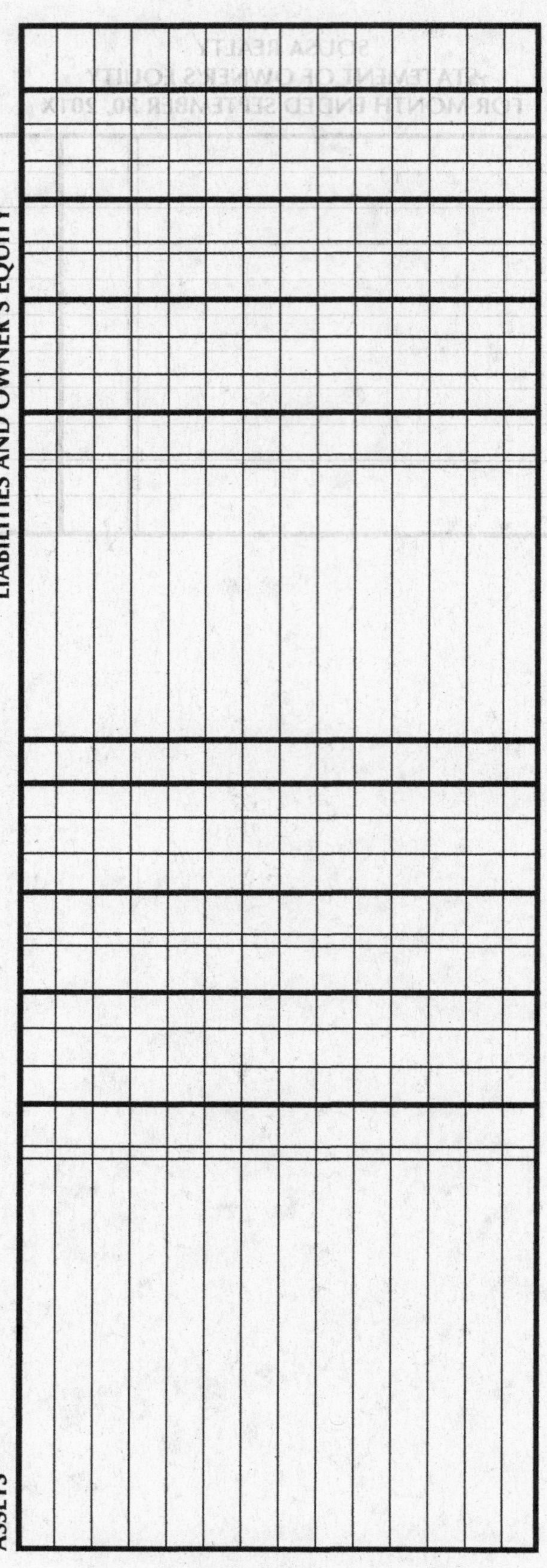

Name ____________________ Class ____________ Date ____________

MINI PRACTICE SET
SOUSA REALTY

(5)

SOUSA REALTY
POST-CLOSING TRIAL BALANCE
SEPTEMBER 30, 201X

	Dr.	Cr.

Name ______________________ Class ______________ Date ______________

MINI PRACTICE SET
SOUSA REALTY

(3)

SOUSA REALTY
INCOME STATEMENT
FOR MONTH ENDED OCTOBER 31, 201X

Name ____________________ Class ____________ Date ____________

MINI PRACTICE SET
SOUSA REALTY

SOUSA REALTY
STATEMENT OF OWNER'S EQUITY
FOR MONTH ENDED OCTOBER 31, 201X

Name ______________________ Class ______________ Date ______________

MINI PRACTICE SET
SOUSA REALTY

SOUSA REALTY
BALANCE SHEET
OCTOBER 31, 201X

ASSETS

LIABILITIES AND OWNER'S EQUITY

Name ______________________ Class ______________ Date ______________

MINI PRACTICE SET
SOUSA REALTY

(5)

SOUSA REALTY
POST-CLOSING TRIAL BALANCE
OCTOBER 31, 201X

	Dr.	Cr.

Name ______________________ Class ______________ Date ______________

CHAPTER 5
SUMMARY PRACTICE TEST:
THE ACCOUNTING CYCLE COMPLETED

Part I

Fill in the blank(s) to complete the statement.

1. After the closing process only ______________ accounts remain with balances.
2. Revenue, Expenses, and Withdrawals are examples of ______________ ______________.
3. ______________ in temporary accounts will not be carried over to the next accounting period.
4. After closing entries are posted, owner's Capital in the ledger will contain the ______________ ______________.
5. Revenue is closed to Income Summary by a(n) ______________ to each revenue account and a(n) ______________ to Income Summary.
6. Expenses are closed to Income Summary by ______________ the individual expenses and ______________ Income Summary.
7. If the balance of Income Summary is a credit, it will be closed by ______________ Income Summary and ______________ owner's Capital.
8. The balance of Withdrawals is closed by a(n) ______________ and the amount transferred to owner's Capital by a(n) ______________.
9. At the end of the closing process, all temporary accounts in the ledger will have a(n) ______________ balance.
10. The ______________ ______________ ______________ ______________ contains a list of permanent accounts after the adjusting and closing entries have been posted to the ledger from a journal.
11. Closing entries can be prepared from a(n) ______________.
12. After closing entries are posted, Income Summary will have a(n) ______________ balance.
13. Journalizing adjustments can be done from the ______________.
14. Cash, Equipment, and Supplies are not part of the ______________ process.
15. Income Summary is a(n) ______________ account.

Part II

The following is a chart of accounts for Al's Auto Shop. From the chart, indicate in Column B (by account number) which accounts will be debited or credited as related to the transactions in Column A.

Name ______________________ Class ______________ Date ______________

CHART OF ACCOUNTS

ASSETS
112 Cash
114 Accounts Receivable
116 Prepaid Rent
118 Auto Supplies
120 Delivery Truck
121 Accumulated Depreciation, Delivery Truck

LIABILITIES
230 Accounts Payable
232 Salaries Payable

OWNER'S EQUITY
340 A. Jones, Capital
341 A. Jones, Withdrawals
342 Income Summary

REVENUE
450 Fees Earned

EXPENSES
560 Salaries Expense
562 Advertising Expense
564 Rent Expense
566 Auto Supplies Expense
568 Depreciation Expense, Delivery Truck

COLUMN A	COLUMN B Debit(s)	Credit(s)
1. Closed balance in revenue account to Income Summary.	________	________
2. Closed balances in individual expenses to Income Summary.	________	________
3. Closed balance in Income Summary to owner's Capital. (Assume that it is a net income.)	________	________
4. Closed Withdrawals to owner's Capital.	________	________
5. Recorded auto supplies used up.	________	________
6. Recorded depreciation on delivery truck.	________	________
7. Brought Salaries Expense up to date (an adjustment).	________	________

Part III

Answer true or false to the following statements.

1. Closing entries are done every other month.
2. Adjustments are journalized before preparing the worksheet.
3. Closing entries can only clear permanent accounts.
4. Income summary is a temporary account.
5. Interim statements can be prepared from worksheets.
6. To close expenses in the closing process, a compound entry is appropriate.
7. Withdrawals is a temporary account on the income statement.
8. Income Summary helps update withdrawals.

Name ______________ Class ______________ Date ______________

9. Accumulated Depreciation is a permanent account on the income statement.
10. Cash, Rent Expense, and Accounts Receivable need to be closed at the end of the period.
11. Closing entries do not relate to the worksheet.
12. Revenue is closed by a credit.
13. Expenses are placed on the debit side of the Income Summary account.
14. A post-closing trial balance closely resembles the ending balance sheet.
15. Accumulated Depreciation never has to be adjusted.
16. Interim statements are always prepared monthly.
17. A post-closing trial balance is prepared before adjustments are journalized.
18. Income Summary is shown on the balance sheet.
19. The process of closing entries will help update owner's Capital.
20. The normal balance of the Income Summary is a debit.
21. The normal balance of the Income Summary is a credit.
22. The income statement is listed in terms of debits and credits.
23. Closing updates only permanent accounts.
24. After the closing process, the balance in Service Revenue is zero.
25. Withdrawals is closed to Income Summary.

SOLUTIONS

Part I

1. permanent
2. temporary accounts
3. Balances
4. ending figure (balance)
5. debit, credit
6. crediting, debiting
7. debiting, crediting
8. credit, debit
9. zero
10. post-closing trial balance
11. worksheet
12. zero
13. worksheet
14. closing
15. temporary

Part II

	Debit	Credit
1.	450	342
2.	342	560, 562, 564, 566, 568
3.	342	340
4.	340	341
5.	566	118
6.	568	121
7.	560	232

Name ______________________ Class ______________ Date ______________

Part III

1. false
2. false
3. false
4. true
5. true
6. true
7. false
8. false
9. false
10. false
11. false
12. false
13. true
14. true
15. false
16. false
17. false
18. false
19. true
20. false
21. false
22. false
23. false
24. true
25. false

Study Guide and Working Papers

Banking Procedures and Control of Cash

Name ______________________ Class ______________ Date ______________

FORMS FOR DEMONSTRATION PROBLEM

(1)

LEE CO.
BANK RECONCILIATION AS OF MARCH 31, 201X

Checkbook Balance		Bank Balance	
Add:		Add:	
Deduct:		Deduct:	
Reconciled Bal.		Reconciled Bal.	

(2)

Date		Account Titles and Description	PR	Dr.	Cr.

Name ______________________ Class ______________ Date ______________

FORMS FOR SET A EXERCISES

6A-1

BANG CO.
BANK RECONCILIATION AS OF FEBRUARY 28, 201X

CHECKBOOK BALANCE		BALANCE PER BANK	
Ending Checkbook Balance		Ending Bank Statement Balance	
Add:		Add:	
Deduct:		Deduct:	
Reconciled Balance		Reconciled Balance	

Date	Account	Dr.	Cr.

6A-2

Date	Account	Dr.	Cr.

6A-3

Date	Account	Dr.	Cr.

Name ______________________ Class ____________ Date ______________

SET A EXERCISES

6A-4

Date		Account	Dr.	Cr.

6A-5

Beg. Change Fund
+Cash Register Total
=Cash should have on hand
–Counted Cash
= Cash Shortage

Date		Account	Dr.	Cr.

Name ______________________ Class ______________ Date ______________

FORMS FOR SET B EXERCISES

6B-1

ZOOM CO.
BANK RECONCILIATION AS OF OCTOBER 31, 201X

CHECKBOOK BALANCE		BALANCE PER BANK	
Ending Checkbook Balance		Ending Bank Statement Balance	
Add:		Add:	
Deduct:		Deduct:	
Reconciled Balance		Reconciled Balance	

Date		Account	Dr.	Cr.

6B-2

Date		Account	Dr.	Cr.

6B-3

Date		Account	Dr.	Cr.

Name ______________________ Class ______________ Date ______________

SET B EXERCISES

6B-4

Date		Account	Dr.	Cr.

6B-5

Beg. Change Fund
+Cash Register Total
=Cash should have on hand
–Counted Cash
= Cash Shortage

Date		Account	Dr.	Cr.

Name ______________ Class ______________ Date ______________

FORMS FOR SET A PROBLEMS

PROBLEM 6A-1

DENIM.COM
BANK RECONCILIATION AS OF JULY 31, 201X

CHECKBOOK BALANCE		BALANCE PER BANK	
Checkbook Balance		Bank Statement Balance	
Add:		Add:	
		Deduct:	
Deduct:			
Reconciled Balance		Reconciled Balance	

Name ____________________ Class ____________ Date ________________

PROBLEM 6A-1 (CONCLUDED)

Date	Account Titles and Description	PR	Dr.	Cr.

Name ____________________ Class ____________ Date ____________

PROBLEM 6A-2

JOSH'S DELI
BANK RECONCILIATION AS OF FEBRUARY 28, 201X

CHECKBOOK BALANCE		**BALANCE PER BANK**	
Checkbook Balance		Bank Statement Balance	
Add:		Add:	
		Deduct:	
Deduct:			
Reconciled Balance		Reconciled Balance	

Name ______________________ Class ______________ Date ______________

PROBLEM 6A-2 (CONCLUDED)

(2)

GENERAL JOURNAL

Date		Account Titles and Description	PR	Dr.	Cr.

Name ______________________ Class ______________ Date ______________

PROBLEM 6A-3

(a, b)

EXULTANT CO.
GENERAL JOURNAL

Date	Account Titles and Description	PR	Dr.	Cr.

Name ______________________ Class ______________ Date ______________

PROBLEM 6A-3 (CONCLUDED)

EXULTANT CO.
AUXILIARY PETTY CASH RECORD

Date	Voucher No.	Description	Receipts	Payment	Category of Payment			
					Postage Expense	Office Supplies Expense	Sundry	
							Account	Amount

Name ______________________ Class ______________ Date ______________

PROBLEM 6A-4

ROCHESTER CO.
GENERAL JOURNAL

PAGE 2

Date		Account Titles and Description	PR	Dr.	Cr.

Name ______________________ Class ______________ Date ______________

PROBLEM 6A-4 (CONCLUDED)

ROCHESTER CO.
AUXILIARY PETTY CASH RECORD

Date	Voucher No.	Description	Receipts	Payment	Category of Payment			
					Postage Expense	Delivery Expense	Sundry	
							Account	Amount

Name ______________________ Class ______________ Date ______________

FORMS FOR SET B PROBLEMS

PROBLEM 6B-1

WORK.COM
BANK RECONCILIATION AS OF JULY 31, 201X

CHECKBOOK BALANCE		**BALANCE PER BANK**	
Checkbook Balance		Bank Statement Balance	
Add:		Add:	
		Deduct:	
Deduct:			
Reconciled Balance		Reconciled Balance	

Name ____________________ Class ____________________ Date ____________________

PROBLEM 6B-1 (CONCLUDED)

Date		Account Titles and Description	PR	Dr.	Cr.

Name ______________________ Class ______________ Date ______________

PROBLEM 6B-2

JACKIE'S DELI
BANK RECONCILIATION AS OF FEBRUARY 28, 201X

CHECKBOOK BALANCE		**BALANCE PER BANK**	
Checkbook Balance		Bank Statement Balance	
Add:		Add:	
	______	Deduct:	______
Deduct:			
	______		______
Reconciled Balance	______	Reconciled Balance	______

Name ____________ Class ____________ Date ____________

PROBLEM 6B-2 (CONCLUDED)

(2)

GENERAL JOURNAL

Date		Account Titles and Description	PR	Dr.	Cr.

Name ______________________ Class ______________ Date ______________

PROBLEM 6B-3

(a, b)

JOLLY CO.
GENERAL JOURNAL

Date	Account Titles and Description	PR	Dr.	Cr.

Name ______________________ Class ______________ Date ______________

PROBLEM 6B-3 (CONCLUDED)

JOLLY CO.
AUXILIARY PETTY CASH RECORD

Date	Voucher No.	Description	Receipts	Payment	Category of Payment			
					Postage Expense	Office Supplies Expense	Sundry	
							Account	Amount

Name ________________ Class ________________ Date ________________

PROBLEM 6B-4

KONA CO.
GENERAL JOURNAL

PAGE 2

Date		Account Titles and Description	PR	Dr.	Cr.

Name ______________________ Class ______________ Date ______________

PROBLEM 6B-4 (CONCLUDED)

KONA CO.
AUXILIARY PETTY CASH RECORD

Date	Voucher No.	Description	Receipts	Payment	Category of Payment			
					Postage Expense	Delivery Expense	Sundry	
							Account	Amount

Name ____________________ Class ____________________ Date ____________________

ON THE JOB CONTINUING PROBLEM

ASSIGNMENT 1

SMITH COMPUTER CENTER
GENERAL JOURNAL

PAGE 3

Date		Account Titles and Description	PR	Dr.	Cr.

Name ______________ Class ______________ Date ______________

AUXILIARY PETTY CASH RECORD

Date	Voucher No.	Description	Receipts	Payment	Category of Payment			
					Postage Expense	Supplies Expense	Sundry	
							Account	Amount

Name ______________ Class ______________ Date ______________

ASSIGNMENT 2

CASH — **ACCOUNT NO. 1000**

Date		Explanation	Post Ref.	Debit	Credit	Balance Debit	Balance Credit
9/30	1X	Balance forward	✓			2 120 00	

PETTY CASH — **ACCOUNT NO. 1010**

Date		Explanation	Post Ref.	Debit	Credit	Balance Debit	Balance Credit

Name ____________________ Class ____________ Date ____________

ACCOUNTS RECEIVABLE ACCOUNT NO. 1020

Date		Explanation	Post Ref.	Debit	Credit	Balance Debit	Balance Credit
9/30	1X	Balance forward	✓			2 7 0 0 00	

PREPAID RENT ACCOUNT NO. 1025

Date		Explanation	Post Ref.	Debit	Credit	Balance Debit	Balance Credit
9/30	1X	Balance forward	✓			5 0 0 00	

SUPPLIES ACCOUNT NO. 1030

Date		Explanation	Post Ref.	Debit	Credit	Balance Debit	Balance Credit
9/30	1X	Balance forward	✓			1 9 2 00	

COMPUTER SHOP EQUIPMENT ACCOUNT NO. 1080

Date		Explanation	Post Ref.	Debit	Credit	Balance Debit	Balance Credit
9/30	1X	Balance forward	✓			3 9 0 0 00	

Name ______________________ Class ______________ Date ______________

ACCUMULATED DEPRECIATION, COMPUTER SHOP EQUIPMENT **ACCOUNT NO. 1081**

Date		Explanation	Post Ref.	Debit	Credit	Balance Debit	Balance Credit
9/30	1X	Balance forward	✓				1 5 0 00

OFFICE EQUIPMENT **ACCOUNT NO. 1090**

Date		Explanation	Post Ref.	Debit	Credit	Balance Debit	Balance Credit
9/30	1X	Balance forward	✓			3 3 0 0 00	

ACCUMULATED DEPRECIATION, OFFICE EQUIPMENT **ACCOUNT NO. 1091**

Date		Explanation	Post Ref.	Debit	Credit	Balance Debit	Balance Credit
9/30	1X	Balance forward	✓				1 1 0 00

ACCOUNTS PAYABLE **ACCOUNT NO. 2000**

Date		Explanation	Post Ref.	Debit	Credit	Balance Debit	Balance Credit
9/30	1X	Balance forward	✓				1 7 0 00

Name ________________ Class ________________ Date ________________

T. FELDMAN, CAPITAL ACCOUNT NO. 3000

Date		Explanation	Post Ref.	Debit	Credit	Balance Debit	Balance Credit
9/30	1X	Balance forward	✓				12 282 00

T. FELDMAN, WITHDRAWALS ACCOUNT NO. 3010

Date		Explanation	Post Ref.	Debit	Credit	Balance Debit	Balance Credit

INCOME SUMMARY ACCOUNT NO. 3020

Date		Explanation	Post Ref.	Debit	Credit	Balance Debit	Balance Credit

Name ______________ Class ______________ Date ______________

SERVICE REVENUE **ACCOUNT NO. 4000**

Date		Explanation	Post Ref.	Debit	Credit	Balance Debit	Balance Credit

ADVERTISING EXPENSE **ACCOUNT NO. 5010**

Date		Explanation	Post Ref.	Debit	Credit	Balance Debit	Balance Credit

RENT EXPENSE **ACCOUNT NO. 5020**

Date		Explanation	Post Ref.	Debit	Credit	Balance Debit	Balance Credit

Name ______________ Class ______________ Date ______________

UTILITIES EXPENSE **ACCOUNT NO. 5030**

Date	Explanation	Post Ref.	Debit	Credit	Balance	
					Debit	Credit

PHONE EXPENSE **ACCOUNT NO. 5040**

Date	Explanation	Post Ref.	Debit	Credit	Balance	
					Debit	Credit

SUPPLIES EXPENSE **ACCOUNT NO. 5050**

Date	Explanation	Post Ref.	Debit	Credit	Balance	
					Debit	Credit

INSURANCE EXPENSE **ACCOUNT NO. 5060**

Date	Explanation	Post Ref.	Debit	Credit	Balance	
					Debit	Credit

Name ____________________ Class ____________ Date ____________

POSTAGE EXPENSE — ACCOUNT NO. 5070

Date	Explanation	Post Ref.	Debit	Credit	Balance Debit	Balance Credit

DEPRECIATION EXPENSE, COMPUTER SHOP EQUIPMENT — ACCOUNT NO. 5080

Date	Explanation	Post Ref.	Debit	Credit	Balance Debit	Balance Credit

DEPRECIATION EXPENSE, OFFICE EQUIPMENT — ACCOUNT NO. 5090

Date	Explanation	Post Ref.	Debit	Credit	Balance Debit	Balance Credit

MISCELLANEOUS EXPENSE — ACCOUNT NO. 5100

Date	Explanation	Post Ref.	Debit	Credit	Balance Debit	Balance Credit

Name ____________________ Class ____________ Date ____________

ASSIGNMENT 3

SMITH COMPUTER CENTER
TRIAL BALANCE
OCTOBER 31, 201X

Name ______________________ Class ______________ Date ______________

ASSIGNMENT 4

SMITH COMPUTER CENTER
BANK RECONCILIATION AS OF SEPTEMBER 30, 201X

CHECKBOOK BALANCE		**BALANCE PER BANK**	
Checkbook Balance		Bank Statement Balance	
Add:		Add:	
		Deduct:	
Deduct:			
Reconciled Balance		Reconciled Balance	

Name ______________________ Class ______________ Date ______________

CHAPTER 6
SUMMARY PRACTICE TEST
BANKING PROCEDURES AND CONTROL OF CASH

Part I

Fill in the blank(s) to complete the statement.

1. Online banking is ______________ due to the internet.
2. Today, use of the ______________ ______________ has greatly increased.
3. All adjustments to the checkbook balance in the reconciliation process will require ______________ ______________.
4. Petty cash is a(n) ______________ found on the balance sheet.
5. The auxiliary petty cash record is not a(n) ______________.
6. A(n) ______________ ______________ is an asset used to make change for customer.
7. A cash overage will be ______________ ______________ on the income statement.
8. ______________ ______________ represents checks not processed by the bank at the time the bank statement was prepared.
9. When a bank credits your account, your balance will ______________.
10. ______________ is a procedure whereby the bank does not return the processed checks.

Part II

Indicate which of the following procedures are involved in each of the transactions below.

a. Recorded in General Journal
b. Recorded in both general journal and auxiliary petty cash record
c. Recorded only in auxiliary petty cash record
d. New check is written
e. Account petty cash is increased

1. EXAMPLE: Check issued to establish petty cash b,d,e
2. Paid donation from petty cash ______
3. Paid postage from petty cash ______
4. Paid past purchases previously charged ______
5. Paid for business luncheon with petty cash ______
6. Issued check to pay for office supplies ______
7. Replenished petty cash ______
8. Paid local donation from petty cash ______
9. Paid for past purchases bought on account ______
10. Replenished petty cash ______

Name ____________________ Class ____________ Date ____________

Part III

Answer true or false to the following statements.

1. Online banking is decreasing today.
2. Petty cash is a liability found on the balance sheet.
3. Checks returned from the bank are placed in alphabetical order.
4. ATMs are being used less today than in the past.
5. Bank service charges represent an expense to the business.
6. The bank statement is the same as the bank reconciliation.
7. The balance in the company cash account will always equal the bank balance before the bank statement is received.
8. Deposit slips are needed in writing checks.
9. A bank uses the signature card when cashing a check.
10. The auxiliary petty cash record is posted monthly.
11. The petty cash account has a debit balance.
12. Replenishment of petty cash requires a new check.
13. The expenses paid from petty cash are journalized at time of replenishment.
14. Internal control only affects large companies.
15. A petty cash voucher records the expense into the ledger.
16. The petty cash fund must be replenished monthly.
17. The petty cash voucher identifies the account that will be charged.
18. The establishment of petty cash may require some judgment as to the amount of petty cash needed.
19. EFT is the same as safekeeping.
20. The drawer is the person who receives the check.
21. A debit memo issued by a bank will increase the depositor's balance.
22. A change fund uses only one denomination.
23. The payer is the person or company the check is payable to.

Part IV

Based on the following situation, prepare a bank reconciliation.

The checkbook balance of Miller Company is $5,263.08. The bank statement shows a bank balance of $7,980. The bank statement shows interest earned of $42 and a service charge of $29.76. There is a deposit in transit of $2,558.22. Outstanding checks total $3,762.90. The bank collected a note for Miller for $4,200. Miller Company forgot to deduct a check for $2,700 during the month.

Name ________________ Class ________________ Date ________________

SOLUTIONS

Part I

1. increasing
2. debit card
3. journal entries
4. asset
5. journal
6. change fund
7. miscellaneous income
8. Checks outstanding
9. increase
10. Truncation

Part II

1. b, d, e
2. c
3. c
4. a, d
5. c
6. a, d
7. b, d
8. c
9. a, d
10. b, d

Part III

1. false
2. false
3. false
4. false
5. true
6. false
7. false
8. false
9. true
10. false
11. true
12. true
13. true
14. false
15. false
16. false
17. true
18. true
19. false
20. false
21. false
22. false
23. false

Part IV

MILLER COMPANY
BANK RECONCILIATION

Checkbook Balance		$5,263.08	Bank Balance	$7,980.00
ADD:			ADD:	
			Deposit	
Interest	$ 42		in Transit	2,558.22
Collection of note	4,200	4,242.00		$10,538.22
		9,505.08		
DEDUCT:			DEDUCT:	
Service Chg.	$ 29.76		Check outstanding	$3,762.90
Error	2,700.00	2,729.76		
Reconciled Balance		$6,775.32	Reconciled Balance	$6,775.32

Study Guide and Working Papers

Calculating Pay and Recording Payroll Taxes: The Beginning of the Payroll Process

Name ______________________ Class ______________ Date ______________

FORMS FOR DEMONSTRATION PROBLEM

REQUIREMENT 1

Use fold-out worksheet for Chapter 7 Demonstration Problem

REQUIREMENTS 2 AND 3

DAVIDSON COMPANY
GENERAL JOURNAL

PAGE 1

Date		Account Titles and Description	PR	Dr.	Cr.

Name ______________________ Class ______________ Date ______________

FORMS FOR SET A EXERCISES

7A-1

Total Wages

a. Paula Anderson ______________________
Olivia Turner ______________________
____
Kellen Gates ______________________
____

Biweekly Earnings

b. John Smith ______________________
Jane Doe ______________________

7A-2

Xu Daoning	William Pierce
Gross Pay $1,650	Gross Pay $1,630
OASDI:	OASDI:
Medicare:	Medicare:
FIT:	FIT:
Net Pay	Net Pay

7A-3

Employee	FICA–OASDI	FICA–Medicare	FUTA Tax	SUTA Tax
O. Barns				
C. Hart				
Q. Roberts				
Total				

7A-4

Employee	FICA–OASDI	FICA–Medicare	FUTA Tax	SUTA Tax
O. Barns				
C. Hart				
Q. Roberts				
Total				

Name ____________ Class ____________ Date ____________

SET A EXERCISES

7A-5

Employee	FICA–OASDI	FICA–Medicare	FUTA Tax	SUTA Tax
O. Barns				
C. Hart				
Q. Roberts				
Total				

7A-6

Date	Account	Debit	Credit

7A-7

Employee	Weekly Pay	Weeks	Total	FUTA Taxable Earnings	FUTA Tax Rate	FUTA Tax
W. Duncan	$690					
S. Ivan	780					
V. North	560					
H. Young	430					
Total						

7A-8

Name ____________________ Class ____________ Date ____________

FORMS FOR SET B EXERCISES

7B-1

Total Wages | Biweekly Earnings

a. Marie Norris ____________
Heidi Rodes ____________
____
Norman Duncan ____________
____

b. George Day ____________
Min Lee ____________

7B-2

Alvin Pang	David Parker
Gross Pay $1,680	Gross Pay $1,600
OASDI:	OASDI:
Medicare:	Medicare:
FIT:	FIT:
Net Pay	Net Pay

7B-3

Employee	FICA–OASDI	FICA–Medicare	FUTA Tax	SUTA Tax
I. Benson				
K. Larry				
Q. Roberts				
Total				

7B-4

Employee	FICA–OASDI	FICA–Medicare	FUTA Tax	SUTA Tax
I. Benson				
K. Larry				
Q. Roberts				
Total				

Name ______________________ Class ____________ Date ______________

SET B EXERCISES

7B-5

Employee	FICA–OASDI	FICA–Medicare	FUTA Tax	SUTA Tax
I. Benson				
K. Larry				
Q. Roberts				
Total				

7B-6

Date	Account	Debit	Credit

7B-7

Employee	Weekly Pay	Weeks	Total	FUTA Taxable Earnings	FUTA Tax Rate	FUTA Tax
O. Barn	$650					
Z. Grande	790					
J. Mathison	580					
E. Walsh	460					
Total						

7B-8

Name ____________________ Class ____________ Date ____________

FORMS FOR SET A PROBLEMS

PROBLEM 7A-1

Employee	Number of Hours Worked	Number of Regular Hours	Hourly Rate	Total Regular Earnings	Overtime Hours	Overtime Rate	Total Overtime Earnings
Jade Martina							
Lauren McBride							
Natala Polino							
Dmitri Wittman							

	Gross Earnings
Jade Martina	
Lauren McBride	
Natala Polino	
Dmitri Wittman	

PROBLEM 7A-2

Use the fold-out payroll register for Problem 7A-2 that accompanied your textbook.

PROBLEM 7A-3

Use the fold-out payroll register for Problem 7A-3 that accompanied your textbook.

PROBLEM 7A-4

REQUIREMENT 1

Use the fold-out payroll register for Problem 7A-4 that accompanied your textbook.

REQUIREMENT 2

Employee	FICA–OASDI	FICA–Medicare	FUTA Tax	SUTA Tax
Avery, Joanna				
Garth, Natashia				
Martinez, Joan				
Seward, Peter				
Total				

Name ____________________ Class ______________ Date ______________

PROBLEM 7A-4 (CONCLUDED)

REQUIREMENT 3

GENERAL JOURNAL

Date		Account Titles and Description	PR	Dr.	Cr.

Name ____________________ Class ____________ Date ____________

FORMS FOR SET B PROBLEMS

PROBLEM 7B-1

Employee	Number of Hours Worked	Number of Regular Hours	Hourly Rate	Total Regular Earnings	Overtime Hours	Overtime Rate	Total Overtime Earnings
Jag Valleria							
Lara Harrison							
Natalie Whittier							
Dmitri Jacobson							

	Gross Earnings
Jag Valleria	
Lara Harrison	
Natalie Whittier	
Dmitri Jacobson	

PROBLEM 7B-2

Use the fold-out payroll register for Problem 7B-2 that accompanied your textbook.

PROBLEM 7B-3

Use the fold-out payroll register for Problem 7B-3 that accompanied your textbook.

PROBLEM 7B-4

REQUIREMENT 1

Use the fold-out payroll register for Problem 7B-4 that accompanied your textbook.

REQUIREMENT 2

Employee	FICA–OASDI	FICA–Medicare	FUTA Tax	SUTA Tax
Ackery, John				
Geary, Nicki				
Martin, Jeff				
Sherard, Paul				
Total				

Name ____________ Class ____________ Date ____________

PROBLEM 7B-4 (CONCLUDED)

REQUIREMENT 3

GENERAL JOURNAL

Date	Account Titles and Description	PR	Dr.	Cr.

Name ____________________ Class ____________________ Date ____________________

ON THE JOB CONTINUING PROBLEM

ASSIGNMENT 1

SMITH COMPUTER CENTER
GENERAL JOURNAL

PAGE 4

Date	Account Titles and Description	PR	Dr.	Cr.

Name ______________________ Class ______________ Date ______________

SMITH COMPUTER CENTER
GENERAL JOURNAL

PAGE 5

Date		Account Titles and Description	PR	Dr.	Cr.

Name ______________________ Class ____________ Date ____________

CASH — ACCOUNT NO. 1000

Date		Explanation	Post Ref.	Debit	Credit	Balance Debit	Balance Credit
10/31	1X	Balance forward	✓			6,485.00	

PETTY CASH — ACCOUNT NO. 1010

Date		Explanation	Post Ref.	Debit	Credit	Balance Debit	Balance Credit
10/31	1X	Balance forward	✓			300.00	

ACCOUNTS RECEIVABLE — ACCOUNT NO. 1020

Date		Explanation	Post Ref.	Debit	Credit	Balance Debit	Balance Credit
10/31	1X	Balance forward	✓			5,400.00	

Name ______________________ Class ______________ Date ______________

PREPAID RENT **ACCOUNT NO. 1025**

Date		Explanation	Post Ref.	Debit	Credit	Balance Debit	Balance Credit
10/31	1X	Balance forward	✓			2 0 0 0 00	

SUPPLIES **ACCOUNT NO. 1030**

Date		Explanation	Post Ref.	Debit	Credit	Balance Debit	Balance Credit
10/31	1X	Balance forward	✓			1 9 2 00	

COMPUTER SHOP EQUIPMENT **ACCOUNT NO. 1080**

Date		Explanation	Post Ref.	Debit	Credit	Balance Debit	Balance Credit
10/31	1X	Balance forward	✓			3 9 0 0 00	

ACCUMULATED DEPRECIATION, COMPUTER SHOP EQUIPMENT **ACCOUNT NO. 1081**

Date		Explanation	Post Ref.	Debit	Credit	Balance Debit	Balance Credit
10/31	1X	Balance forward	✓				1 5 0 00

Name ____________ Class ____________ Date ____________

OFFICE EQUIPMENT ACCOUNT NO. 1090

Date		Explanation	Post Ref.	Debit	Credit	Balance Debit	Balance Credit
10/31	1X	Balance forward	✓			3 3 0 0 00	

ACCUMULATED DEPRECIATION, OFFICE EQUIPMENT ACCOUNT NO. 1091

Date		Explanation	Post Ref.	Debit	Credit	Balance Debit	Balance Credit
10/31	1X	Balance forward	✓				1 1 0 00

ACCOUNTS PAYABLE ACCOUNT NO. 2000

Date		Explanation	Post Ref.	Debit	Credit	Balance Debit	Balance Credit
10/31	1X	Balance forward	✓				5 0 00

WAGES PAYABLE ACCOUNT NO. 2010

Date		Explanation	Post Ref.	Debit	Credit	Balance Debit	Balance Credit

Name ______________________ Class ______________ Date ______________

FICA—OASDI PAYABLE ACCOUNT NO. 2020

Date		Explanation	Post Ref.	Debit	Credit	Balance	
						Debit	Credit

FICA—MEDICARE PAYABLE ACCOUNT NO. 2030

Date		Explanation	Post Ref.	Debit	Credit	Balance	
						Debit	Credit

FIT PAYABLE ACCOUNT NO. 2040

Date		Explanation	Post Ref.	Debit	Credit	Balance	
						Debit	Credit

SIT PAYABLE ACCOUNT NO. 2050

Date		Explanation	Post Ref.	Debit	Credit	Balance	
						Debit	Credit

Name ______________________ Class ______________ Date ______________

T. FELDMAN, CAPITAL ACCOUNT NO. 3000

Date		Explanation	Post Ref.	Debit	Credit	Balance Debit	Balance Credit
10/31	1X	Balance forward	✓				12 2 8 2 00

T. FELDMAN, WITHDRAWALS ACCOUNT NO. 3010

Date		Explanation	Post Ref.	Debit	Credit	Balance Debit	Balance Credit
10/31	1X	Balance forward	✓			9 1 5 00	

SERVICE REVENUE ACCOUNT NO. 4000

Date		Explanation	Post Ref.	Debit	Credit	Balance Debit	Balance Credit
10/31	1X	Balance forward	✓				10 0 0 0 00

ADVERTISING EXPENSE ACCOUNT NO. 5010

Date		Explanation	Post Ref.	Debit	Credit	Balance Debit	Balance Credit

RENT EXPENSE ACCOUNT NO. 5020

Date		Explanation	Post Ref.	Debit	Credit	Balance Debit	Balance Credit

Name ____________ Class ____________ Date ____________

UTILITIES EXPENSE **ACCOUNT NO. 5030**

Date		Explanation	Post Ref.	Debit	Credit	Balance Debit	Balance Credit

PHONE EXPENSE **ACCOUNT NO. 5040**

Date		Explanation	Post Ref.	Debit	Credit	Balance Debit	Balance Credit

SUPPLIES EXPENSE **ACCOUNT NO. 5050**

Date		Explanation	Post Ref.	Debit	Credit	Balance Debit	Balance Credit
10/31	1X	Balance forward	✓			45 00	

INSURANCE EXPENSE **ACCOUNT NO. 5060**

Date		Explanation	Post Ref.	Debit	Credit	Balance Debit	Balance Credit

POSTAGE EXPENSE **ACCOUNT NO. 5070**

Date		Explanation	Post Ref.	Debit	Credit	Balance Debit	Balance Credit
10/31	1X	Balance forward	✓			40 00	

Name ______________________ Class ______________ Date ______________

DEPRECIATION EXPENSE C. S. EQUIPMENT ACCOUNT NO. 5080

Date		Explanation	Post Ref.	Debit	Credit	Balance Debit	Balance Credit

DEPRECIATION EXPENSE OFFICE EQUIPMENT ACCOUNT NO. 5090

Date		Explanation	Post Ref.	Debit	Credit	Balance Debit	Balance Credit

MISCELLANEOUS EXPENSE ACCOUNT NO. 5100

Date		Explanation	Post Ref.	Debit	Credit	Balance Debit	Balance Credit
10/31	1X	Balance forward	✓			15 00	

WAGES EXPENSE ACCOUNT NO. 5110

Date		Explanation	Post Ref.	Debit	Credit	Balance Debit	Balance Credit

Name ______________________ Class ______________ Date ______________

ASSIGNMENT 2

SMITH COMPUTER CENTER
TRIAL BALANCE
NOVEMBER 30, 201X

	Dr.	Cr.

Name ______________________________ Class ________________ Date ________________

CHAPTER 7
SUMMARY PRACTICE TEST:
CALCULATING PAY AND RECORDING PAYROLL TAXES: THE BEGINNING OF THE PAYROLL PROCESS

PART I

Fill in the blank(s) to complete the statement.

1. ______________ ______________ is gross pay less deductions.
2. Form ______________ aids the employer in knowing how much to deduct for federal income tax.
3. The base for OASDI-Medicare will ______________ ______________ from year to year.
4. ______________ ______________ of the employer's tax guide has tables available for deductions for FIT.
5. ______________ ______________ ______________ protects employees against losses due to injury or death incurred while on the job.
6. The two primary records used to keep track of payroll information are the ______________ ______________ and ______________ ______________ ______________.
7. Payroll tax expense includes ______________, ______________, ______________, and ______________.
8. ______________ ______________ is paid every two weeks.
9. A(n) ______________ employee will only be paid for the hours actually worked.
10. An employer must pay FUTA on wages earned by each employee up to a maximum of $______________.

Part II

Answer true or false to the following.

1. OASDI is the tax form for SUTA.
2. Employers only pay FUTA and SUTA.
3. Employers pay a higher FICA-OASDI tax rate than employees do.
4. Gross pay plus deductions equals net pay.
5. Form W-4 aids in calculating FICA-OASDI.
6. The employer will match the employee's contribution for FICA (OASDI and Medicare).
7. The maximum tax credit for state unemployment tax is .8%.
8. A company may have different types of employees.
9. The Wage-Bracket Table makes it more difficult to calculate the amount of deductions for FIT.
10. A calendar year has no effect on taxes for FICA-Social Security.

Name ____________ Class ____________ Date ____________

Part III

Complete the chart below (use table in text as needed). Use the following information: Before this payroll Pete Bloom had earned $105,800. This week Pete earned $2,000 for the past two weeks. Assume an OASDI rate of Social Security of 6.2% up to $117,000. Medicare, 1.45%. FIT is $246.00. The state income tax is 7 percent.

GROSS PAY	TAXABLE FICA	DEDUCTIONS				NET PAY
		FICA		FIT	SIT	
		OASDI	Med.			

SOLUTIONS

Part I

1. Net Pay
2. W-4
3. not change
4. Circular E
5. Workers' Compensation Insurance
6. payroll register, employee earnings record
7. FICA-OASDI, FICA-Medicare, FUTA, SUTA
8. Biweekly payroll
9. hourly
10. 7,000

Part II

1. false
2. true
3. false
4. false
5. false
6. true
7. false
8. true
9. false
10. false

Part III

OASDI	$2,000 x .062 =	$124.00	
Medicare	2,000 x .0145 =	29.00	
FIT		246.00	$2,000.00
SIT	2,000 x .07	140.00	– 539.00
Total deductions		$539.00	$1,461.00

Study Guide and Working Papers

Paying the Payroll, Depositing Payroll Taxes, and Filing the Required Quarterly and Annual Tax Forms: The Conclusion of the Payroll Process

Name ____________________ Class ____________ Date ____________

FORMS FOR DEMONSTRATION PROBLEM

REQUIREMENT 1

Name ______________________ Class ______________ Date ______________

FORMS FOR DEMONSTRATION PROBLEM

REQUIREMENT 2

Form **941 for 201X: Employer's QUARTERLY Federal Tax Return** 950114
(Rev. January 2014) Department of the Treasury — Internal Revenue Service OMB No. 1545-0029

Employer identification number (EIN) [ ][ ] – [ ][ ][ ][ ][ ][ ][ ]

Name *(not your trade name)* ______________________

Trade name *(if any)* ______________________

Address ______________________
Number Street Suite or room number

____
City State ZIP code

____
Foreign country name Foreign province/county Foreign postal code

Report for this Quarter of 201X
(Check one.)

- [ ] **1:** January, February, March
- [ ] **2:** April, May, June
- [ ] **3:** July, August, September
- [ ] **4:** October, November, December

Instructions and prior year forms are available at *www.irs.gov/form941.*

Read the separate instructions before you complete Form 941. Type or print within the boxes.

Part 1: Answer these questions for this quarter.

1	**Number of employees who received wages, tips, or other compensation for the pay period including:** ***Mar. 12*** **(Quarter 1),** ***June 12*** **(Quarter 2),** ***Sept. 12*** **(Quarter 3), or** ***Dec. 12*** **(Quarter 4)**	1	
2	**Wages, tips, and other compensation**	2	.
3	**Federal income tax withheld from wages, tips, and other compensation**	3	.
4	**If no wages, tips, and other compensation are subject to social security or Medicare tax**		☐ **Check and go to line 6.**

		Column 1		Column 2
5a	**Taxable social security wages** . .	.	× .124 =	.
5b	**Taxable social security tips** . . .	.	× .124 =	.
5c	**Taxable Medicare wages & tips.** .	.	× .029 =	.
5d	**Taxable wages & tips subject to Additional Medicare Tax withholding**	.	× .009 =	.

5e	**Add Column 2 from lines 5a, 5b, 5c, and 5d**	5e	.
5f	**Section 3121(q) Notice and Demand—Tax due on unreported tips** (see instructions) . .	5f	.
6	**Total taxes before adjustments.** Add lines 3, 5e, and 5f	6	.
7	**Current quarter's adjustment for fractions of cents**	7	.
8	**Current quarter's adjustment for sick pay**	8	.
9	**Current quarter's adjustments for tips and group-term life insurance**	9	.
10	**Total taxes after adjustments.** Combine lines 6 through 9	10	.
11	**Total deposits for this quarter, including overpayment applied from a prior quarter and overpayments applied from Form 941-X, 941-X (PR), 944-X, 944-X (PR), or 944-X (SP) filed in the current quarter**	11	.
12	**Balance due.** If line 10 is more than line 11, enter the difference and see instructions . . .	12	0 .
13	**Overpayment.** If line 11 is more than line 10, enter the difference [.] Check one: ☐ Apply to next return. ☐ Send a refund.		

► **You MUST complete both pages of Form 941 and SIGN it.** Next ►

For Privacy Act and Paperwork Reduction Act Notice, see the back of the Payment Voucher. Cat. No. 17001Z Form **941** (Rev. 1-2014)

Name ______________________ Class ____________ Date ____________

FORMS FOR DEMONSTRATION PROBLEM
REQUIREMENT 2 (CONCLUDED)

Name *(not your trade name)* | Employer identification number (EIN) 950214

Part 2: Tell us about your deposit schedule and tax liability for this quarter.

If you are unsure about whether you are a monthly schedule depositor or a semiweekly schedule depositor, see Pub. 15 (Circular E), section 11.

14 Check one: ☐ **Line 10 on this return is less than $2,500 or line 10 on the return for the prior quarter was less than $2,500, and you did not incur a $100,000 next-day deposit obligation during the current quarter.** If line 10 for the prior quarter was less than $2,500 but line 10 on this return is $100,000 or more, you must provide a record of your federal tax liability. If you are a monthly schedule depositor, complete the deposit schedule below; if you are a semiweekly schedule depositor, attach Schedule B (Form 941). Go to Part 3.

☐ **You were a monthly schedule depositor for the entire quarter.** Enter your tax liability for each month and total liability for the quarter, then go to Part 3.

Tax liability: Month 1 ______ .

Month 2 ______ .

Month 3 ______ .

Total liability for quarter ______ . **Total must equal line 10.**

☐ **You were a semiweekly schedule depositor for any part of this quarter.** Complete Schedule B (Form 941), Report of Tax Liability for Semiweekly Schedule Depositors, and attach it to Form 941.

Part 3: Tell us about your business. If a question does NOT apply to your business, leave it blank.

15 If your business has closed or you stopped paying wages . . . . ☐ Check here, and

enter the final date you paid wages ___ / ___ / ___ .

16 If you are a seasonal employer and you do not have to file a return for every quarter of the year . . ☐ Check here.

Part 4: May we speak with your third-party designee?

Do you want to allow an employee, a paid tax preparer, or another person to discuss this return with the IRS? See the instructions for details.

☐ Yes. Designee's name and phone number ______ ______

Select a 5-digit Personal Identification Number (PIN) to use when talking to the IRS. ☐☐☐☐☐

☐ No.

Part 5: Sign here. You MUST complete both pages of Form 941 and SIGN it.

Under penalties of perjury, I declare that I have examined this return, including accompanying schedules and statements, and to the best of my knowledge and belief, it is true, correct, and complete. Declaration of preparer (other than taxpayer) is based on all information of which preparer has any knowledge.

X **Sign your name here** ______ Print your name here ______

Print your title here ______

Date ___ / ___ / ___ Best daytime phone ______

Paid Preparer Use Only Check if you are self-employed . . . ☐

Preparer's name		PTIN	
Preparer's signature		Date	/ /
Firm's name (or yours if self-employed)		EIN	
Address		Phone	
City	State	ZIP code	

Name ______________________ Class ______________ Date ______________

FORMS FOR DEMONSTRATION PROBLEM

REQUIREMENT 3

Form **940 for 201X: Employer's Annual Federal Unemployment (FUTA) Tax Return** 850113

Department of the Treasury — Internal Revenue Service

OMB No. 1545-0028

Employer identification number (EIN) __ __ – __ __ __ __ __ __ __

Name *(not your trade name)*

Trade name *(if any)*

Address

Number Street Suite or room number

City State ZIP code

Foreign country name Foreign province/county Foreign postal code

Type of Return
(Check all that apply.)

- ☐ **a.** Amended
- ☐ **b.** Successor employer
- ☐ **c.** No payments to employees in 201X
- ☐ **d.** Final: Business closed or stopped paying wages

Instructions and prior-year forms are available at *www.irs.gov/form940.*

Read the separate instructions before you complete this form. Please type or print within the boxes.

Part 1: Tell us about your return. If any line does NOT apply, leave it blank.

1a **If you had to pay state unemployment tax in one state only, enter the state abbreviation** . 1a ☐☐

1b **If you had to pay state unemployment tax in more than one state, you are a multi-state employer** . . . . 1b ☐ Check here. Complete Schedule A (Form 940).

2 **If you paid wages in a state that is subject to CREDIT REDUCTION** . . . . 2 ☐ Check here. Complete Schedule A (Form 940).

Part 2: Determine your FUTA tax before adjustments for 201X. If any line does NOT apply, leave it blank.

3 **Total payments to all employees** . . . . 3 ______ .

4 **Payments exempt from FUTA tax** . . . . 4 ______ .

Check all that apply: 4a ☐ Fringe benefits 4b ☐ Group-term life insurance 4c ☐ Retirement/Pension 4d ☐ Dependent care 4e ☐ Other

5 **Total of payments made to each employee in excess of $7,000** . . . . 5 ______ .

6 **Subtotal** (line 4 + line 5 = line 6) . . . . 6 ______ .

7 **Total taxable FUTA wages** (line 3 – line 6 = line 7) (see instructions) . . . . . . 7 ______ .

8 **FUTA tax before adjustments** (line 7 x .006 = line 8) . . . . 8 ______ .

Part 3: Determine your adjustments. If any line does NOT apply, leave it blank.

9 **If ALL of the taxable FUTA wages you paid were excluded from state unemployment tax, multiply line 7 by .054** (line 7 × .054 = line 9). Go to line 12 . . . . 9 ______ .

10 **If SOME of the taxable FUTA wages you paid were excluded from state unemployment tax, OR you paid ANY state unemployment tax late** (after the due date for filing Form 940), complete the worksheet in the instructions. Enter the amount from line 7 of the worksheet . . 10 ______ .

11 **If credit reduction applies,** enter the total from Schedule A (Form 940) . . . . 11 ______ .

Part 4: Determine your FUTA tax and balance due or overpayment for 201X. If any line does NOT apply, leave it blank.

12 **Total FUTA tax after adjustments** (lines 8 + 9 + 10 + 11 = line 12) . . . . 12 ______ .

13 **FUTA tax deposited for the year, including any overpayment applied from a prior year** . 13 ______ .

14 **Balance due** (If line 12 is more than line 13, enter the excess on line 14.)

- If line 14 is more than $500, you must deposit your tax.
- If line 14 is $500 or less, you may pay with this return. (see instructions) . . . . . 14 ______ .

15 **Overpayment** (If line 13 is more than line 12, enter the excess on line 15 and check a box below.) . . . . 15 ______ .

► You **MUST** complete both pages of this form and **SIGN** it.

Check one: ☐ Apply to next return. ☐ Send a refund.

Next ►

For Privacy Act and Paperwork Reduction Act Notice, see the back of Form 940-V, Payment Voucher. Cat. No. 11234O Form **940** (2013)

Name ______________________ Class ______________ Date ______________

FORMS FOR DEMONSTRATION PROBLEM

REQUIREMENT 3 (CONCLUDED)

850212

Name *(not your trade name)* | **Employer identification number (EIN)**

Part 5: Report your FUTA tax liability by quarter only if line 12 is more than $500. If not, go to Part 6.

16 Report the amount of your FUTA tax liability for each quarter; do NOT enter the amount you deposited. If you had no liability for a quarter, leave the line blank.

16a 1st quarter (January 1 – March 31) . . . . **16a** ______ .

16b 2nd quarter (April 1 – June 30) . . . . **16b** ______ .

16c 3rd quarter (July 1 – September 30) . . . . **16c** ______ .

16d 4th quarter (October 1 – December 31) . . . . **16d** ______ .

17 Total tax liability for the year (lines 16a + 16b + 16c + 16d = line 17) **17** ______ . **Total must equal line 12.**

Part 6: May we speak with your third-party designee?

Do you want to allow an employee, a paid tax preparer, or another person to discuss this return with the IRS? See the instructions for details.

☐ **Yes.** Designee's name and phone number

Select a 5-digit Personal Identification Number (PIN) to use when talking to IRS

☐ **No.**

Part 7: Sign here. You MUST complete both pages of this form and SIGN it.

Under penalties of perjury, I declare that I have examined this return, including accompanying schedules and statements, and to the best of my knowledge and belief, it is true, correct, and complete, and that no part of any payment made to a state unemployment fund claimed as a credit was, or is to be, deducted from the payments made to employees. Declaration of preparer (other than taxpayer) is based on all information of which preparer has any knowledge.

✗ Sign your name here

Print your name here

Print your title here

Date / /

Best daytime phone

Paid Preparer Use Only

Check if you are self-employed . ☐

Preparer's name

PTIN

Preparer's signature

Date / /

Firm's name (or yours if self-employed)

EIN

Address

Phone

City

State

ZIP code

Name ______________ Class ______________ Date ______________

FORMS FOR SET A EXERCISES

8A-1

Date		Account	Debit	Credit

8A-2

	941 Tax Deposit Due Date
a. Monthly depositor, owing $1,500 tax for the first quarter.	
b. Monthly depositor, owing $5,000 tax for the month of July.	
c. Monthly depositor, owing $110,000 tax as of Tuesday.	
d. Semiweekly depositor, owing $110,000 tax as of Tuesday.	
e. Semiweekly depositor, owing $20,000 tax as of Friday.	

8A-3

		Column 1		Column 2
Line 1	Number of employees who received wages, tips, or other compensation			______
Line 2	Wages, tips, and other compensation			______
Line 3	Federal income tax withheld from wages, tips, and other compensation			______
Line 4	If no wages, tips, and other compensation are subject to social security or Medicare tax			___ Check
Line 5a	Taxable social security wages		x .124 =	______
Line 5b	Taxable social security tips	______	x .124 =	______
Line 5c	Taxable Medicare wages & tips	______	x .029 =	______
Line 5d	Taxable wages & tips subject to additional Medicare Tax	______	x .009 =	______
Line 5e	Add Column 2 from Lines 5a, 5b, 5c, and 5d			______
Line 5f	Section 3121(q) Notice and Demand—Tax due on unreported tips			______
Line 6	Total taxes before adjustments. Add lines 3, 5e, and 5f			______

Name ____________ Class ____________ Date ____________

SET A EXERCISES

8A-4

Date		Account		Debit	Credit

8A-5

Line 3 Total payments to all employees

Line 4 Payments exempt from FUTA tax ____________

Line 5 Total of payments made to each employee in excess of $7,000 ____________

Line 6 Subtotal (line 4 + line 5 = line 6)

Line 7 Total taxable FUTA wages (line 3 – line 6 = line 7)

Line 8 FUTA tax before adjustments (line 7 x .006 = line 8)

Total annual payroll for the year

Payments made in excess of $7,000 FUTA tax limit

Total FUTA liability before any adjustments

8A-6

Monthly or semiweekly for 201C?

8A-7

Monthly or semiweekly for 201C?

8A-8

Date		Account		Debit	Credit

Name ______________________ Class ______________ Date ______________

FORMS FOR SET B EXERCISES

8B-1

Date		Account		Debit	Credit

8B-2

	941 Tax Deposit Due Date
a. Monthly depositor, owing $1,850 tax for the third quarter.	
b. Monthly depositor, owing $4,100 tax for the month of May.	
c. Monthly depositor, owing $121,000 tax as of Thursday.	
d. Semiweekly depositor, owing $121,000 tax as of Friday.	
e. Semiweekly depositor, owing $32,000 tax as of Friday.	

8B-3

Line 1 Number of employees who received wages, tips, or other compensation ________

Line 2 Wages, tips, and other compensation ________

Line 3 Federal income tax withheld from wages, tips, and other compensation ________

Line 4 If no wages, tips, and other compensation are subject to social security or Medicare tax ___ Check

Line 5a Taxable social security wages ________ x .124 = ________

Line 5b Taxable social security tips ________ x .124 = ________

Line 5c Taxable Medicare wages & tips ________ x .029 = ________

Line 5d Taxable wages & tips subject to additional Medicare Tax ________ x .009 = ________

Line 5e Add Column 2 from Lines 5a, 5b, 5c, and 5d ________

Line 5f Section 3121(q) Notice and Demand—Tax due on unreported tips ________

Line 6 Total taxes before adjustments. Add lines 3, 5e, and 5f ________

Name ____________________ Class ____________________ Date ____________________

SET B EXERCISES

8B-4

Date		Account	Debit	Credit

8B-5

Line 3 Total payments to all employees ____________

Line 4 Payments exempt from FUTA tax ____________

Line 5 Total of payments made to each employee in excess of $7,000 ____________

Line 6 Subtotal (line 4 + line 5 = line 6) ____________

Line 7 Total taxable FUTA wages (line 3 – line 6 = line 7) ____________

Line 8 FUTA tax before adjustments (line 7 x .006 = line 8) ____________

Total annual payroll for the year ____________

Payments made in excess of $7,000 FUTA limit ____________

Total FUTA liability before any adjustments ____________

8B-6

Monthly or semiweekly for 201C? ____________

8B-7

Monthly or semiweekly for 201C? ____________

8B-8

Date		Account	Debit	Credit

Name ______________________ Class ______________ Date ______________

FORMS FOR SET A PROBLEMS

PROBLEM 8A-1

Employee	Taxable FUTA Earnings	Taxable SUTA Earnings	FUTA Tax	SUTA Tax
January				
Steven Koy				
Juanita Lane				
Alison Pickens				
February				
Steven Koy				
Juanita Lane				
Alison Pickens				
March				
Steven Koy				
Juanita Lane				
Alison Pickens				

Name ______________________ Class ______________ Date ______________

PROBLEM 8A-1 (CONTINUED)

REQUIREMENT 1

Record payroll tax expense.

Date	Account Titles and Description	PR	Dr.	Cr.

Name ____________________ Class ____________ Date ____________

PROBLEM 8A-1 (CONCLUDED)

REQUIREMENT 2

Record payment of each tax liability.

Date	Account Titles and Description	PR	Dr.	Cr.

Name ____________ Class ____________ Date ____________

PROBLEM 8A-2

Form **941 for 201X: Employer's QUARTERLY Federal Tax Return** 950114

(Rev. January 2014) Department of the Treasury — Internal Revenue Service OMB No. 1545-0029

Employer identification number (EIN) [ ][ ] – [ ][ ][ ][ ][ ][ ][ ]

Name *(not your trade name)*

Trade name *(if any)*

Address

Number Street Suite or room number

City State ZIP code

Foreign country name Foreign province/county Foreign postal code

Report for this Quarter of 201X
(Check one.)

☐ 1: January, February, March

☐ 2: April, May, June

☐ 3: July, August, September

☐ 4: October, November, December

Instructions and prior year forms are available at *www.irs.gov/form941.*

Read the separate instructions before you complete Form 941. Type or print within the boxes.

Part 1: Answer these questions for this quarter.

1 **Number of employees who received wages, tips, or other compensation for the pay period including: *Mar. 12* (Quarter 1), *June 12* (Quarter 2), *Sept. 12* (Quarter 3), or *Dec. 12* (Quarter 4)** . . . 1 ______

2 **Wages, tips, and other compensation** . . . 2 ______ .

3 **Federal income tax withheld from wages, tips, and other compensation** . . . 3 ______ .

4 **If no wages, tips, and other compensation are subject to social security or Medicare tax** ☐ **Check and go to line 6.**

	Column 1		Column 2
5a **Taxable social security wages** . .	.	× .124 =	.
5b **Taxable social security tips** . .	.	× .124 =	.
5c **Taxable Medicare wages & tips** . .	.	× .029 =	.
5d **Taxable wages & tips subject to Additional Medicare Tax withholding**	.	× .009 =	.

5e **Add Column 2 from lines 5a, 5b, 5c, and 5d** . . . 5e ______ .

5f **Section 3121(q) Notice and Demand—Tax due on unreported tips** (see instructions) . . 5f ______ .

6 **Total taxes before adjustments.** Add lines 3, 5e, and 5f . . . 6 ______ .

7 **Current quarter's adjustment for fractions of cents** . . . 7 ______ .

8 **Current quarter's adjustment for sick pay** . . . 8 ______ .

9 **Current quarter's adjustments for tips and group-term life insurance** . . . 9 ______ .

10 **Total taxes after adjustments.** Combine lines 6 through 9 . . . 10 ______ .

11 **Total deposits for this quarter, including overpayment applied from a prior quarter and overpayments applied from Form 941-X, 941-X (PR), 944-X, 944-X (PR), or 944-X (SP) filed in the current quarter** . . . 11 ______ .

12 **Balance due.** If line 10 is more than line 11, enter the difference and see instructions . . . 12 0 .

13 **Overpayment.** If line 11 is more than line 10, enter the difference ______ . Check one: ☐ Apply to next return. ☐ Send a refund.

▶ **You MUST complete both pages of Form 941 and SIGN it.** Next

For Privacy Act and Paperwork Reduction Act Notice, see the back of the Payment Voucher. Cat. No. 17001Z Form **941** (Rev. 1-2014)

Name ____________ Class ____________ Date ____________

PROBLEM 8A-2 (CONCLUDED)

950214

Name *(not your trade name)* ____________ **Employer identification number (EIN)** ____________

Part 2: Tell us about your deposit schedule and tax liability for this quarter.

If you are unsure about whether you are a monthly schedule depositor or a semiweekly schedule depositor, see Pub. 15 (Circular E), section 11.

14 Check one: ☐ **Line 10 on this return is less than $2,500 or line 10 on the return for the prior quarter was less than $2,500, and you did not incur a $100,000 next-day deposit obligation during the current quarter.** If line 10 for the prior quarter was less than $2,500 but line 10 on this return is $100,000 or more, you must provide a record of your federal tax liability. If you are a monthly schedule depositor, complete the deposit schedule below; if you are a semiweekly schedule depositor, attach Schedule B (Form 941). Go to Part 3.

☐ **You were a monthly schedule depositor for the entire quarter.** Enter your tax liability for each month and total liability for the quarter, then go to Part 3.

Tax liability: Month 1 ________ .

Month 2 ________ .

Month 3 ________ .

Total liability for quarter ________ . **Total must equal line 10.**

☐ **You were a semiweekly schedule depositor for any part of this quarter.** Complete Schedule B (Form 941), Report of Tax Liability for Semiweekly Schedule Depositors, and attach it to Form 941.

Part 3: Tell us about your business. If a question does NOT apply to your business, leave it blank.

15 If your business has closed or you stopped paying wages . . . . ☐ Check here, and

enter the final date you paid wages ___ / ___ / ___ .

16 If you are a seasonal employer and you do not have to file a return for every quarter of the year . . ☐ Check here.

Part 4: May we speak with your third-party designee?

Do you want to allow an employee, a paid tax preparer, or another person to discuss this return with the IRS? See the instructions for details.

☐ Yes. Designee's name and phone number ____________ ____________

Select a 5-digit Personal Identification Number (PIN) to use when talking to the IRS. ☐☐☐☐☐

☐ No.

Part 5: Sign here. You MUST complete both pages of Form 941 and SIGN it.

Under penalties of perjury, I declare that I have examined this return, including accompanying schedules and statements, and to the best of my knowledge and belief, it is true, correct, and complete. Declaration of preparer (other than taxpayer) is based on all information of which preparer has any knowledge.

X **Sign your name here** ____________

Print your name here ____________

Print your title here ____________

Date ___ / ___ / ___

Best daytime phone ____________

Paid Preparer Use Only

Check if you are self-employed . . . ☐

Preparer's name ____________ PTIN ____________

Preparer's signature ____________ Date ___ / ___ / ___

Firm's name (or yours if self-employed) ____________ EIN ____________

Address ____________ Phone ____________

City ____________ State ____________ ZIP code ____________

Name ______________________ Class ______________ Date ______________

PROBLEM 8A-3

REQUIREMENT 1

Karen Becker

Calculation for December OASDI tax ______________________________

REQUIREMENT 2

Date	Account	Debit	Credit

Name ______________________ Class ______________ Date ______________

PROBLEM 8A-3 (CONTINUED)

REQUIREMENT 3

Date	Account	Debit	Credit

Name ____________ Class ____________ Date ____________

PROBLEM 8A-3 (CONTINUED)

REQUIREMENT 4

950114

Form **941 for 201X: Employer's QUARTERLY Federal Tax Return**
(Rev. January 2014) Department of the Treasury — Internal Revenue Service OMB No. 1545-0029

Employer identification number (EIN) ☐☐ – ☐☐☐☐☐☐☐

Name *(not your trade name)* ____________

Trade name *(if any)* ____________

Address ____________
Number Street Suite or room number

____
City State ZIP code

____
Foreign country name Foreign province/county Foreign postal code

Report for this Quarter of 201X
(Check one.)

- ☐ **1:** January, February, March
- ☐ **2:** April, May, June
- ☐ **3:** July, August, September
- ☐ **4:** October, November, December

Instructions and prior year forms are available at *www.irs.gov/form941.*

Read the separate instructions before you complete Form 941. Type or print within the boxes.

Part 1: Answer these questions for this quarter.

1	**Number of employees who received wages, tips, or other compensation for the pay period including:** *Mar. 12* (Quarter 1), *June 12* (Quarter 2), *Sept. 12* (Quarter 3), or *Dec. 12* (Quarter 4)	1	
2	**Wages, tips, and other compensation**	2	.
3	**Federal income tax withheld from wages, tips, and other compensation**	3	.
4	**If no wages, tips, and other compensation are subject to social security or Medicare tax**	☐ **Check and go to line 6.**	

		Column 1		Column 2
5a	**Taxable social security wages**	.	× .124 =	.
5b	**Taxable social security tips**	.	× .124 =	.
5c	**Taxable Medicare wages & tips**	.	× .029 =	.
5d	**Taxable wages & tips subject to Additional Medicare Tax withholding**	.	× .009 =	.

5e	**Add Column 2 from lines 5a, 5b, 5c, and 5d**	5e	.
5f	**Section 3121(q) Notice and Demand—Tax due on unreported tips** (see instructions)	5f	.
6	**Total taxes before adjustments.** Add lines 3, 5e, and 5f	6	.
7	**Current quarter's adjustment for fractions of cents**	7	.
8	**Current quarter's adjustment for sick pay**	8	.
9	**Current quarter's adjustments for tips and group-term life insurance**	9	.
10	**Total taxes after adjustments.** Combine lines 6 through 9	10	.
11	**Total deposits for this quarter, including overpayment applied from a prior quarter and overpayments applied from Form 941-X, 941-X (PR), 944-X, 944-X (PR), or 944-X (SP) filed in the current quarter**	11	.
12	**Balance due.** If line 10 is more than line 11, enter the difference and see instructions	12	0 .
13	**Overpayment.** If line 11 is more than line 10, enter the difference ____ . Check one: ☐ Apply to next return. ☐ Send a refund.		

► **You MUST complete both pages of Form 941 and SIGN it.** Next ►

For Privacy Act and Paperwork Reduction Act Notice, see the back of the Payment Voucher. Cat. No. 17001Z Form **941** (Rev. 1-2014)

Name ______________ Class ______________ Date ______________

PROBLEM 8A-3 (CONCLUDED)

Name (not your trade name) | Employer identification number (EIN) 950214

Part 2: Tell us about your deposit schedule and tax liability for this quarter.

If you are unsure about whether you are a monthly schedule depositor or a semiweekly schedule depositor, see Pub. 15 (Circular E), section 11.

14 Check one: ☐ **Line 10 on this return is less than $2,500 or line 10 on the return for the prior quarter was less than $2,500, and you did not incur a $100,000 next-day deposit obligation during the current quarter.** If line 10 for the prior quarter was less than $2,500 but line 10 on this return is $100,000 or more, you must provide a record of your federal tax liability. If you are a monthly schedule depositor, complete the deposit schedule below; if you are a semiweekly schedule depositor, attach Schedule B (Form 941). Go to Part 3.

☐ **You were a monthly schedule depositor for the entire quarter.** Enter your tax liability for each month and total liability for the quarter, then go to Part 3.

Tax liability: Month 1 ______ .

Month 2 ______ .

Month 3 ______ .

Total liability for quarter ______ . **Total must equal line 10.**

☐ **You were a semiweekly schedule depositor for any part of this quarter.** Complete Schedule B (Form 941), Report of Tax Liability for Semiweekly Schedule Depositors, and attach it to Form 941.

Part 3: Tell us about your business. If a question does NOT apply to your business, leave it blank.

15 If your business has closed or you stopped paying wages . . . . ☐ Check here, and

enter the final date you paid wages ___ / ___ / ___

16 If you are a seasonal employer and you do not have to file a return for every quarter of the year . . ☐ Check here.

Part 4: May we speak with your third-party designee?

Do you want to allow an employee, a paid tax preparer, or another person to discuss this return with the IRS? See the instructions for details.

☐ Yes. Designee's name and phone number ______ ______

Select a 5-digit Personal Identification Number (PIN) to use when talking to the IRS. ☐☐☐☐☐

☐ No.

Part 5: Sign here. You MUST complete both pages of Form 941 and SIGN it.

Under penalties of perjury, I declare that I have examined this return, including accompanying schedules and statements, and to the best of my knowledge and belief, it is true, correct, and complete. Declaration of preparer (other than taxpayer) is based on all information of which preparer has any knowledge.

X **Sign your name here** ______ Print your name here ______

Print your title here ______

Date ___ / ___ / ___ Best daytime phone ______

Paid Preparer Use Only Check if you are self-employed . . . ☐

Preparer's name ______ PTIN ______

Preparer's signature ______ Date ___ / ___ / ___

Firm's name (or yours if self-employed) ______ EIN ______

Address ______ Phone ______

City ______ State ______ ZIP code ______

Name ______ Class ______ Date ______

PROBLEM 8A-4

Form **940 for 201X: Employer's Annual Federal Unemployment (FUTA) Tax Return**
Department of the Treasury — Internal Revenue Service

850113
OMB No. 1545-0028

Employer identification number (EIN) ☐☐ – ☐☐☐☐☐☐☐

Name *(not your trade name)* ______

Trade name *(if any)* ______

Address ______
Number Street Suite or room number

City State ZIP code

Foreign country name Foreign province/county Foreign postal code

Type of Return
(Check all that apply.)

☐ **a.** Amended
☐ **b.** Successor employer
☐ **c.** No payments to employees in 201X
☐ **d.** Final: Business closed or stopped paying wages

Instructions and prior-year forms are available at *www.irs.gov/form940.*

Read the separate instructions before you complete this form. Please type or print within the boxes.

Part 1: Tell us about your return. If any line does NOT apply, leave it blank.

1a **If you had to pay state unemployment tax in one state only, enter the state abbreviation** . 1a ☐☐

1b **If you had to pay state unemployment tax in more than one state, you are a multi-state employer** . . . . 1b ☐ Check here. Complete Schedule A (Form 940).

2 **If you paid wages in a state that is subject to CREDIT REDUCTION** . . . . . 2 ☐ Check here. Complete Schedule A (Form 940).

Part 2: Determine your FUTA tax before adjustments for 201X. If any line does NOT apply, leave it blank.

3 **Total payments to all employees** . . . . . 3 ______ .

4 **Payments exempt from FUTA tax** . . . . . 4 ______ .

Check all that apply: 4a ☐ Fringe benefits 4c ☐ Retirement/Pension 4e ☐ Other
4b ☐ Group-term life insurance 4d ☐ Dependent care

5 **Total of payments made to each employee in excess of $7,000** . . . . . 5 ______ .

6 **Subtotal** (line 4 + line 5 = line 6) . . . . . 6 ______ .

7 **Total taxable FUTA wages** (line 3 – line 6 = line 7) (see instructions) . . . . . 7 ______ .

8 **FUTA tax before adjustments** (line 7 x .006 = line 8) . . . . . 8 ______ .

Part 3: Determine your adjustments. If any line does NOT apply, leave it blank.

9 **If ALL of the taxable FUTA wages you paid were excluded from state unemployment tax, multiply line 7 by .054** (line 7 × .054 = line 9). Go to line 12 . . . . . 9 ______ .

10 **If SOME of the taxable FUTA wages you paid were excluded from state unemployment tax, OR you paid ANY state unemployment tax late** (after the due date for filing Form 940), complete the worksheet in the instructions. Enter the amount from line 7 of the worksheet . . 10 ______ .

11 **If credit reduction applies,** enter the total from Schedule A (Form 940) . . . . . 11 ______ .

Part 4: Determine your FUTA tax and balance due or overpayment for 201X. If any line does NOT apply, leave it blank.

12 **Total FUTA tax after adjustments** (lines 8 + 9 + 10 + 11 = line 12) . . . . . 12 ______ .

13 **FUTA tax deposited for the year, including any overpayment applied from a prior year** . 13 ______ .

14 **Balance due** (If line 12 is more than line 13, enter the excess on line 14.)
- If line 14 is more than $500, you must deposit your tax.
- If line 14 is $500 or less, you may pay with this return. (see instructions) . . . . . 14 ______ .

15 **Overpayment** (If line 13 is more than line 12, enter the excess on line 15 and check a box below.) . . . . . 15 ______ .

▶ You **MUST** complete both pages of this form and **SIGN** it. Check one: ☐ Apply to next return. ☐ Send a refund.

Next ▶

For Privacy Act and Paperwork Reduction Act Notice, see the back of Form 940-V, Payment Voucher. Cat. No. 11234O Form **940** (2013)

Name ________________ Class ________________ Date ________________

PROBLEM 8A-4 (CONCLUDED)

850212

Name *(not your trade name)* | Employer identification number (EIN)

Part 5: Report your FUTA tax liability by quarter only if line 12 is more than $500. If not, go to Part 6.

16 Report the amount of your FUTA tax liability for each quarter; do NOT enter the amount you deposited. If you had no liability for a quarter, leave the line blank.

16a 1st quarter (January 1 – March 31) . . . . **16a** ________ .

16b 2nd quarter (April 1 – June 30) . . . . **16b** ________ .

16c 3rd quarter (July 1 – September 30) . . . . **16c** ________ .

16d 4th quarter (October 1 – December 31) . . . . **16d** ________ .

17 Total tax liability for the year (lines 16a + 16b + 16c + 16d = line 17) **17** ________ . **Total must equal line 12.**

Part 6: May we speak with your third-party designee?

Do you want to allow an employee, a paid tax preparer, or another person to discuss this return with the IRS? See the instructions for details.

☐ **Yes.** Designee's name and phone number

Select a 5-digit Personal Identification Number (PIN) to use when talking to IRS

☐ **No.**

Part 7: Sign here. You MUST complete both pages of this form and SIGN it.

Under penalties of perjury, I declare that I have examined this return, including accompanying schedules and statements, and to the best of my knowledge and belief, it is true, correct, and complete, and that no part of any payment made to a state unemployment fund claimed as a credit was, or is to be, deducted from the payments made to employees. Declaration of preparer (other than taxpayer) is based on all information of which preparer has any knowledge.

X Sign your name here

Print your name here

Print your title here

Date / /

Best daytime phone

Paid Preparer Use Only

Check if you are self-employed . ☐

Preparer's name

PTIN

Preparer's signature

Date / /

Firm's name (or yours if self-employed)

EIN

Address

Phone

City

State

ZIP code

Name ____________________ Class ____________________ Date ____________________

FORMS FOR SET B PROBLEMS

PROBLEM 8B-1

Employee	Taxable FUTA Earnings	Taxable SUTA Earnings	FUTA Tax	SUTA Tax
January				
Saul Hantona				
Jade Alaymo				
Ariana Santana				
February				
Saul Hantona				
Jade Alaymo				
Ariana Santana				
March				
Saul Hantona				
Jade Alaymo				
Ariana Santana				

PROBLEM 8B-1 (CONTINUED)

REQUIREMENT 1

Record payroll tax expense.

Date		Account Titles and Description	PR	Dr.	Cr.

Name ______________________ Class ______________ Date ______________

PROBLEM 8B-1 (CONCLUDED)

REQUIREMENT 2

Record payment of each tax liability.

Date	Account Titles and Description	PR	Dr.	Cr.

Name ____________ Class ____________ Date ____________

PROBLEM 8B-2

Form **941 for 201X: Employer's QUARTERLY Federal Tax Return** 950114

(Rev. January 2014) Department of the Treasury — Internal Revenue Service OMB No. 1545-0029

Employer identification number (EIN) [ ][ ] – [ ][ ][ ][ ][ ][ ][ ]

Name *(not your trade name)* ____________

Trade name *(if any)* ____________

Address ____________
Number Street Suite or room number

City State ZIP code

Foreign country name Foreign province/county Foreign postal code

Report for this Quarter of 201X
(Check one.)

- ☐ **1:** January, February, March
- ☐ **2:** April, May, June
- ☐ **3:** July, August, September
- ☐ **4:** October, November, December

Instructions and prior year forms are available at *www.irs.gov/form941.*

Read the separate instructions before you complete Form 941. Type or print within the boxes.

Part 1: Answer these questions for this quarter.

1	**Number of employees who received wages, tips, or other compensation for the pay period including:** ***Mar. 12*** **(Quarter 1),** ***June 12*** **(Quarter 2),** ***Sept. 12*** **(Quarter 3), or** ***Dec. 12*** **(Quarter 4)**			1	
2	**Wages, tips, and other compensation**			2	.
3	**Federal income tax withheld from wages, tips, and other compensation** . . .			3	.
4	**If no wages, tips, and other compensation are subject to social security or Medicare tax**				☐ **Check and go to line 6.**
		Column 1		**Column 2**	
5a	**Taxable social security wages** . .	.	× .124 =	.	
5b	**Taxable social security tips** . . .	.	× .124 =	.	
5c	**Taxable Medicare wages & tips.** .	.	× .029 =	.	
5d	**Taxable wages & tips subject to Additional Medicare Tax withholding**	.	× .009 =	.	
5e	**Add Column 2 from lines 5a, 5b, 5c, and 5d**			5e	.
5f	**Section 3121(q) Notice and Demand—Tax due on unreported tips** (see instructions) . .			5f	.
6	**Total taxes before adjustments.** Add lines 3, 5e, and 5f			6	.
7	**Current quarter's adjustment for fractions of cents**			7	.
8	**Current quarter's adjustment for sick pay**			8	.
9	**Current quarter's adjustments for tips and group-term life insurance**			9	.
10	**Total taxes after adjustments.** Combine lines 6 through 9			10	.
11	**Total deposits for this quarter, including overpayment applied from a prior quarter and overpayments applied from Form 941-X, 941-X (PR), 944-X, 944-X (PR), or 944-X (SP) filed in the current quarter** .			11	.
12	**Balance due.** If line 10 is more than line 11, enter the difference and see instructions . . .			12	0 .
13	**Overpayment.** If line 11 is more than line 10, enter the difference	.		Check one:	☐ Apply to next return. ☐ Send a refund.

► **You MUST complete both pages of Form 941 and SIGN it.** Next ►

For Privacy Act and Paperwork Reduction Act Notice, see the back of the Payment Voucher. Cat. No. 17001Z Form **941** (Rev. 1-2014)

Name ____________ Class ____________ Date ____________

PROBLEM 8B-2 (CONCLUDED)

950214

Name *(not your trade name)* | **Employer identification number (EIN)**

Part 2: Tell us about your deposit schedule and tax liability for this quarter.

If you are unsure about whether you are a monthly schedule depositor or a semiweekly schedule depositor, see Pub. 15 (Circular E), section 11.

14 **Check one:** ☐ **Line 10 on this return is less than $2,500 or line 10 on the return for the prior quarter was less than $2,500, and you did not incur a $100,000 next-day deposit obligation during the current quarter.** If line 10 for the prior quarter was less than $2,500 but line 10 on this return is $100,000 or more, you must provide a record of your federal tax liability. If you are a monthly schedule depositor, complete the deposit schedule below; if you are a semiweekly schedule depositor, attach Schedule B (Form 941). Go to Part 3.

☐ **You were a monthly schedule depositor for the entire quarter.** Enter your tax liability for each month and total liability for the quarter, then go to Part 3.

Tax liability: **Month 1** ____ .

Month 2 ____ .

Month 3 ____ .

Total liability for quarter ____ . **Total must equal line 10.**

☐ **You were a semiweekly schedule depositor for any part of this quarter.** Complete Schedule B (Form 941), Report of Tax Liability for Semiweekly Schedule Depositors, and attach it to Form 941.

Part 3: Tell us about your business. If a question does NOT apply to your business, leave it blank.

15 **If your business has closed or you stopped paying wages** . . . . ☐ Check here, and

enter the final date you paid wages ____ / / ____.

16 **If you are a seasonal employer and you do not have to file a return for every quarter of the year** . . ☐ Check here.

Part 4: May we speak with your third-party designee?

Do you want to allow an employee, a paid tax preparer, or another person to discuss this return with the IRS? See the instructions for details.

☐ Yes. Designee's name and phone number ____ ____

Select a 5-digit Personal Identification Number (PIN) to use when talking to the IRS. ☐☐☐☐☐

☐ No.

Part 5: Sign here. You MUST complete both pages of Form 941 and SIGN it.

Under penalties of perjury, I declare that I have examined this return, including accompanying schedules and statements, and to the best of my knowledge and belief, it is true, correct, and complete. Declaration of preparer (other than taxpayer) is based on all information of which preparer has any knowledge.

X **Sign your name here** ____

Print your name here ____

Print your title here ____

Date ____ / / ____

Best daytime phone ____

Paid Preparer Use Only

Check if you are self-employed . . . ☐

Preparer's name		PTIN	
Preparer's signature		Date	/ /
Firm's name (or yours if self-employed)		EIN	
Address		Phone	
City	State	ZIP code	

Name ______________________ Class ____________ Date ____________

PROBLEM 8B-3

REQUIREMENT 1

Amber Bixby

Calculation for December OASDI tax ______________________

REQUIREMENT 2

Date	Account	Debit	Credit

Name ______________________ Class ______________ Date ______________

PROBLEM 8B-3 (CONTINUED)

REQUIREMENT 3

Date		Account	Debit	Credit

Name ____________ Class ____________ Date ____________

PROBLEM 8B-3 (CONTINUED)

REQUIREMENT 4

Form **941 for 201X: Employer's QUARTERLY Federal Tax Return** 950114
(Rev. January 2014) Department of the Treasury — Internal Revenue Service OMB No. 1545-0029

Employer identification number (EIN) [ ][ ] – [ ][ ][ ][ ][ ][ ][ ]

Name *(not your trade name)* ____________

Trade name *(if any)* ____________

Address ____________
Number Street Suite or room number
____
City State ZIP code
____
Foreign country name Foreign province/county Foreign postal code

Report for this Quarter of 201X
(Check one.)

☐ **1:** January, February, March

☐ **2:** April, May, June

☐ **3:** July, August, September

☐ **4:** October, November, December

Instructions and prior year forms are available at *www.irs.gov/form941.*

Read the separate instructions before you complete Form 941. Type or print within the boxes.

Part 1: Answer these questions for this quarter.

1 **Number of employees who received wages, tips, or other compensation for the pay period including:** ***Mar. 12*** **(Quarter 1),** ***June 12*** **(Quarter 2),** ***Sept. 12*** **(Quarter 3), or** ***Dec. 12*** **(Quarter 4)** . . . 1 ______

2 **Wages, tips, and other compensation** . . . . 2 ______ .

3 **Federal income tax withheld from wages, tips, and other compensation** . . . . . . 3 ______ .

4 **If no wages, tips, and other compensation are subject to social security or Medicare tax** ☐ **Check and go to line 6.**

		Column 1		Column 2
5a	**Taxable social security wages** . .	.	× .124 =	.
5b	**Taxable social security tips** . . .	.	× .124 =	.
5c	**Taxable Medicare wages & tips** . .	.	× .029 =	.
5d	**Taxable wages & tips subject to Additional Medicare Tax withholding**	.	× .009 =	.

5e **Add Column 2 from lines 5a, 5b, 5c, and 5d** . . . . 5e ______ .

5f **Section 3121(q) Notice and Demand—Tax due on unreported tips** (see instructions) . . 5f ______ .

6 **Total taxes before adjustments.** Add lines 3, 5e, and 5f . . . . . . 6 ______ .

7 **Current quarter's adjustment for fractions of cents** . . . . . . 7 ______ .

8 **Current quarter's adjustment for sick pay** . . . . 8 ______ .

9 **Current quarter's adjustments for tips and group-term life insurance** . . . . . 9 ______ .

10 **Total taxes after adjustments.** Combine lines 6 through 9 . . . . . . 10 ______ .

11 **Total deposits for this quarter, including overpayment applied from a prior quarter and overpayments applied from Form 941-X, 941-X (PR), 944-X, 944-X (PR), or 944-X (SP) filed in the current quarter** . . . . 11 ______ .

12 **Balance due.** If line 10 is more than line 11, enter the difference and see instructions . . . 12 0 .

13 **Overpayment.** If line 11 is more than line 10, enter the difference ______ . Check one: ☐ Apply to next return. ☐ Send a refund.

► **You MUST complete both pages of Form 941 and SIGN it.** Next ►

For Privacy Act and Paperwork Reduction Act Notice, see the back of the Payment Voucher. Cat. No. 17001Z Form **941** (Rev. 1-2014)

Name ______________ Class ______________ Date ______________

PROBLEM 8B-3 (CONCLUDED)

950214

Name *(not your trade name)* | **Employer identification number (EIN)**

Part 2: Tell us about your deposit schedule and tax liability for this quarter.

If you are unsure about whether you are a monthly schedule depositor or a semiweekly schedule depositor, see Pub. 15 (Circular E), section 11.

14 Check one: ☐ **Line 10 on this return is less than $2,500 or line 10 on the return for the prior quarter was less than $2,500, and you did not incur a $100,000 next-day deposit obligation during the current quarter.** If line 10 for the prior quarter was less than $2,500 but line 10 on this return is $100,000 or more, you must provide a record of your federal tax liability. If you are a monthly schedule depositor, complete the deposit schedule below; if you are a semiweekly schedule depositor, attach Schedule B (Form 941). Go to Part 3.

☐ **You were a monthly schedule depositor for the entire quarter.** Enter your tax liability for each month and total liability for the quarter, then go to Part 3.

Tax liability: Month 1 ______ .

Month 2 ______ .

Month 3 ______ .

Total liability for quarter ______ . **Total must equal line 10.**

☐ **You were a semiweekly schedule depositor for any part of this quarter.** Complete Schedule B (Form 941), Report of Tax Liability for Semiweekly Schedule Depositors, and attach it to Form 941.

Part 3: Tell us about your business. If a question does NOT apply to your business, leave it blank.

15 If your business has closed or you stopped paying wages ☐ Check here, and

enter the final date you paid wages ___ / ___ / ___ .

16 If you are a seasonal employer and you do not have to file a return for every quarter of the year ☐ Check here.

Part 4: May we speak with your third-party designee?

Do you want to allow an employee, a paid tax preparer, or another person to discuss this return with the IRS? See the instructions for details.

☐ Yes. Designee's name and phone number ______ ______

Select a 5-digit Personal Identification Number (PIN) to use when talking to the IRS. ☐☐☐☐☐

☐ No.

Part 5: Sign here. You MUST complete both pages of Form 941 and SIGN it.

Under penalties of perjury, I declare that I have examined this return, including accompanying schedules and statements, and to the best of my knowledge and belief, it is true, correct, and complete. Declaration of preparer (other than taxpayer) is based on all information of which preparer has any knowledge.

X **Sign your name here** ______

Print your name here ______

Print your title here ______

Date ___ / ___ / ___

Best daytime phone ______

Paid Preparer Use Only

Check if you are self-employed ☐

Preparer's name ______ PTIN ______

Preparer's signature ______ Date ___ / ___ / ___

Firm's name (or yours if self-employed) ______ EIN ______

Address ______ Phone ______

City ______ State ______ ZIP code ______

Name ____________________ Class ____________________ Date ____________________

PROBLEM 8B-4

Form **940 for 201X: Employer's Annual Federal Unemployment (FUTA) Tax Return** 850113

Department of the Treasury — Internal Revenue Service

OMB No. 1545-0028

Employer identification number (EIN) ☐☐ – ☐☐☐☐☐☐☐

Name *(not your trade name)*

Trade name *(if any)*

Address

Number Street Suite or room number

City State ZIP code

Foreign country name Foreign province/county Foreign postal code

Type of Return
(Check all that apply.)

☐ **a.** Amended

☐ **b.** Successor employer

☐ **c.** No payments to employees in 201X

☐ **d.** Final: Business closed or stopped paying wages

Instructions and prior-year forms are available at *www.irs.gov/form940.*

Read the separate instructions before you complete this form. Please type or print within the boxes.

Part 1: Tell us about your return. If any line does NOT apply, leave it blank.

1a **If you had to pay state unemployment tax in one state only, enter the state abbreviation** . 1a ☐☐

1b **If you had to pay state unemployment tax in more than one state, you are a multi-state employer** . . . . 1b ☐ Check here. Complete Schedule A (Form 940).

2 **If you paid wages in a state that is subject to CREDIT REDUCTION** . . . . 2 ☐ Check here. Complete Schedule A (Form 940).

Part 2: Determine your FUTA tax before adjustments for 201X. If any line does NOT apply, leave it blank.

3 **Total payments to all employees** . . . . 3 .

4 **Payments exempt from FUTA tax** . . . 4 .

Check all that apply: 4a ☐ Fringe benefits 4c ☐ Retirement/Pension 4e ☐ Other

4b ☐ Group-term life insurance 4d ☐ Dependent care

5 **Total of payments made to each employee in excess of $7,000** . . . . 5 .

6 **Subtotal** (line 4 + line 5 = line 6) . . . . 6 .

7 **Total taxable FUTA wages** (line 3 – line 6 = line 7) (see instructions) . . . . 7 .

8 **FUTA tax before adjustments** (line 7 x .006 = line 8) . . . . 8 .

Part 3: Determine your adjustments. If any line does NOT apply, leave it blank.

9 **If ALL of the taxable FUTA wages you paid were excluded from state unemployment tax, multiply line 7 by .054** (line 7 × .054 = line 9). Go to line 12 . . . . 9 .

10 **If SOME of the taxable FUTA wages you paid were excluded from state unemployment tax, OR you paid ANY state unemployment tax late** (after the due date for filing Form 940), complete the worksheet in the instructions. Enter the amount from line 7 of the worksheet . . 10 .

11 **If credit reduction applies,** enter the total from Schedule A (Form 940) . . . . 11 .

Part 4: Determine your FUTA tax and balance due or overpayment for 201X. If any line does NOT apply, leave it blank.

12 **Total FUTA tax after adjustments** (lines 8 + 9 + 10 + 11 = line 12) . . . . 12 .

13 **FUTA tax deposited for the year, including any overpayment applied from a prior year** . 13 .

14 **Balance due** (If line 12 is more than line 13, enter the excess on line 14.)

- If line 14 is more than $500, you must deposit your tax.
- If line 14 is $500 or less, you may pay with this return. (see instructions) . . . . 14 .

15 **Overpayment** (If line 13 is more than line 12, enter the excess on line 15 and check a box below.) . . . . 15 .

► You **MUST** complete both pages of this form and **SIGN** it. Check one: ☐ Apply to next return. ☐ Send a refund.

Next ►

For Privacy Act and Paperwork Reduction Act Notice, see the back of Form 940-V, Payment Voucher. Cat. No. 11234O Form **940** (2013)

Name ______ Class ______ Date ______

PROBLEM 8B-4 (CONCLUDED)

850212

Name *(not your trade name)* | **Employer identification number (EIN)**

Part 5: Report your FUTA tax liability by quarter only if line 12 is more than $500. If not, go to Part 6.

16 Report the amount of your FUTA tax liability for each quarter; do NOT enter the amount you deposited. If you had no liability for a quarter, leave the line blank.

16a 1st quarter (January 1 – March 31) . . . . **16a** ______ .

16b 2nd quarter (April 1 – June 30) . . . . **16b** ______ .

16c 3rd quarter (July 1 – September 30) . . . . **16c** ______ .

16d 4th quarter (October 1 – December 31) . . . . **16d** ______ .

17 Total tax liability for the year (lines 16a + 16b + 16c + 16d = line 17) **17** ______ . **Total must equal line 12.**

Part 6: May we speak with your third-party designee?

Do you want to allow an employee, a paid tax preparer, or another person to discuss this return with the IRS? See the instructions for details.

☐ **Yes.** Designee's name and phone number ______ ______

Select a 5-digit Personal Identification Number (PIN) to use when talking to IRS ☐☐☐☐☐

☐ **No.**

Part 7: Sign here. You MUST complete both pages of this form and SIGN it.

Under penalties of perjury, I declare that I have examined this return, including accompanying schedules and statements, and to the best of my knowledge and belief, it is true, correct, and complete, and that no part of any payment made to a state unemployment fund claimed as a credit was, or is to be, deducted from the payments made to employees. Declaration of preparer (other than taxpayer) is based on all information of which preparer has any knowledge.

✗ Sign your name here ______

Print your name here ______

Print your title here ______

Date ___ / ___ / ___

Best daytime phone ______

Paid Preparer Use Only

Check if you are self-employed . ☐

Preparer's name ______ PTIN ______

Preparer's signature ______ Date ___ / ___ / ___

Firm's name (or yours if self-employed) ______ EIN ______

Address ______ Phone ______

City ______ State ______ ZIP code ______

Name ______________________ Class ______________ Date ______________

ON THE JOB CONTINUING PROBLEM
SMITH COMPUTER CENTER

ASSIGNMENT 1

Use the fold-out payroll register provided for this assignment, which includes the first three pay periods. Prepare the payroll register.

ASSIGNMENT 2

Record the December payrolls and the payment of the payrolls in the general journal. Post journal entries to the general ledger.

SMITH COMPUTER CENTER
GENERAL JOURNAL

PAGE 5

Date		Account Titles and Description	PR	Dr.	Cr.

Name ______________________ Class ______________ Date ______________

ON THE JOB CONTINUING PROBLEM
SMITH COMPUTER CENTER

ASSIGNMENT 3

Record payroll tax expense for the fourth quarter in the general journal. Post to the ledger.

ASSIGNMENT 4

Record the payment of each tax liability in the general journal and post to the ledger.

SMITH COMPUTER CENTER
GENERAL JOURNAL

PAGE 6

Date	Account Titles and Description	PR	Dr.	Cr.

Name ______________________ Class ______________ Date ______________

CASH — ACCOUNT NO. 1000

Date		Explanation	Post Ref.	Debit	Credit	Balance Debit	Balance Credit
11/30	1X	Balance forward	✓			8 1 1 0 00	

PETTY CASH — ACCOUNT NO. 1010

Date		Explanation	Post Ref.	Debit	Credit	Balance Debit	Balance Credit
11/30	1X	Balance forward	✓			3 0 0 00	

ACCOUNTS RECEIVABLE — ACCOUNT NO. 1020

Date		Explanation	Post Ref.	Debit	Credit	Balance Debit	Balance Credit
11/30	1X	Balance forward	✓			15 5 7 5 00	

Name ______________________ Class ______________ Date ______________

PREPAID RENT **ACCOUNT NO. 1025**

Date		Explanation	Post Ref.	Debit	Credit	Balance Debit	Balance Credit
11/30	1X	Balance forward	✓			2 0 0 0 00	

SUPPLIES **ACCOUNT NO. 1030**

Date		Explanation	Post Ref.	Debit	Credit	Balance Debit	Balance Credit
11/30	1X	Balance forward	✓			1 9 2 00	

COMPUTER SHOP EQUIPMENT **ACCOUNT NO. 1080**

Date		Explanation	Post Ref.	Debit	Credit	Balance Debit	Balance Credit
11/30	1X	Balance forward	✓			5 7 0 0 00	

ACCUMULATED DEPRECIATION, COMPUTER SHOP EQUIPMENT **ACCOUNT NO. 1081**

Date		Explanation	Post Ref.	Debit	Credit	Balance Debit	Balance Credit
11/30	1X	Balance forward	✓				1 5 0 00

Name ____________________ Class ____________________ Date ____________________

OFFICE EQUIPMENT — ACCOUNT NO. 1090

Date		Explanation	Post Ref.	Debit	Credit	Balance Debit	Balance Credit
11/30	1X	Balance forward	✓			3 850 00	

ACCUMULATED DEPRECIATION, OFFICE EQUIPMENT — ACCOUNT NO. 1091

Date		Explanation	Post Ref.	Debit	Credit	Balance Debit	Balance Credit
11/30	1X	Balance forward	✓				1 1 0 00

ACCOUNTS PAYABLE — ACCOUNT NO. 2000

Date		Explanation	Post Ref.	Debit	Credit	Balance Debit	Balance Credit
11/30	1X	Balance forward	✓				2 570 00

WAGES PAYABLE — ACCOUNT NO. 2010

Date		Explanation	Post Ref.	Debit	Credit	Balance Debit	Balance Credit

Name ____________________ Class ____________ Date ____________

FICA—OASDI PAYABLE ACCOUNT NO. 2020

Date	Explanation	Post Ref.	Debit	Credit	Balance	
					Debit	Credit

FICA—MEDICARE PAYABLE ACCOUNT NO. 2030

Date	Explanation	Post Ref.	Debit	Credit	Balance	
					Debit	Credit

FIT PAYABLE ACCOUNT NO. 2040

Date	Explanation	Post Ref.	Debit	Credit	Balance	
					Debit	Credit

SIT PAYABLE ACCOUNT NO. 2050

Date	Explanation	Post Ref.	Debit	Credit	Balance	
					Debit	Credit

Name ______________________ Class ______________ Date ______________

FUTA TAX PAYABLE **ACCOUNT NO. 2060**

Date	Explanation	Post Ref.	Debit	Credit	Balance	
					Debit	Credit

SUTA TAX PAYABLE **ACCOUNT NO. 2070**

Date	Explanation	Post Ref.	Debit	Credit	Balance	
					Debit	Credit

Name ______________ Class ______________ Date ______________

T. FELDMAN, CAPITAL ACCOUNT NO. 3000

Date		Explanation	Post Ref.	Debit	Credit	Balance Debit	Balance Credit
11/30	1X	Balance forward	✓				12 2 8 2 00

T. FELDMAN, WITHDRAWALS ACCOUNT NO. 3010

Date		Explanation	Post Ref.	Debit	Credit	Balance Debit	Balance Credit
11/30	1X	Balance forward	✓			9 1 5 00	

SERVICE REVENUE ACCOUNT NO. 4000

Date		Explanation	Post Ref.	Debit	Credit	Balance Debit	Balance Credit
11/30	1X	Balance forward	✓				21 8 0 0 00

ADVERTISING EXPENSE ACCOUNT NO. 5010

Date		Explanation	Post Ref.	Debit	Credit	Balance Debit	Balance Credit

RENT EXPENSE ACCOUNT NO. 5020

Date		Explanation	Post Ref.	Debit	Credit	Balance Debit	Balance Credit

Name ____________________ Class ____________________ Date ____________________

UTILITIES EXPENSE ACCOUNT NO. 5030

Date		Explanation	Post Ref.	Debit	Credit	Balance Debit	Balance Credit

PHONE EXPENSE ACCOUNT NO. 5040

Date		Explanation	Post Ref.	Debit	Credit	Balance Debit	Balance Credit
11/30	1X	Balance forward	✓			170 00	

SUPPLIES EXPENSE ACCOUNT NO. 5050

Date		Explanation	Post Ref.	Debit	Credit	Balance Debit	Balance Credit
11/30	1X	Balance forward	✓			45 00	

INSURANCE EXPENSE ACCOUNT NO. 5060

Date		Explanation	Post Ref.	Debit	Credit	Balance Debit	Balance Credit

POSTAGE EXPENSE ACCOUNT NO. 5070

Date		Explanation	Post Ref.	Debit	Credit	Balance Debit	Balance Credit
11/30	1X	Balance forward	✓			40 00	

Name ______________________ Class ______________ Date ______________

DEPRECIATION EXPENSE C. S. EQUIPMENT ACCOUNT NO. 5080

Date		Explanation	Post Ref.	Debit	Credit	Balance Debit	Balance Credit

DEPRECIATION EXPENSE OFFICE EQUIPMENT ACCOUNT NO. 5090

Date		Explanation	Post Ref.	Debit	Credit	Balance Debit	Balance Credit

MISCELLANEOUS EXPENSE ACCOUNT NO. 5100

Date		Explanation	Post Ref.	Debit	Credit	Balance Debit	Balance Credit
11/30	1X	Balance forward	✓			1 5 00	

WAGES EXPENSE ACCOUNT NO. 5110

Date		Explanation	Post Ref.	Debit	Credit	Balance Debit	Balance Credit

PAYROLL TAX EXPENSE ACCOUNT NO. 5120

Date		Explanation	Post Ref.	Debit	Credit	Balance Debit	Balance Credit

Name ______________________ Class ______________ Date ______________

ON THE JOB CONTINUING PROBLEM

ASSIGNMENT 5

Form **941 for 201X: Employer's QUARTERLY Federal Tax Return** 950114
(Rev. January 2014) Department of the Treasury — Internal Revenue Service OMB No. 1545-0029

Employer identification number (EIN) [ ][ ] – [ ][ ][ ][ ][ ][ ][ ]

Name *(not your trade name)* ____________________

Trade name *(if any)* ____________________

Address ____________________
Number Street Suite or room number

____
City State ZIP code

____
Foreign country name Foreign province/county Foreign postal code

Report for this Quarter of 201X
(Check one.)

- [ ] **1:** January, February, March
- [ ] **2:** April, May, June
- [ ] **3:** July, August, September
- [ ] **4:** October, November, December

Instructions and prior year forms are available at *www.irs.gov/form941.*

Read the separate instructions before you complete Form 941. Type or print within the boxes.

Part 1: Answer these questions for this quarter.

1	**Number of employees who received wages, tips, or other compensation for the pay period including:** ***Mar. 12*** **(Quarter 1),** ***June 12*** **(Quarter 2),** ***Sept. 12*** **(Quarter 3), or** ***Dec. 12*** **(Quarter 4)**			1	
2	**Wages, tips, and other compensation**			2	.
3	**Federal income tax withheld from wages, tips, and other compensation**			3	.
4	**If no wages, tips, and other compensation are subject to social security or Medicare tax**				☐ **Check and go to line 6.**
		Column 1		**Column 2**	
5a	**Taxable social security wages**	.	× .124 =	.	
5b	**Taxable social security tips**	.	× .124 =	.	
5c	**Taxable Medicare wages & tips**	.	× .029 =	.	
5d	**Taxable wages & tips subject to Additional Medicare Tax withholding**	.	× .009 =	.	
5e	**Add Column 2 from lines 5a, 5b, 5c, and 5d**			5e	.
5f	**Section 3121(q) Notice and Demand—Tax due on unreported tips** (see instructions)			5f	.
6	**Total taxes before adjustments.** Add lines 3, 5e, and 5f			6	.
7	**Current quarter's adjustment for fractions of cents**			7	.
8	**Current quarter's adjustment for sick pay**			8	.
9	**Current quarter's adjustments for tips and group-term life insurance**			9	.
10	**Total taxes after adjustments.** Combine lines 6 through 9			10	.
11	**Total deposits for this quarter, including overpayment applied from a prior quarter and overpayments applied from Form 941-X, 941-X (PR), 944-X, 944-X (PR), or 944-X (SP) filed in the current quarter**			11	.
12	**Balance due.** If line 10 is more than line 11, enter the difference and see instructions			12	0 .
13	**Overpayment.** If line 11 is more than line 10, enter the difference	.	Check one:	☐ Apply to next return.	☐ Send a refund.

▶ **You MUST complete both pages of Form 941 and SIGN it.** Next ▶

For Privacy Act and Paperwork Reduction Act Notice, see the back of the Payment Voucher. Cat. No. 17001Z Form **941** (Rev. 1-2014)

Name ______________ Class ______________ Date ______________

ON THE JOB CONTINUING PROBLEM

ASSIGNMENT 5 (CONCLUDED)

950214

Name *(not your trade name)* | Employer identification number (EIN)

Part 2: Tell us about your deposit schedule and tax liability for this quarter.

If you are unsure about whether you are a monthly schedule depositor or a semiweekly schedule depositor, see Pub. 15 (Circular E), section 11.

14 Check one: ☐ **Line 10 on this return is less than $2,500 or line 10 on the return for the prior quarter was less than $2,500, and you did not incur a $100,000 next-day deposit obligation during the current quarter.** If line 10 for the prior quarter was less than $2,500 but line 10 on this return is $100,000 or more, you must provide a record of your federal tax liability. If you are a monthly schedule depositor, complete the deposit schedule below; if you are a semiweekly schedule depositor, attach Schedule B (Form 941). Go to Part 3.

☐ **You were a monthly schedule depositor for the entire quarter.** Enter your tax liability for each month and total liability for the quarter, then go to Part 3.

Tax liability: Month 1 ______ .

Month 2 ______ .

Month 3 ______ .

Total liability for quarter ______ . **Total must equal line 10.**

☐ **You were a semiweekly schedule depositor for any part of this quarter.** Complete Schedule B (Form 941), Report of Tax Liability for Semiweekly Schedule Depositors, and attach it to Form 941.

Part 3: Tell us about your business. If a question does NOT apply to your business, leave it blank.

15 If your business has closed or you stopped paying wages . . . . ☐ Check here, and

enter the final date you paid wages ___ / ___ / ___ .

16 If you are a seasonal employer and you do not have to file a return for every quarter of the year . . ☐ Check here.

Part 4: May we speak with your third-party designee?

Do you want to allow an employee, a paid tax preparer, or another person to discuss this return with the IRS? See the instructions for details.

☐ Yes. Designee's name and phone number ______ ______

Select a 5-digit Personal Identification Number (PIN) to use when talking to the IRS. ☐☐☐☐☐

☐ No.

Part 5: Sign here. You MUST complete both pages of Form 941 and SIGN it.

Under penalties of perjury, I declare that I have examined this return, including accompanying schedules and statements, and to the best of my knowledge and belief, it is true, correct, and complete. Declaration of preparer (other than taxpayer) is based on all information of which preparer has any knowledge.

X **Sign your name here** ______

Print your name here ______

Print your title here ______

Date ___ / ___ / ___

Best daytime phone ______

Paid Preparer Use Only Check if you are self-employed . . . ☐

Preparer's name		PTIN	
Preparer's signature		Date	/ /
Firm's name (or yours if self-employed)		EIN	
Address		Phone	
City		State	ZIP code

Name ____________________ Class ________ Date ____________

ON THE JOB CONTINUING PROBLEM

ASSIGNMENT 6

Form **940 for 201X: Employer's Annual Federal Unemployment (FUTA) Tax Return** 850113

Department of the Treasury — Internal Revenue Service OMB No. 1545-0028

Employer identification number (EIN) [ ][ ] – [ ][ ][ ][ ][ ][ ][ ]

Name *(not your trade name)* ____________________

Trade name *(if any)* ____________________

Address ____________________

Number Street Suite or room number

City State ZIP code

Foreign country name Foreign province/county Foreign postal code

Type of Return
(Check all that apply.)

- ☐ **a.** Amended
- ☐ **b.** Successor employer
- ☐ **c.** No payments to employees in 201X
- ☐ **d.** Final: Business closed or stopped paying wages

Instructions and prior-year forms are available at *www.irs.gov/form940.*

Read the separate instructions before you complete this form. Please type or print within the boxes.

Part 1: Tell us about your return. If any line does NOT apply, leave it blank.

1a **If you had to pay state unemployment tax in one state only, enter the state abbreviation** . **1a** [ ][ ]

1b **If you had to pay state unemployment tax in more than one state, you are a multi-state employer** . . . . . **1b** ☐ Check here. Complete Schedule A (Form 940).

2 **If you paid wages in a state that is subject to CREDIT REDUCTION** . . . . . **2** ☐ Check here. Complete Schedule A (Form 940).

Part 2: Determine your FUTA tax before adjustments for 201X. If any line does NOT apply, leave it blank.

3 **Total payments to all employees** . . . . . **3** ______ .

4 **Payments exempt from FUTA tax** . . . . . **4** ______ .

Check all that apply: **4a** ☐ Fringe benefits **4c** ☐ Retirement/Pension **4e** ☐ Other
4b ☐ Group-term life insurance **4d** ☐ Dependent care

5 **Total of payments made to each employee in excess of $7,000** . . . . . **5** ______ .

6 **Subtotal** (line 4 + line 5 = line 6) . . . . . **6** ______ .

7 **Total taxable FUTA wages** (line 3 – line 6 = line 7) (see instructions) . . . . . **7** ______ .

8 **FUTA tax before adjustments** (line 7 x .006 = line 8) . . . . . **8** ______ .

Part 3: Determine your adjustments. If any line does NOT apply, leave it blank.

9 **If ALL of the taxable FUTA wages you paid were excluded from state unemployment tax, multiply line 7 by .054** (line 7 × .054 = line 9). Go to line 12 . . . . . **9** ______ .

10 **If SOME of the taxable FUTA wages you paid were excluded from state unemployment tax, OR you paid ANY state unemployment tax late** (after the due date for filing Form 940), complete the worksheet in the instructions. Enter the amount from line 7 of the worksheet . . **10** ______ .

11 **If credit reduction applies,** enter the total from Schedule A (Form 940) . . . . . **11** ______ .

Part 4: Determine your FUTA tax and balance due or overpayment for 201X. If any line does NOT apply, leave it blank.

12 **Total FUTA tax after adjustments** (lines 8 + 9 + 10 + 11 = line 12) . . . . . **12** ______ .

13 **FUTA tax deposited for the year, including any overpayment applied from a prior year** . **13** ______ .

14 **Balance due** (If line 12 is more than line 13, enter the excess on line 14.)
- If line 14 is more than $500, you must deposit your tax.
- If line 14 is $500 or less, you may pay with this return. (see instructions) . . . . . **14** ______ .

15 **Overpayment** (If line 13 is more than line 12, enter the excess on line 15 and check a box below.) . . . . . **15** ______ .

► You **MUST** complete both pages of this form and **SIGN** it. Check one: ☐ Apply to next return. ☐ Send a refund.

Next ►

For Privacy Act and Paperwork Reduction Act Notice, see the back of Form 940-V, Payment Voucher. Cat. No. 11234O Form **940** (2013)

Name ________________ Class ________ Date ________

ON THE JOB CONTINUING PROBLEM (CONCLUDED)

ASSIGNMENT 6 (CONCLUDED)

850212

Name (not your trade name) | Employer identification number (EIN)

Part 5: Report your FUTA tax liability by quarter only if line 12 is more than $500. If not, go to Part 6.

16 Report the amount of your FUTA tax liability for each quarter; do NOT enter the amount you deposited. If you had no liability for a quarter, leave the line blank.

16a 1st quarter (January 1 – March 31) . . . . **16a** ________ .

16b 2nd quarter (April 1 – June 30) . . . . **16b** ________ .

16c 3rd quarter (July 1 – September 30) . . . . **16c** ________ .

16d 4th quarter (October 1 – December 31) . . . . **16d** ________ .

17 Total tax liability for the year (lines 16a + 16b + 16c + 16d = line 17) **17** ________ . **Total must equal line 12.**

Part 6: May we speak with your third-party designee?

Do you want to allow an employee, a paid tax preparer, or another person to discuss this return with the IRS? See the instructions for details.

☐ **Yes.** Designee's name and phone number

Select a 5-digit Personal Identification Number (PIN) to use when talking to IRS

☐ **No.**

Part 7: Sign here. You MUST complete both pages of this form and SIGN it.

Under penalties of perjury, I declare that I have examined this return, including accompanying schedules and statements, and to the best of my knowledge and belief, it is true, correct, and complete, and that no part of any payment made to a state unemployment fund claimed as a credit was, or is to be, deducted from the payments made to employees. Declaration of preparer (other than taxpayer) is based on all information of which preparer has any knowledge.

✗ Sign your name here

Print your name here

Print your title here

Date / /

Best daytime phone

Paid Preparer Use Only

Check if you are self-employed . ☐

Preparer's name | PTIN

Preparer's signature | Date / /

Firm's name (or yours if self-employed) | EIN

Address | Phone

City | State | ZIP code

Name ______________________ Class ____________ Date ______________

CHAPTER 8
SUMMARY PRACTICE TEST:
PAYING THE PAYROLL, DEPOSITING PAYROLL TAXES, AND FILING THE REQUIRED QUARTERLY AND ANNUAL TAX FORMS

Part I

Fill in the blank(s) to complete the statement.

1. Form 941 is completed ______________.

2. The payroll tax expense for the employer is made up of ______________, ______________, ______________, and FUTA.

3. Data from the ______________ ______________ will provide the needed information to record the payroll in the general journal.

4. SUTA is usually paid ______________.

5. FUTA Payable is a ______________ found on the ______________ ______________.

6. Form 941 summarizes the taxes owed for ______________ and ______________.

7. ______________ ______________ ______________ will tell if a deposit is to be made monthly or semiweekly for FIT and Social Security.

8. Form ______________ is prepared quarterly to summarize tax liabilities for FICA (Social Security and Medicare) and FIT.

9. The ______________ ______________ ______________ is required to be given to employees by January 31 following the year employed.

10. ______________ does not have a merit rating like SUTA.

Part II

Answer true or false to the following.

1. Prepaid Workers' Compensation Insurance is a liability.

2. Payroll taxes are recorded as assets for a business.

3. Payroll Tax Expense is made up of FICA, SUTA, and FIT.

4. The frequency of deposits relating to Form 941 is based on the amount of payroll tax liability in the look-back period.

5. The normal balance of FIT payable is a debit.

6. The individual earnings record provides the data to prepare W-2s.

7. A tax calendar provides little help to the employer involving the payment of tax liabilities.

8. Form 941 is completed twice a year.

9. A year-end adjusting entry is needed for workers' compensation.

10. Form 940 reports state unemployment taxes payable for all employees.

Name ______________________ Class ______________ Date ______________

Part III

Complete the following table:

ACCOUNT	CATEGORY	FOUND ON WHICH REPORT
1. Salaries Payable		
2. FUTA Payable		
3. SUTA Payable		
4. OASDI Tax Payable—Medicare		
5. FIT Payable		
6. Office Salaries Expense		

Part IV

Complete the following table:

	4 QUARTERS LOOK-BACK PERIOD LIABILITY	PAYROLL PAID WEEKLY	TAX PAID BY:
Sit. A	$40,000	October	?
Sit. B	75,000		
		on Wed.	?
		on Thurs.	?
		on Fri.	?
		on Sat.	?
		on Sun.	?
		on Mon.	?
		on Tues.	?

Why is the depositor in situation A classified as a monthly depositor while in situation B the depositor is classified as semiweekly?

SOLUTIONS

Part I

1. quarterly
2. FICA (OASDI), FICA (Medicare), SUTA
3. payroll register
4. quarterly
5. liability, balance sheet
6. FICA (OASDI and Medicare), FIT
7. Payroll tax liability in look-back period
8. 941
9. Wage and Tax Statement
10. FUTA

Name ______________________ Class ______________ Date ______________

Part II

1.	false	**6.**	true
2.	false	**7.**	false
3.	false	**8.**	false
4.	true	**9.**	true
5.	false	**10.**	false

Part III

1. Liability; Balance Sheet
2. Liability; Balance Sheet
3. Liability; Balance Sheet
4. Liability; Balance Sheet
5. Liability; Balance Sheet
6. Expense; Income Statement

Part IV

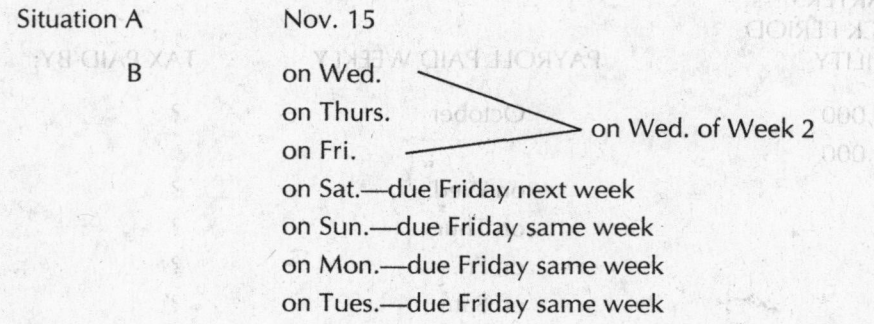

Situation A — Nov. 15

B
on Wed.
on Thurs. } on Wed. of Week 2
on Fri.
on Sat.—due Friday next week
on Sun.—due Friday same week
on Mon.—due Friday same week
on Tues.—due Friday same week

The depositor in situation A is classified as a monthly depositor because its tax liability of $40,000 during the look-back period was less than the $50,000 limit.

On the other hand, the depositor in situation B owed $75,000 during the look-back period. Since this is greater than the $50,000 limit, it was classified as a semiweekly depositor.

Study Guide and Working Papers

Sales and Cash Receipts

Name ______________________ Class ______________ Date ______________

FORMS FOR DEMONSTRATION PROBLEM

REQUIREMENT 1

KIM'S RUNNING SHOP
GENERAL JOURNAL

PAGE 6

Date		Account Titles and Description	PR	Dr.	Cr.

Name ______________________ Class ______________ Date ______________

FORMS FOR DEMONSTRATION PROBLEM

REQUIREMENT 2

PARTIAL GENERAL LEDGER

CASH — ACCOUNT NO. 110

Date 201X		Explanation	Post Ref.	Debit	Credit	Balance Debit	Balance Credit
June	1	Balance	✓			4 0 0 0 00	

ACCOUNTS RECEIVABLE — ACCOUNT NO. 120

Date 201X		Explanation	Post Ref.	Debit	Credit	Balance Debit	Balance Credit
June	1	Balance	✓			1 4 0 0 00	

DISPLAY EQUIPMENT — ACCOUNT NO. 130

Date 201X		Explanation	Post Ref.	Debit	Credit	Balance Debit	Balance Credit
June	1	Balance	✓			9 0 0 00	

M. KIM, CAPITAL — ACCOUNT NO. 310

Date 201X		Explanation	Post Ref.	Debit	Credit	Balance Debit	Balance Credit
June	1	Balance	✓				8 0 0 0 00

Name ____________________ Class ____________________ Date ____________________

FORMS FOR DEMONSTRATION PROBLEM

PARTIAL GENERAL LEDGER

SALES — **ACCOUNT NO. 410**

Date 201X		Explanation	Post Ref.	Debit	Credit	Balance Debit	Balance Credit
June	1	Balance	✓				2 0 0 0 00

SALES DISCOUNTS — **ACCOUNT NO. 420**

Date 201X		Explanation	Post Ref.	Debit	Credit	Balance Debit	Balance Credit

SALES RETURNS AND ALLOWANCES — **ACCOUNT NO. 440**

Date 201X		Explanation	Post Ref.	Debit	Credit	Balance Debit	Balance Credit

Name ______________________ Class ______________ Date ______________

FORMS FOR DEMONSTRATION PROBLEM

ACCOUNTS RECEIVABLE SUBSIDIARY LEDGER

NAME **ROGER FLYNN**
ADDRESS **81 FOSTER RD., BEVERLY, MA 09125**

Date 201X		Explanation	Post Ref.	Debit	Credit	Dr. Balance
June	1	Balance	✓			200 00

NAME **BOB JEY**
ADDRESS **10 RONG RD., BEVERLY, MA 01215**

Date 201X		Explanation	Post Ref.	Debit	Credit	Dr. Balance
June	1	Balance	✓			400 00

Name ____________ Class ____________ Date ____________

FORMS FOR DEMONSTRATION PROBLEM

ACCOUNTS RECEIVABLE SUBSIDIARY LEDGER

NAME JOE LANTZ

ADDRESS 81 FOSTER RD., BEVERLY, MA 09125

Date 201X		Explanation	Post Ref.	Debit	Credit	Dr. Balance
June	1	Balance	✓			800 00

NAME VALERIE TOG

ADDRESS 10 RONG RD., BEVERLY, MA 01215

Date 201X		Explanation	Post Ref.	Debit	Credit	Dr. Balance

Name ______________________ Class ______________ Date ______________

FORMS FOR DEMONSTRATION PROBLEM

REQUIREMENT 3

KIM'S RUNNING SHOP
SCHEDULE OF ACCOUNTS RECEIVABLE
JUNE 30, 201X

Name ______________________ Class ______________ Date ______________

FORMS FOR SET A EXERCISES

9A-1

GENERAL JOURNAL

PAGE 1

Date 201X		Account Titles and Description	PR	Dr.	Cr.
Sept.	18	Accounts Receivable, Twilight Co.		640 00	
		Sales			640 00
		Sold merchandise to Twilight Co.			
	19	Accounts Receivable, Falcon Co.		850 00	
		Sales			850 00
		Sold merchandise to Falcon Co.			

Twilight Co.

Accounts Receivable 112

Falcon Co.

Sales 411

Name ____________________ Class ____________ Date ____________

9A-2

GENERAL JOURNAL

PAGE 1

Date		Account Titles and Description	PR	Dr.	Cr.

Cart Co.

Accounts Receivable 112

Sales 411

French Co.

Sales Returns & Allowances 412

Sales Discounts 413

Name ____________ Class ____________ Date ____________

SET A EXERCISES

9A-3

Date	Account	PR	Dr.	Cr.

9A-4

AVA CO.
GENERAL JOURNAL

PAGE 1

Date	Account Titles and Description	PR	Dr.	Cr.

Name ____________ Class ____________ Date ____________

SET A EXERCISES

9A-4 (CONCLUDED)

GENERAL JOURNAL (CONTINUED) PAGE 1

Date		Account Titles and Description	PR	Dr.	Cr.

ACCOUNTS RECEIVABLE SUBSIDIARY LEDGER

Charleston Co.

William Co.

PARTIAL GENERAL LEDGER

Cash 111

Accounts Receivable 113

Ava Roberts, Capital 311

Sales 411

Sales Returns & Allowances 412

Sales Discount 413

AVA CO.
SCHEDULE OF ACCOUNTS RECEIVABLE
October 31, 201X

9A-5

Name ______________________ Class ______________ Date ______________

FORMS FOR SET B EXERCISES

9B-1

GENERAL JOURNAL

PAGE 1

Date 201X		Account Titles and Description	PR	Dr.	Cr.
May	18	Accounts Receivable, Henry Co.		590 00	
		Sales			590 00
		Sold merchandise to Henry Co.			
	19	Accounts Receivable, Lincoln Co.		890 00	
		Sales			890 00
		Sold merchandise to Lincoln Co.			

Henry Co.

Accounts Receivable 112

Lincoln Co.

Sales 411

Name ________________ Class ________________ Date ________________

9B-2

GENERAL JOURNAL

PAGE 1

Date		Account Titles and Description	PR	Dr.	Cr.

Market Co.

Accounts Receivable 112

Sales 411

Ralph Co.

Sales Returns & Allowances 412

Sales Discounts 413

Name ____________________ Class ____________ Date ____________

SET B EXERCISES

9B-3

Date	Account	PR	Dr.	Cr.

9B-4

AUTUMN CO.
GENERAL JOURNAL

PAGE 1

Date	Account Titles and Description	PR	Dr.	Cr.

Name ______________ Class ______________ Date ______________

SET B EXERCISES

9B-4 (CONCLUDED)

GENERAL JOURNAL (CONTINUED)

PAGE 1

Date		Account Titles and Description	PR	Dr.	Cr.

ACCOUNTS RECEIVABLE SUBSIDIARY LEDGER

Clearview Co.

Nathan Co.

PARTIAL GENERAL LEDGER

Cash 111

Accounts Receivable 113

Andrew Rodgers, Capital 311

Sales 411

Sales Returns & Allowances 412

Sales Discount 413

AUTUMN CO.
SCHEDULE OF ACCOUNTS RECEIVABLE
August 31, 201X

9B-5

Name ______________________ Class ____________ Date ______________

FORMS FOR SET A PROBLEMS

PROBLEM 9A-1
REQUIREMENT 1

FONTINA AND STUFF
GENERAL JOURNAL

PAGE 1

Date		Account Titles and Description	PR	Dr.	Cr.

Name ______________________ Class ______________ Date ______________

PROBLEM 9A-1 (CONTINUED)

REQUIREMENT 2

ACCOUNTS RECEIVABLE SUBSIDIARY LEDGER

NAME DUTCH CO.

ADDRESS 942 MOSE ST., REVERE, MA 01938

Date		Explanation	Post Ref.	Debit	Credit	Dr. Balance

NAME FRAN CO.

ADDRESS 8 JOSS AVE., LYNN, MA 01947

Date		Explanation	Post Ref.	Debit	Credit	Dr. Balance

NAME GROOM CO.

ADDRESS 10 LOST RD., TOPSFIELD, MA 01998

Date		Explanation	Post Ref.	Debit	Credit	Dr. Balance

Name ______________________ Class ____________ Date ____________

PROBLEM 9A-1 (CONTINUED)

FONTINA AND STUFF
GENERAL LEDGER

ACCOUNTS RECEIVABLE — **ACCOUNT NO. 112**

Date	Explanation	Post Ref.	Debit	Credit	Balance Debit	Balance Credit

CHEESE SALES — **ACCOUNT NO. 410**

Date	Explanation	Post Ref.	Debit	Credit	Balance Debit	Balance Credit

GROCERY SALES — **ACCOUNT NO. 411**

Date	Explanation	Post Ref.	Debit	Credit	Balance Debit	Balance Credit

SALES RETURNS AND ALLOWANCES — **ACCOUNT NO. 412**

Date	Explanation	Post Ref.	Debit	Credit	Balance Debit	Balance Credit

Name ____________________ Class ____________ Date ____________

PROBLEM 9A-1 (CONCLUDED)

REQUIREMENT 3

FONTINA AND STUFF
SCHEDULE OF ACCOUNTS RECEIVABLE
FEBRUARY 28, 201X

PROBLEM 9A-2

REQUIREMENT 1

JEFF'S AUTO SUPPLY
GENERAL JOURNAL

PAGE 2

Date	Account Titles and Description	PR	Dr.	Cr.

Name ______________________ Class ______________ Date ______________

PROBLEM 9A-2 (CONTINUED)

REQUIREMENT 2

ACCOUNTS RECEIVABLE SUBSIDIARY LEDGER

NAME **LANCE BLACK**

ADDRESS **9 ROE ST., BARTLETT, NH 01382**

Date		Explanation	Post Ref.	Debit	Credit	Dr. Balance
		Balance				

NAME **R. DICK**

ADDRESS **22 REESE ST., LACONIA, NH 04321**

Date		Explanation	Post Ref.	Debit	Credit	Dr. Balance

NAME **J. METCALF**

ADDRESS **12 ASTER RD., MERRIMACK, NH 02134**

Date		Explanation	Post Ref.	Debit	Credit	Dr. Balance

Name ______________________ Class ______________ Date ______________

PROBLEM 9A-2 (CONTINUED)

JEFF'S AUTO SUPPLY
PARTIAL GENERAL LEDGER

ACCOUNTS RECEIVABLE ACCOUNT NO. 110

Date		Explanation	Post Ref.	Debit	Credit	Balance	
						Debit	Credit

SALES TAX PAYABLE ACCOUNT NO. 210

Date		Explanation	Post Ref.	Debit	Credit	Balance	
						Debit	Credit

AUTO PARTS SALES ACCOUNT NO. 410

Date		Explanation	Post Ref.	Debit	Credit	Balance	
						Debit	Credit

SALES RETURNS AND ALLOWANCES ACCOUNT NO. 420

Date		Explanation	Post Ref.	Debit	Credit	Balance	
						Debit	Credit

Name ______________________ Class ______________ Date ______________

PROBLEM 9A-2 (CONCLUDED)

REQUIREMENT 3

JEFF'S AUTO SUPPLY
SCHEDULE OF ACCOUNTS RECEIVABLE
FEBRUARY 28, 201X

Name ____________________ Class __________ Date __________

PROBLEM 9A-3

REQUIREMENT 1

PAYNE'S SNEAKER SHOP
GENERAL JOURNAL

PAGE 2

Date		Account Titles and Description	PR	Dr.	Cr.

Name ______________________ Class ______________ Date ______________

PROBLEM 9A-3 (CONTINUED)

PAYNE'S SNEAKER SHOP
GENERAL JOURNAL

PAGE 3

Date	Account Titles and Description	PR	Dr.	Cr.

Name ______________________ Class ______________ Date ______________

PROBLEM 9A-3 (CONTINUED)

REQUIREMENT 2

ACCOUNTS RECEIVABLE SUBSIDIARY LEDGER

NAME **B. DURANT**

ADDRESS **1822 RIVER RD., MEMPHIS, TN 09111**

Date		Explanation	Post Ref.	Debit	Credit	Dr. Balance

NAME **RON LANHAM**

ADDRESS **18 MASS. AVE., SAN DIEGO, CA 01999**

Date		Explanation	Post Ref.	Debit	Credit	Dr. Balance

NAME **PENNY PRY**

ADDRESS **918 MOORE DR., HOMEWOOD, IL 60430**

Date		Explanation	Post Ref.	Debit	Credit	Dr. Balance

Name ______________________ Class ______________ Date ______________

PROBLEM 9A-3 (CONTINUED)

NAME JIM ZAMARA

ADDRESS 2 CHESTNUT ST., SWAMPSCOTT, MA 01970

Date		Explanation	Post Ref.	Debit	Credit	Dr. Balance

PAYNE'S SNEAKER SHOP
PARTIAL GENERAL LEDGER

CASH **ACCOUNT NO. 10**

Date		Explanation	Post Ref.	Debit	Credit	Balance Debit	Balance Credit

Name ______________ Class ______________ Date ______________

PROBLEM 9A-3 (CONTINUED)

ACCOUNTS RECEIVABLE — ACCOUNT NO. 12

Date	Explanation	Post Ref.	Debit	Credit	Balance Debit	Balance Credit

SNEAKER RACK EQUIPMENT — ACCOUNT NO. 14

Date	Explanation	Post Ref.	Debit	Credit	Balance Debit	Balance Credit

JARED PAYNE, CAPITAL — ACCOUNT NO. 30

Date	Explanation	Post Ref.	Debit	Credit	Balance Debit	Balance Credit

Name _______________ Class _______________ Date _______________

PROBLEM 9A-3 (CONTINUED)

SALES **ACCOUNT NO. 40**

Date	Explanation	Post Ref.	Debit	Credit	Balance	
					Debit	Credit

SALES DISCOUNT **ACCOUNT NO. 42**

Date 201X	Explanation	Post Ref.	Debit	Credit	Balance	
					Debit	Credit

SALES RETURNS & ALLOWANCES **ACCOUNT NO. 44**

Date 201X	Explanation	Post Ref.	Debit	Credit	Balance	
					Debit	Credit

Name ______________ Class ______________ Date ______________

PROBLEM 9A-3 (CONCLUDED)

REQUIREMENT 3

PAYNE'S SNEAKER SHOP
SCHEDULE OF ACCOUNTS RECEIVABLE
MARCH 31, 201X

Name ______________________ Class ______________ Date ______________

PROBLEM 9A-4

REQUIREMENT 1

CHEVY'S COSMETIC MARKET
GENERAL JOURNAL

PAGE 1

Date		Account Titles and Description	PR	Dr.	Cr.

Name ______________ Class ______________ Date ______________

PROBLEM 9A-4 (CONTINUED)

CHEVY'S COSMETIC MARKET
GENERAL JOURNAL

PAGE 2

Date		Account Titles and Description	PR	Dr.	Cr.

Name ______________________ Class ______________ Date ______________

PROBLEM 9A-4 (CONTINUED)

ACCOUNTS RECEIVABLE SUBSIDIARY LEDGER

NAME **LOIS KOZAK CO.**

ADDRESS **2 RYAN RD., BUFFALO, NY 09113**

Date		Explanation	Post Ref.	Debit	Credit	Debit Balance

Name ______________ Class ______________ Date ______________

PROBLEM 9A-4 (CONTINUED)

ACCOUNTS RECEIVABLE SUBSIDIARY LEDGER

NAME ANN MARIE MAXWELL CO.

ADDRESS 4 REEL RD., LANCASTER, PA 04332

Date		Explanation	Post Ref.	Debit	Credit	Debit Balance

NAME DAVID PARNELL CO.

ADDRESS 14 BONE DR., ENGLEWOOD CLIFFS, NJ 07632

Date		Explanation	Post Ref.	Debit	Credit	Debit Balance

NAME EVERETTE TENNIS CO.

ADDRESS 2 MARION RD., BOSTON, MA 01981

Date		Explanation	Post Ref.	Debit	Credit	Debit Balance

Name ______________________ Class ______________ Date ______________

PROBLEM 9A-4 (CONTINUED)

CHEVY'S COSMETIC MARKET
GENERAL LEDGER

CASH — **ACCOUNT NO. 10**

Date	Explanation	Post Ref.	Debit	Credit	Balance Debit	Balance Credit

ACCOUNTS RECEIVABLE — **ACCOUNT NO. 12**

Date	Explanation	Post Ref.	Debit	Credit	Balance Debit	Balance Credit

Name ______________________ Class ______________ Date ______________

PROBLEM 9A-4 (CONTINUED)

SALES TAX PAYABLE **ACCOUNT NO. 20**

Date		Explanation	Post Ref.	Debit	Credit	Balance Debit	Balance Credit

CHEVY CANTON, CAPITAL **ACCOUNT NO. 30**

Date		Explanation	Post Ref.	Debit	Credit	Balance Debit	Balance Credit

LIPSTICK SALES **ACCOUNT NO. 40**

Date		Explanation	Post Ref.	Debit	Credit	Balance Debit	Balance Credit

Name ____________ Class ____________ Date ____________

PROBLEM 9A-4 (CONCLUDED)

SALES RETURNS & ALLOWANCES, LIPSTICK **ACCOUNT NO. 42**

Date		Explanation	Post Ref.	Debit	Credit	Balance	
						Debit	Credit

EYE SHADOW SALES **ACCOUNT NO. 44**

Date		Explanation	Post Ref.	Debit	Credit	Balance	
						Debit	Credit

REQUIREMENT 2

CHEVY'S COSMETIC MARKET
SCHEDULE OF ACCOUNTS RECEIVABLE
MAY 31, 201X

Name ______________________ Class ______________ Date ______________

FORMS FOR SET B PROBLEMS

PROBLEM 9B-1
REQUIREMENT 1

MACCHIATO AND MORE
GENERAL JOURNAL

PAGE 1

Date	Account Titles and Description	PR	Dr.	Cr.

Name ______________ Class ______________ Date ______________

PROBLEM 9B-1 (CONTINUED)

REQUIREMENT 2

ACCOUNTS RECEIVABLE SUBSIDIARY LEDGER

NAME DUTCH CO.

ADDRESS 942 MOSE ST., REVERE, MA 01938

Date		Explanation	Post Ref.	Debit	Credit	Dr. Balance

NAME FRAN CO.

ADDRESS 8 JOSS AVE., LYNN, MA 01947

Date		Explanation	Post Ref.	Debit	Credit	Dr. Balance

NAME GROOM CO.

ADDRESS 10 LOST RD., TOPSFIELD, MA 01998

Date		Explanation	Post Ref.	Debit	Credit	Dr. Balance

Name ____________ Class ____________ Date ____________

PROBLEM 9B-1 (CONTINUED)

MACCHIATO AND MORE
GENERAL LEDGER

ACCOUNTS RECEIVABLE ACCOUNT NO. 112

Date		Explanation	Post Ref.	Debit	Credit	Balance	
						Debit	Credit

COFFEE SALES ACCOUNT NO. 410

Date		Explanation	Post Ref.	Debit	Credit	Balance	
						Debit	Credit

GROCERY SALES ACCOUNT NO. 411

Date		Explanation	Post Ref.	Debit	Credit	Balance	
						Debit	Credit

SALES RETURNS AND ALLOWANCES ACCOUNT NO. 412

Date		Explanation	Post Ref.	Debit	Credit	Balance	
						Debit	Credit

Name ______________________ Class ______________ Date ______________

PROBLEM 9B-1 (CONCLUDED)

REQUIREMENT 3

MACCHIATO AND MORE
SCHEDULE OF ACCOUNTS RECEIVABLE
JUNE 30, 201X

PROBLEM 9B-2

REQUIREMENT 1

JACK'S AUTO SUPPLY
GENERAL JOURNAL

PAGE 2

Date	Account Titles and Description	PR	Dr.	Cr.

Name ____________ Class ____________ Date ____________

PROBLEM 9B-2 (CONTINUED)

REQUIREMENT 2

ACCOUNTS RECEIVABLE SUBSIDIARY LEDGER

NAME LANCE CORNER

ADDRESS 9 ROE ST., BARTLETT, NH 01382

Date		Explanation	Post Ref.	Debit	Credit	Dr. Balance
		Balance				

NAME R. NONACK

ADDRESS 22 REESE ST., LACONIA, NH 04321

Date		Explanation	Post Ref.	Debit	Credit	Dr. Balance

NAME J. SETH

ADDRESS 12 ASTER RD., MERRIMACK, NH 02134

Date		Explanation	Post Ref.	Debit	Credit	Dr. Balance

Name ______________________ Class ______________ Date ______________

PROBLEM 9B-2 (CONTINUED)

JACK'S AUTO SUPPLY
PARTIAL GENERAL LEDGER

ACCOUNTS RECEIVABLE ACCOUNT NO. 110

Date		Explanation	Post Ref.	Debit	Credit	Balance Debit	Balance Credit

SALES TAX PAYABLE ACCOUNT NO. 210

Date		Explanation	Post Ref.	Debit	Credit	Balance Debit	Balance Credit

AUTO PARTS SALES ACCOUNT NO. 410

Date		Explanation	Post Ref.	Debit	Credit	Balance Debit	Balance Credit

SALES RETURNS AND ALLOWANCES ACCOUNT NO. 420

Date		Explanation	Post Ref.	Debit	Credit	Balance Debit	Balance Credit

Name ____________ Class ____________ Date ____________

PROBLEM 9B-2 (CONCLUDED)

REQUIREMENT 3

JACK'S AUTO SUPPLY
SCHEDULE OF ACCOUNTS RECEIVABLE
JANUARY 31, 201X

Name ______________________ Class ______________ Date ______________

PROBLEM 9B-3

REQUIREMENT 1

PENEY'S SNEAKER SHOP
GENERAL JOURNAL

PAGE 2

Date		Account Titles and Description	PR	Dr.	Cr.

Name ______________________ Class ______________ Date ______________

PROBLEM 9B-3 (CONTINUED)

PENEY'S SNEAKER SHOP
GENERAL JOURNAL

PAGE 3

Date	Account Titles and Description	PR	Dr.	Cr.

Name ______________ Class ______________ Date ______________

PROBLEM 9B-3 (CONTINUED)

REQUIREMENT 2

ACCOUNTS RECEIVABLE SUBSIDIARY LEDGER

NAME B. DONOVAN

ADDRESS 1822 RIVER RD., MEMPHIS, TN 09111

Date		Explanation	Post Ref.	Debit	Credit	Dr. Balance

NAME RON LITTLER

ADDRESS 18 MASS. AVE., SAN DIEGO, CA 01999

Date		Explanation	Post Ref.	Debit	Credit	Dr. Balance

NAME PAGE PRY

ADDRESS 918 MOORE DR., HOMEWOOD, IL 60430

Date		Explanation	Post Ref.	Debit	Credit	Dr. Balance

PROBLEM 9B-3 (CONTINUED)

NAME JIM ZAMORA

ADDRESS 2 CHESTNUT ST., SWAMPSCOTT, MA 01970

Date		Explanation	Post Ref.	Debit	Credit	Dr. Balance

PENEY'S SNEAKER SHOP
PARTIAL GENERAL LEDGER

CASH **ACCOUNT NO. 10**

Date		Explanation	Post Ref.	Debit	Credit	Balance	
						Debit	Credit

Name ______________ Class ______________ Date ______________

PROBLEM 9B-3 (CONTINUED)

ACCOUNTS RECEIVABLE **ACCOUNT NO. 12**

Date	Explanation	Post Ref.	Debit	Credit	Balance Debit	Balance Credit

SNEAKER RACK EQUIPMENT **ACCOUNT NO. 14**

Date	Explanation	Post Ref.	Debit	Credit	Balance Debit	Balance Credit

MAX PENEY, CAPITAL **ACCOUNT NO. 30**

Date	Explanation	Post Ref.	Debit	Credit	Balance Debit	Balance Credit

Name ______________________ Class ______________ Date ______________

PROBLEM 9B-3 (CONTINUED)

SALES **ACCOUNT NO. 40**

Date	Explanation	Post Ref.	Debit	Credit	Balance Debit	Balance Credit

SALES DISCOUNT **ACCOUNT NO. 42**

Date 201X	Explanation	Post Ref.	Debit	Credit	Balance Debit	Balance Credit

SALES RETURNS & ALLOWANCES **ACCOUNT NO. 44**

Date 201X	Explanation	Post Ref.	Debit	Credit	Balance Debit	Balance Credit

Name ______________________ Class ______________ Date ______________

PROBLEM 9B-3 (CONCLUDED)

REQUIREMENT 3

PENEY'S SNEAKER SHOP
SCHEDULE OF ACCOUNTS RECEIVABLE
AUGUST 31, 201X

Name ____________________ Class ____________________ Date ____________________

PROBLEM 9B-4
REQUIREMENT 1

AL'S COSMETIC MARKET
GENERAL JOURNAL

PAGE 1

Date	Account Titles and Description	PR	Dr.	Cr.

Name ______________________ Class ______________ Date ______________

PROBLEM 9B-4 (CONTINUED)

AL'S COSMETIC MARKET
GENERAL JOURNAL

PAGE 2

Date	Account Titles and Description	PR	Dr.	Cr.

Name ______________________ Class ______________ Date ______________

PROBLEM 9B-4 (CONTINUED)

ACCOUNTS RECEIVABLE SUBSIDIARY LEDGER

NAME ALEXANDER KOZLOSKY CO.

ADDRESS 2 RYAN RD., BUFFALO, NY 09113

Date		Explanation	Post Ref.	Debit	Credit	Debit Balance

Name ______________ Class ______________ Date ______________

PROBLEM 9B-4 (CONTINUED)

ACCOUNTS RECEIVABLE SUBSIDIARY LEDGER

NAME DOUGLAS SABIN CO.

ADDRESS 4 REEL RD., LANCASTER, PA 04332

Date		Explanation	Post Ref.	Debit	Credit	Debit Balance

NAME JOHN TOBIN CO.

ADDRESS 14 BONE DR., ENGLEWOOD CLIFFS, NJ 07632

Date		Explanation	Post Ref.	Debit	Credit	Debit Balance

NAME EDWARD WEASE CO.

ADDRESS 2 MARION RD., BOSTON, MA 01981

Date		Explanation	Post Ref.	Debit	Credit	Debit Balance

Name ______________________ Class ______________ Date ______________

PROBLEM 9B-4 (CONTINUED)

AL'S COSMETIC MARKET
GENERAL LEDGER

CASH — **ACCOUNT NO. 10**

Date		Explanation	Post Ref.	Debit	Credit	Balance Debit	Balance Credit

ACCOUNTS RECEIVABLE — **ACCOUNT NO. 12**

Date		Explanation	Post Ref.	Debit	Credit	Balance Debit	Balance Credit

Name ____________________ Class ____________________ Date ____________________

PROBLEM 9B-4 (CONTINUED)

SALES TAX PAYABLE **ACCOUNT NO. 20**

Date		Explanation	Post Ref.	Debit	Credit	Balance Debit	Balance Credit

AL FRANKLIN, CAPITAL **ACCOUNT NO. 30**

Date		Explanation	Post Ref.	Debit	Credit	Balance Debit	Balance Credit

LIPSTICK SALES **ACCOUNT NO. 40**

Date		Explanation	Post Ref.	Debit	Credit	Balance Debit	Balance Credit

Name ______________________ Class ______________ Date ______________

PROBLEM 9B-4 (CONCLUDED)

SALES RETURNS & ALLOWANCES, LIPSTICK — ACCOUNT NO. 42

Date		Explanation	Post Ref.	Debit	Credit	Balance	
						Debit	Credit

EYE SHADOW SALES — ACCOUNT NO. 44

Date		Explanation	Post Ref.	Debit	Credit	Balance	
						Debit	Credit

REQUIREMENT 2

AL'S COSMETIC MARKET
SCHEDULE OF ACCOUNTS RECEIVABLE
DECEMBER 31, 201X

Name ______________________ Class ______________ Date ______________

ON THE JOB CONTINUING PROBLEM

ASSIGNMENT 1

SMITH COMPUTER CENTER
GENERAL JOURNAL

PAGE 4

Date		Account Titles and Description	PR	Dr.	Cr.

Name ________________________ Class ______________ Date ______________

ASSIGNMENT 2

CASH **ACCOUNT NO. 1000**

Date		Explanation	Post Ref.	Debit	Credit	Balance	
						Debit	Credit
1/1	1X	Balance Forward	✓			5 861 76	

Name ______________________ Class ______________ Date ______________

SMITH COMPUTER CENTER
PARTIAL GENERAL LEDGER

ACCOUNTS RECEIVABLE — ACCOUNT NO. 1020

Date		Explanation	Post Ref.	Debit	Credit	Balance Debit	Balance Credit
1/1	1X	Balance Forward	✓			15 5 7 5 00	

SALES — ACCOUNT NO. 4010

Date		Explanation	Post Ref.	Debit	Credit	Balance Debit	Balance Credit

SALES RETURNS & ALLOWANCES — ACCOUNT NO. 4020

Date		Explanation	Post Ref.	Debit	Credit	Balance Debit	Balance Credit

Name ______________________ Class ______________ Date ______________

SALES DISCOUNTS **ACCOUNT NO. 4030**

Date		Explanation	Post Ref.	Debit	Credit	Balance Debit	Balance Credit

ACCOUNTS RECEIVABLE SUBSIDIARY LEDGER

NAME **PHIL'S PHOTOGRAPHY** **ACCOUNT NO. 100**

ADDRESS **1010 MOCKINGBIRD LANE, CARLSBAD, CA 92008**

Date		Explanation	Post Ref.	Debit	Credit	Dr. Balance
1/1	1X	Balance forward	✓			3775 00

NAME **WORLDWIDE PROFESSIONALS** **ACCOUNT NO. 101**

ADDRESS **144 CANTATA, IRVINE, CA 92606**

Date		Explanation	Post Ref.	Debit	Credit	Dr. Balance
1/1	1X	Balance	✓			7400 00

Name ______ Class ______ Date ______

ACCOUNTS RECEIVABLE SUBSIDIARY LEDGER

NAME ALL STAR SPORTS, INC. **ACCOUNT NO.** 103

ADDRESS 1717 JORDAN ST., SAN CLEMENTE, CA 91607

Date		Explanation	Post Ref.	Debit	Credit	Dr. Balance
1/1	1X	Balance	✓			4 4 0 0 00

NAME DR. MICHAEL TURIONO **ACCOUNT NO.** 104

ADDRESS 600 NEWPORT BEACH, NEWPORT, CA 91600

Date		Explanation	Post Ref.	Debit	Credit	Dr. Balance

Name ______________________ Class ______________ Date ______________

ASSIGNMENT 3

SMITH COMPUTER CENTER
SCHEDULE OF ACCOUNTS RECEIVABLE
1/31/1X

Name ______________________ Class ______________ Date ______________

CHAPTER 9
SUMMARY PRACTICE TEST
SALES AND CASH RECEIPTS

Part I

Fill in the blank(s) to complete the statement.

1. The normal balance of sales returns and allowances is ____________.
2. ____________ ____________ and ____________ is a contra-revenue account.
3. Sales is a(n) ____________ account.
4. A discount period is less time than the ____________ ____________.
5. A debit to accounts receivable and a credit to sales records the sale of merchandise ____________ ____________.
6. The ____________ ____________ ____________ ____________ lists in alphabetical order an account for each customer.
7. ____________ ____________ in the general ledger is called the controlling account.
8. The collection of a sale on account is posted to the ____________ and ____________.
9. Issuing ____________ ____________ results in a debit to sales returns and allowancs and a credit to accounts receivable.
10. The normal balance of Sales Discounts is ____________.
11. Sales Tax Payable is a(n) ____________ in the general ledger.
12. Cash sales result in a(n) ____________ to cash and a ____________ to sales.
13. Sales Returns and Allowances is a(n) ____________ ____________ account.
14. A sale on account is posted to the ____________ and the ____________.
15. No ____________ ____________ are taken on sales tax.
16. A(n) ____________ ____________ ____________ ____________ lists the ending balances from the accounts receivable ledger.

Part II

Complete the following chart:

	Transaction	Dr.	Cr.
1.	Sale for cash	____________	____________
2.	Issued credit memo	____________	____________
3.	Sale on account	____________	____________
4.	Received cash payment less discount	____________	____________

Partial Chart of Accounts

10 Cash
20 Accounts Receivable
40 Sales
42 Sales Discount
44 Sales Returns and Allowances

Name ______________________ Class ______________________ Date ______________________

Part III

Answer true or false to the following statements.

1. A schedule of accounts receivable shows what customers do not owe.
2. A perpetual system would keep continual track of inventory.
3. Sales Discount policies can never change.
4. Sales Tax Payable is an asset.
5. Sales Discount is a contra asset.
6. Issuing a credit memorandum results in Sales Returns and Allowances decreasing with Accounts Receivable increasing.
7. The sum of the accounts in the accounts receivable subsidiary ledger is equal to the balance in the controlling account at the end of the month.
8. The buyer issues the credit memo.
9. The accounts receivable subsidiary ledger is listed in numerical order.
10. Sales Discount is a contra-revenue account.
11. Net sales = gross sales – SRA – SD.
12. The normal balance of Accounts Receivable is a debit.
13. Discounts are taken on sales tax.
14. 2/10, N/30 means a cash discount is good for 30 days.
15. The accounts receivable subsidiary ledger is always located in the general ledger.
16. Gross profit plus operating expenses equals net income.
17. A credit period is longer than the discount period.
18. In the accounts receivable subsidiary ledger each account is debited to record amounts customers owe.
19. Sales Tax Payable is an asset.

SOLUTIONS

Part I

1. debit
2. Sales Returns, Allowances
3. revenue
4. credit period
5. on account
6. accounts receivable subsidiary ledger
7. Accounts Receivable
8. general ledger, accounts receivable subsidiary ledger
9. credit memorandum
10. debit
11. liability
12. debit, credit
13. contra-revenue
14. general ledger, accounts receivable subsidiary ledger
15. sales discounts
16. schedule of accounts receivable

Name ______________________ Class ______________ Date ______________

Part II

	Dr.	Cr.
1.	10	40
2.	44	20
3.	20	40
4.	10	20
	42	

Part III

1. false
2. true
3. false
4. false
5. false
6. false
7. true
8. false
9. false
10. true
11. true
12. true
13. false
14. false
15. false
16. false
17. true
18. true
19. false

Study Guide and Working Papers

Purchases and Cash Payments

Name ______________________ Class ______________ Date ______________

FORMS FOR DEMONSTRATION PROBLEM

REQUIREMENT 1

DALE'S ELECTRONICS SHOP
GENERAL JOURNAL

PAGE 2

Date		Account Titles and Description	PR	Dr.	Cr.

Name ____________________ Class ____________ Date ____________

FORMS FOR DEMONSTRATION PROBLEM

PARTIAL GENERAL LEDGER

ELECTRONIC SUPPLIES — **ACCOUNT NO. 112**

Date	Explanation	Post Ref.	Debit	Credit	Balance Debit	Balance Credit

ELECTRONIC EQUIPMENT — **ACCOUNT NO. 120**

Date	Explanation	Post Ref.	Debit	Credit	Balance Debit	Balance Credit

ACCOUNTS PAYABLE — **ACCOUNT NO. 210**

Date	Explanation	Post Ref.	Debit	Credit	Balance Debit	Balance Credit

PURCHASES — **ACCOUNT NO. 510**

Date	Explanation	Post Ref.	Debit	Credit	Balance Debit	Balance Credit

PURCHASES RETURNS AND ALLOWANCES — **ACCOUNT NO. 512**

Date	Explanation	Post Ref.	Debit	Credit	Balance Debit	Balance Credit

Name ______________________ Class ______________ Date ______________

FORMS FOR DEMONSTRATION PROBLEM

ACCOUNTS PAYABLE SUBSIDARY LEDGER

NAME **HOPE CO.**

ADDRESS **112 FLYING HIGHWAY, TRENTON, NJ 00861**

Date 201X		Explanation	Post Ref.	Debit	Credit	Cr. Balance

NAME **MATTY CO.**

ADDRESS **118 WANG RD., SAUGUS, MA 01432**

Date 201X		Explanation	Post Ref.	Debit	Credit	Cr. Balance

NAME **MIA CO.**

ADDRESS **112 FLYING HIGHWAY, TRENTON, NJ 00861**

Date 201X		Explanation	Post Ref.	Debit	Credit	Cr. Balance

NAME **SAM CO.**

ADDRESS **118 WANG RD., SAUGUS, MA 01432**

Date 201X		Explanation	Post Ref.	Debit	Credit	Cr. Balance

Name ______________________ Class ____________ Date ______________

FORMS FOR DEMONSTRATION PROBLEM

REQUIREMENT 2

DALE'S ELECTRONICS SHOP
SCHEDULE OF ACCOUNTS PAYABLE
NOVEMBER 30, 201X

REQUIREMENT 3

Date	Account Titles and Description	PR	Dr.	Cr.

FORMS FOR SET A EXERCISES

10A-1

Page 2

Date 201X		Account Titles and Description	PR	Dr.	Cr.
Jun.	3	Purchases		940 00	
		Accounts Payable, Cortland.com			940 00
		Purchased merchandise on account			
	4	Purchases		620 00	
		Accounts Payable, Harold.com			620 00
		Purchased merchandise on account			
	8	Equipment		190 00	
		Accounts Payable, Nickel.com			190 00
		Bought equipment on account			

Cortland.com

Harold.com

Nickel.com

Equipment 120

Accounts Payable 210

Purchases 510

Name ______________________ Class ______________ Date ______________

10A-2

PAGE 1

Date		Accounts		Debit	Credit

Roger Co.

Accounts Payable 211

Purchases Returns and Allowances 513

Name ______________ Class ______________ Date ______________

SET A EXERCISES

10A-3

PAGE 2

Date		Account Titles and Description	PR	Dr.	Cr.

ACCOUNTS PAYABLE SUBSIDIARY LEDGER

A. Jordan

	500

B. Thomas

	200

J. Wright

	400

B. Campbell

	100

PARTIAL GENERAL LEDGER

Cash 110

3,100	

Accounts Payable 210

	1,200

Purchases Discount 511

Advertising Expense 610

Name ____________________ Class ____________________ Date ____________________

SET A EXERCISES

10A-4

JACOB'S CLOTHING
SCHEDULE OF ACCOUNTS PAYABLE
APRIL 30, 201X

Accounts Payable 210

10A-5

Accounts Affected	Category	↑↓	Rules

10A-6

Name ______________________ Class ______________ Date ______________

FORM FOR EXERCISES 10A-7, 10A-8, 10A-9, 10A-10

Date		Account Titles and Description	PR	Dr.	Cr.

Name ______________________ Class ______________ Date ______________

FORM FOR EXERCISES 10A-7, 10A-8, 10A-9, 10A-10

Date		Account Titles and Description	PR	Dr.	Cr.

CALCULATIONS PAGE

Name ____________________ Class ____________________ Date ____________________

FORMS FOR SET B EXERCISES

10B-1

Page 2

Date 201X		Account Titles and Description	PR	Dr.	Cr.
Jun.	3	Purchases		930 00	
		Accounts Payable, Eve.com			930 00
		Purchased merchandise on account			
	4	Purchases		610 00	
		Accounts Payable, Jack.com			610 00
		Purchased merchandise on account			
	8	Equipment		220 00	
		Accounts Payable, Noel.com			220 00
		Bought equipment on account			

Eve.com

Equipment 120

Jack.com

Accounts Payable 210

Noel.com

Purchases 510

Name ____________________ Class ____________ Date ____________

10B-2

PAGE 1

Date		Accounts	Debit	Credit

Line Co.	

Accounts Payable 211	

Purchases Returns and Allowances 513	

Name ______________________ Class ____________ Date ____________

SET B EXERCISES

10B-3

PAGE 2

Date	Account Titles and Description	PR	Dr.	Cr.

ACCOUNTS PAYABLE SUBSIDIARY LEDGER

A. Jae	
	1,400

B. Miller	
	800

J. Hall	
	1,100

B. Parker	
	250

PARTIAL GENERAL LEDGER

Cash 110	
3,600	

Accounts Payable 210	
	3,550

Purchases Discount 511	

Advertising Expense 610	

Name ____________ Class ____________ Date ____________

SET B EXERCISES

10B-4

CODY'S CLOTHING
SCHEDULE OF ACCOUNTS PAYABLE
APRIL 30, 201X

Accounts Payable 210

10B-5

Accounts Affected	Category	↑ ↓	Rules

10B-6

Name ______________________ Class ______________ Date ______________

FORM FOR EXERCISES 10B-7, 10B-8, 10B-9, 10B-10

Date		Account Titles and Description	PR	Dr.	Cr.

Name ____________________ Class ____________________ Date ____________________

FORM FOR EXERCISES 10B-7, 10B-8, 10B-9, 10B-10

Date		Account Titles and Description	PR	Dr.	Cr.

CALCULATIONS PAGE

Name ______________________ Class ______________ Date ______________

FORMS FOR SET A PROBLEMS

PROBLEM 10A-1

ROBERT'S SKATE SHOP
GENERAL JOURNAL

PAGE 2

Date		Account Titles and Description	PR	Dr.	Cr.

Name ______________________ Class ____________ Date ______________

PROBLEM 10A-1 (CONTINUED)

ACCOUNTS PAYABLE SUBSIDIARY LEDGER

NAME KINGSTON CO.
ADDRESS 12 SMITH ST., DEARBORN, MI 09113

Date		Explanation	Post Ref.	Debit	Credit	Cr. Balance

NAME ROLO CO.
ADDRESS 1 RANTOUL RD., CHARLOTTE, NC 01114

Date		Explanation	Post Ref.	Debit	Credit	Cr. Balance

NAME WALES CO.
ADDRESS 2 WEST RD., LYNN, MA 01471

Date		Explanation	Post Ref.	Debit	Credit	Cr. Balance

PARTIAL GENERAL LEDGER

STORE SUPPLIES **ACCOUNT NO. 115**

Date		Explanation	Post Ref.	Debit	Credit	Balance	
						Debit	Credit

Name ______________________ Class ______________ Date ______________

PROBLEM 10A-1 (CONCLUDED)

STORE EQUIPMENT **ACCOUNT NO. 121**

Date		Explanation	Post Ref.	Debit	Credit	Balance Debit	Balance Credit

ACCOUNTS PAYABLE **ACCOUNT NO. 210**

Date		Explanation	Post Ref.	Debit	Credit	Balance Debit	Balance Credit

PURCHASES **ACCOUNT NO. 510**

Date		Explanation	Post Ref.	Debit	Credit	Balance Debit	Balance Credit

Name ______________________ Class ______________ Date ______________

PROBLEM 10A-2

REQUIREMENT 1

RILEY'S NATURAL FOOD STORE

PAGE 2

Date	Account Titles and Description	PR	Dr.	Cr.

Name ____________ Class ____________ Date ____________

PROBLEM 10A-2 (CONTINUED)

REQUIREMENT 2

ACCOUNTS PAYABLE SUBSIDIARY LEDGER

NAME ARIS CO.

ADDRESS 11 LYNNWAY AVE., NEWPORT, RI 03112

Date		Explanation	Post Ref.	Debit	Credit	Cr. Balance

NAME BROWN CO.

ADDRESS 21 RIVER ST., ANAHEIM, CA 43110

Date		Explanation	Post Ref.	Debit	Credit	Cr. Balance

NAME MOOSE CO.

ADDRESS 10 ASTER RD., DUBUQUE, IA 80021

Date		Explanation	Post Ref.	Debit	Credit	Cr. Balance

NAME READY CO.

ADDRESS 22 GERALD RD., SMITH, CO 43138

Date		Explanation	Post Ref.	Debit	Credit	Cr. Balance

Name ____________ Class ____________ Date ____________

PROBLEM 10A-2 (CONTINUED)

PARTIAL GENERAL LEDGER

STORE SUPPLIES — ACCOUNT NO. 110

Date		Explanation	Post Ref.	Debit	Credit	Balance Debit	Balance Credit

OFFICE EQUIPMENT — ACCOUNT NO. 120

Date		Explanation	Post Ref.	Debit	Credit	Balance Debit	Balance Credit

ACCOUNTS PAYABLE — ACCOUNT NO. 210

Date		Explanation	Post Ref.	Debit	Credit	Balance Debit	Balance Credit

PURCHASES — ACCOUNT NO. 510

Date		Explanation	Post Ref.	Debit	Credit	Balance Debit	Balance Credit

Name ____________ Class ____________ Date ____________

PROBLEM 10A-2 (CONCLUDED)

PURCHASES RETURNS AND ALLOWANCES **ACCOUNT NO. 512**

Date		Explanation	Post Ref.	Debit	Credit	Balance	
						Debit	Credit

REQUIREMENT 3

RILEY'S NATURAL FOOD STORE
SCHEDULE OF ACCOUNTS PAYABLE
APRIL 30, 201X

Name ____________________ Class ____________ Date ____________

PROBLEM 10A-3

REQUIREMENT 1

PAGE 5

Date	Account Titles and Description	PR	Dr.	Cr.

Name ______________________ Class ______________ Date ______________

PROBLEM 10A-3 (CONTINUED)

REQUIREMENT 2

ACCOUNTS PAYABLE SUBSIDIARY LEDGER

NAME **ANDERSEN CO.**

ADDRESS **1 REACH RD., IPSWICH, MA 01932**

Date		Explanation	Post Ref.	Debit	Credit	Cr. Balance

NAME **HENDERSON CO.**

ADDRESS **1 RALPH RD., REVERE, MA 01321**

Date		Explanation	Post Ref.	Debit	Credit	Cr. Balance

NAME **SQUASH CO.**

ADDRESS **7 PLYMOUTH AVE., GLENN, NH 01218**

Date		Explanation	Post Ref.	Debit	Credit	Cr. Balance

NAME **XHOSA CO.**

ADDRESS **22 REY RD., BOCA RATON, FL 99132**

Date		Explanation	Post Ref.	Debit	Credit	Cr. Balance

Name ______________________ Class ______________ Date ______________

PROBLEM 10A-3 (CONTINUED)

PARTIAL GENERAL LEDGER

CASH ACCOUNT NO. 110

Date	Explanation	Post Ref.	Debit	Credit	Balance	
					Debit	Credit

DELIVERY TRUCK ACCOUNT NO. 150

Date 201X	Explanation	Post Ref.	Debit	Credit	Balance	
					Debit	Credit

ACCOUNTS PAYABLE ACCOUNT NO. 210

Date	Explanation	Post Ref.	Debit	Credit	Balance	
					Debit	Credit

COMPUTER PURCHASES ACCOUNT NO. 510

Date 201X	Explanation	Post Ref.	Debit	Credit	Balance	
					Debit	Credit

Name ______________________ Class ______________ Date ______________

PROBLEM 10A-3 (CONCLUDED)

COMPUTER PURCHASES DISCOUNT **ACCOUNT NO. 511**

Date	Explanation	Post Ref.	Debit	Credit	Balance Debit	Balance Credit

RENT EXPENSE **ACCOUNT NO. 610**

Date	Explanation	Post Ref.	Debit	Credit	Balance Debit	Balance Credit

UTILITIES EXPENSE **ACCOUNT NO. 620**

Date	Explanation	Post Ref.	Debit	Credit	Balance Debit	Balance Credit

REQUIREMENT 3

DREW COMPUTER CENTER
SCHEDULE OF ACCOUNTS PAYABLE
MARCH 31, 201X

Name ______________________ Class ______________ Date ______________

PROBLEM 10A-4

REQUIREMENT 1

ABBY'S TOY HOUSE
GENERAL JOURNAL

PAGE 1

Date		Account Titles and Description	PR	Dr.	Cr.

Name ______________________ Class ______________ Date ______________

PROBLEM 10A-4 (CONTINUED)

PAGE 2

Date		Account Titles and Description	PR	Dr.	Cr.

Name ______________________ Class ______________ Date ______________

PROBLEM 10A-4 (CONTINUED)

PAGE 3

Date		Account Titles and Description	PR	Dr.	Cr.

Name ____________________ Class ____________________ Date ____________________

PROBLEM 10A-4 (CONTINUED)

PAGE 4

Date	Account Titles and Description	PR	Dr.	Cr.

Name ______________________ Class ______________________ Date ______________________

PROBLEM 10A-4 (CONTINUED)

PAGE 5

Date		Account Titles and Description	PR	Dr.	Cr.

Name ______________________ Class ______________ Date ______________

PROBLEM 10A-4 (CONTINUED)

REQUIREMENT 2

ACCOUNTS PAYABLE SUBSIDIARY LEDGER

NAME MORRIS CURTIS COMPANY

ADDRESS 87 GARFIELD AVE., REVERE, MA 01245

Date		Explanation	Post Ref.	Debit	Credit	Cr. Balance

NAME SAM KATZ GARAGE

ADDRESS 22 REGIS RD., BOSTON, MA 01950

Date		Explanation	Post Ref.	Debit	Credit	Cr. Balance

NAME MILDRED MANN

ADDRESS 22 RETTER ST., SAN DIEGO, CA 01211

Date		Explanation	Post Ref.	Debit	Credit	Cr. Balance

NAME SANYA BURGER

ADDRESS 2 SPRING ST., WEERS, ND 02118

Date		Explanation	Post Ref.	Debit	Credit	Cr. Balance

Name ______________________ Class ______________ Date ______________

PROBLEM 10A-4 (CONTINUED)

ACCOUNTS RECEIVABLE SUBSIDIARY LEDGER

NAME DAVID PLOUFFE

ADDRESS 24 RYAN RD., BUIKE, OH 02183

Date		Explanation	Post Ref.	Debit	Credit	Dr. Balance

NAME ROBERT COOPER

ADDRESS 2 SMITH RD., DALLAS, TX 22210

Date		Explanation	Post Ref.	Debit	Credit	Dr. Balance

NAME ALISON REACH

ADDRESS 1 SCHOOL ST., CLEVELAND, OH 22441

Date		Explanation	Post Ref.	Debit	Credit	Dr. Balance

Name ______ Class ______ Date ______

PROBLEM 10A-4 (CONTINUED)

NAME **BELLA FALCO COMPANY**

ADDRESS **18 VEEK RD., CHESTER, CT 80111**

Date		Explanation	Post Ref.	Debit	Credit	Dr. Balance

GENERAL LEDGER

CASH **ACCOUNT NO. 110**

Date		Explanation	Post Ref.	Debit	Credit	Balance	
						Debit	Credit

Name ______________________ Class ____________ Date ____________

PROBLEM 10A-4 (CONTINUED)

ACCOUNTS RECEIVABLE — ACCOUNT NO. 112

Date	Explanation	Post Ref.	Debit	Credit	Balance Debit	Balance Credit

PREPAID RENT — ACCOUNT NO. 114

Date	Explanation	Post Ref.	Debit	Credit	Balance Debit	Balance Credit

DELIVERY TRUCK — ACCOUNT NO. 121

Date	Explanation	Post Ref.	Debit	Credit	Balance Debit	Balance Credit

Name ______________________ Class __________ Date __________

PROBLEM 10A-4 (CONTINUED)

ACCOUNTS PAYABLE **ACCOUNT NO. 210**

Date	Explanation	Post Ref.	Debit	Credit	Balance Debit	Balance Credit

A. GRAY, CAPITAL **ACCOUNT NO. 310**

Date	Explanation	Post Ref.	Debit	Credit	Balance Debit	Balance Credit

TOY SALES **ACCOUNT NO. 410**

Date	Explanation	Post Ref.	Debit	Credit	Balance Debit	Balance Credit

Name ______________ Class ______________ Date ______________

PROBLEM 10A-4 (CONTINUED)

SALES RETURNS AND ALLOWANCES **ACCOUNT NO. 412**

Date		Explanation	Post Ref.	Debit	Credit	Balance	
						Debit	Credit

SALES DISCOUNTS **ACCOUNT NO. 414**

Date		Explanation	Post Ref.	Debit	Credit	Balance	
						Debit	Credit

TOY PURCHASES **ACCOUNT NO. 510**

Date		Explanation	Post Ref.	Debit	Credit	Balance	
						Debit	Credit

PURCHASES RETURNS AND ALLOWANCES **ACCOUNT NO. 512**

Date		Explanation	Post Ref.	Debit	Credit	Balance	
						Debit	Credit

Name ______________________ Class ______________ Date ______________

PROBLEM 10A-4 (CONTINUED)

PURCHASES DISCOUNT — **ACCOUNT NO. 514**

Date	Explanation	Post Ref.	Debit	Credit	Balance	
					Debit	Credit

SALARIES EXPENSE — **ACCOUNT NO. 610**

Date	Explanation	Post Ref.	Debit	Credit	Balance	
					Debit	Credit

CLEANING EXPENSE — **ACCOUNT NO. 612**

Date	Explanation	Post Ref.	Debit	Credit	Balance	
					Debit	Credit

Name ______________________ Class ______________ Date ______________

PROBLEM 10A-4 (CONCLUDED)

REQUIREMENT 3

ABBY'S TOY HOUSE
SCHEDULE OF ACCOUNTS RECEIVABLE
DECEMBER 31, 201X

ABBY'S TOY HOUSE
SCHEDULE OF ACCOUNTS PAYABLE
DECEMBER 31, 201X

Name ______________________ Class ______________ Date ______________

PROBLEM 10A-5

PAGE 3

Date		Account Titles and Description	PR	Dr.	Cr.

Name ____________ Class ____________ Date ____________

PROBLEM 10A-5 (CONCLUDED)

PAGE 4

Date		Account Titles and Description	PR	Dr.	Cr.

Name ____________ Class ____________ Date ____________

FORMS FOR SET B PROBLEMS

PROBLEM 10B-1

RASHEED'S SKATE SHOP
GENERAL JOURNAL

PAGE 2

Date		Account Titles and Description	PR	Dr.	Cr.

Name ______________________ Class ______________ Date ______________

PROBLEM 10B-1 (CONTINUED)

ACCOUNTS PAYABLE SUBSIDIARY LEDGER

NAME ANDOVER CO.

ADDRESS 12 SMITH ST., DEARBORN, MI 09113

Date		Explanation	Post Ref.	Debit	Credit	Cr. Balance

NAME LAKEVILLE CO.

ADDRESS 1 RANTOUL RD., CHARLOTTE, NC 01114

Date		Explanation	Post Ref.	Debit	Credit	Cr. Balance

NAME NEWBURY CO.

ADDRESS 2 WEST RD., LYNN, MA 01471

Date		Explanation	Post Ref.	Debit	Credit	Cr. Balance

PARTIAL GENERAL LEDGER

STORE SUPPLIES **ACCOUNT NO. 115**

Date		Explanation	Post Ref.	Debit	Credit	Balance	
						Debit	Credit

Name ______________________ Class ______________ Date ______________

PROBLEM 10B-1 (CONCLUDED)

STORE EQUIPMENT **ACCOUNT NO. 121**

Date	Explanation	Post Ref.	Debit	Credit	Balance	
					Debit	Credit

ACCOUNTS PAYABLE **ACCOUNT NO. 210**

Date	Explanation	Post Ref.	Debit	Credit	Balance	
					Debit	Credit

PURCHASES **ACCOUNT NO. 510**

Date	Explanation	Post Ref.	Debit	Credit	Balance	
					Debit	Credit

Name ______________________ Class ______________________ Date ______________________

PROBLEM 10B-2

REQUIREMENT 1

TRINA'S NATURAL FOOD STORE

PAGE 2

Date	Account Titles and Description	PR	Dr.	Cr.

Name ______________________ Class ______________ Date ______________

PROBLEM 10B-2 (CONTINUED)

REQUIREMENT 2

ACCOUNTS PAYABLE SUBSIDIARY LEDGER

NAME ANTION CO.

ADDRESS 11 LYNNWAY AVE., NEWPORT, RI 03112

Date		Explanation	Post Ref.	Debit	Credit	Cr. Balance

NAME BLOCK CO.

ADDRESS 21 RIVER ST., ANAHEIM, CA 43110

Date		Explanation	Post Ref.	Debit	Credit	Cr. Balance

NAME MIDDEN CO.

ADDRESS 10 ASTER RD., DUBUQUE, IA 80021

Date		Explanation	Post Ref.	Debit	Credit	Cr. Balance

NAME REX CO.

ADDRESS 22 GERALD RD., SMITH, CO 43138

Date		Explanation	Post Ref.	Debit	Credit	Cr. Balance

Name ____________ Class ____________ Date ____________

PROBLEM 10B-2 (CONTINUED)

PARTIAL GENERAL LEDGER

STORE SUPPLIES — ACCOUNT NO. 110

Date		Explanation	Post Ref.	Debit	Credit	Balance Debit	Balance Credit

OFFICE EQUIPMENT — ACCOUNT NO. 120

Date		Explanation	Post Ref.	Debit	Credit	Balance Debit	Balance Credit

ACCOUNTS PAYABLE — ACCOUNT NO. 210

Date		Explanation	Post Ref.	Debit	Credit	Balance Debit	Balance Credit

PURCHASES — ACCOUNT NO. 510

Date		Explanation	Post Ref.	Debit	Credit	Balance Debit	Balance Credit

Name ______________________ Class __________ Date __________

PROBLEM 10B-2 (CONCLUDED)

PURCHASES RETURNS AND ALLOWANCES — ACCOUNT NO. 512

Date		Explanation	Post Ref.	Debit	Credit	Balance Debit	Balance Credit

REQUIREMENT 3

TRINA'S NATURAL FOOD STORE
SCHEDULE OF ACCOUNTS PAYABLE
OCTOBER 31, 201X

Name ______________________ Class ______________________ Date ______________________

PROBLEM 10B-3

REQUIREMENT 1

PAGE 5

Date		Account Titles and Description	PR	Dr.	Cr.

Name ______________________ Class ______________ Date ______________

PROBLEM 10B-3 (CONTINUED)

REQUIREMENT 2

ACCOUNTS PAYABLE SUBSIDIARY LEDGER

NAME ANDERSEN CO.

ADDRESS 1 REACH RD., IPSWICH, MA 01932

Date		Explanation	Post Ref.	Debit	Credit	Cr. Balance

NAME HACK CO.

ADDRESS 1 RALPH RD., REVERE, MA 01321

Date		Explanation	Post Ref.	Debit	Credit	Cr. Balance

NAME SOIL CO.

ADDRESS 7 PLYMOUTH AVE., GLENN, NH 01218

Date		Explanation	Post Ref.	Debit	Credit	Cr. Balance

NAME XYDIAS CO.

ADDRESS 22 REY RD., BOCA RATON, FL 99132

Date		Explanation	Post Ref.	Debit	Credit	Cr. Balance

Name ______________________ Class ______________ Date ______________

PROBLEM 10B-3 (CONTINUED)

PARTIAL GENERAL LEDGER

CASH — **ACCOUNT NO. 110**

Date		Explanation	Post Ref.	Debit	Credit	Balance Debit	Balance Credit

DELIVERY TRUCK — **ACCOUNT NO. 150**

Date 201X		Explanation	Post Ref.	Debit	Credit	Balance Debit	Balance Credit

ACCOUNTS PAYABLE — **ACCOUNT NO. 210**

Date		Explanation	Post Ref.	Debit	Credit	Balance Debit	Balance Credit

COMPUTER PURCHASES — **ACCOUNT NO. 510**

Date 201X		Explanation	Post Ref.	Debit	Credit	Balance Debit	Balance Credit

Name ____________________ Class ____________ Date ____________

PROBLEM 10B-3 (CONCLUDED)

COMPUTER PURCHASES DISCOUNT ACCOUNT NO. 511

Date		Explanation	Post Ref.	Debit	Credit	Balance	
						Debit	Credit

RENT EXPENSE ACCOUNT NO. 610

Date		Explanation	Post Ref.	Debit	Credit	Balance	
						Debit	Credit

UTILITIES EXPENSE ACCOUNT NO. 620

Date		Explanation	Post Ref.	Debit	Credit	Balance	
						Debit	Credit

REQUIREMENT 3

JOHNSON COMPUTER CENTER
SCHEDULE OF ACCOUNTS PAYABLE
MAY 31, 201X

Name ______________________ Class ____________ Date ____________

PROBLEM 10B-4

REQUIREMENT 1

ABBY'S TOY HOUSE
GENERAL JOURNAL

PAGE 1

Date	Account Titles and Description	PR	Dr.	Cr.

Name ______________ Class ______________ Date ______________

PROBLEM 10B-4 (CONTINUED)

PAGE 2

Date	Account Titles and Description	PR	Dr.	Cr.

Name ______________________ Class ______________________ Date ______________________

PROBLEM 10B-4 (CONTINUED)

PAGE 3

Date		Account Titles and Description	PR	Dr.	Cr.

Name ______________________ Class ______________ Date ______________

PROBLEM 10B-4 (CONTINUED)

PAGE 4

Date		Account Titles and Description	PR	Dr.	Cr.

Name ______________________ Class ______________ Date ______________

PROBLEM 10B-4 (CONTINUED)

PAGE 5

Date		Account Titles and Description	PR	Dr.	Cr.

Name ______________________ Class ______________ Date ______________

PROBLEM 10B-4 (CONTINUED)

REQUIREMENT 2

ACCOUNTS PAYABLE SUBSIDIARY LEDGER

NAME MORRIS CURTIS COMPANY

ADDRESS 87 GARFIELD AVE., REVERE, MA 01245

Date		Explanation	Post Ref.	Debit	Credit	Cr. Balance

NAME SAM KATZ GARAGE

ADDRESS 22 REGIS RD., BOSTON, MA 01950

Date		Explanation	Post Ref.	Debit	Credit	Cr. Balance

NAME MICHAEL KEISER

ADDRESS 22 RETTER ST., SAN DIEGO, CA 01211

Date		Explanation	Post Ref.	Debit	Credit	Cr. Balance

NAME MILLARD FILMORE

ADDRESS 2 SPRING ST., WEERS, ND 02118

Date		Explanation	Post Ref.	Debit	Credit	Cr. Balance

Name ______________________ Class ______________ Date ______________

PROBLEM 10B-4 (CONTINUED)

ACCOUNTS RECEIVABLE SUBSIDIARY LEDGER

NAME DAVID PLOUFFE

ADDRESS 24 RYAN RD., BUIKE, OH 02183

Date		Explanation	Post Ref.	Debit	Credit	Dr. Balance

NAME JOHN DRAYTON

ADDRESS 2 SMITH RD., DALLAS, TX 22210

Date		Explanation	Post Ref.	Debit	Credit	Dr. Balance

NAME AIMEE RAYPOLE

ADDRESS 1 SCHOOL ST., CLEVELAND, OH 22441

Date		Explanation	Post Ref.	Debit	Credit	Dr. Balance

Name ______________ Class ______________ Date ______________

PROBLEM 10B-4 (CONTINUED)

NAME **BELLA FALCO COMPANY**

ADDRESS **18 VEEK RD., CHESTER, CT 80111**

Date	Explanation	Post Ref.	Debit	Credit	Dr. Balance

GENERAL LEDGER

CASH **ACCOUNT NO. 110**

Date	Explanation	Post Ref.	Debit	Credit	Balance	
					Debit	Credit

Name ______________________ Class ______________ Date ______________

PROBLEM 10B-4 (CONTINUED)

ACCOUNTS RECEIVABLE — ACCOUNT NO. 112

Date	Explanation	Post Ref.	Debit	Credit	Balance Debit	Balance Credit

PREPAID RENT — ACCOUNT NO. 114

Date	Explanation	Post Ref.	Debit	Credit	Balance Debit	Balance Credit

DELIVERY TRUCK — ACCOUNT NO. 121

Date	Explanation	Post Ref.	Debit	Credit	Balance Debit	Balance Credit

Name ____________________ Class ____________ Date ____________

PROBLEM 10B-4 (CONTINUED)

ACCOUNTS PAYABLE **ACCOUNT NO. 210**

Date	Explanation	Post Ref.	Debit	Credit	Balance	
					Debit	Credit

A. ELLEN, CAPITAL **ACCOUNT NO. 310**

Date	Explanation	Post Ref.	Debit	Credit	Balance	
					Debit	Credit

TOY SALES **ACCOUNT NO. 410**

Date	Explanation	Post Ref.	Debit	Credit	Balance	
					Debit	Credit

Name ______________________ Class ______________ Date ______________

PROBLEM 10B-4 (CONTINUED)

SALES RETURNS AND ALLOWANCES **ACCOUNT NO. 412**

Date	Explanation	Post Ref.	Debit	Credit	Balance Debit	Balance Credit

SALES DISCOUNTS **ACCOUNT NO. 414**

Date	Explanation	Post Ref.	Debit	Credit	Balance Debit	Balance Credit

TOY PURCHASES **ACCOUNT NO. 510**

Date	Explanation	Post Ref.	Debit	Credit	Balance Debit	Balance Credit

PURCHASES RETURNS AND ALLOWANCES **ACCOUNT NO. 512**

Date	Explanation	Post Ref.	Debit	Credit	Balance Debit	Balance Credit

Name ______________________ Class ______________ Date ______________

PROBLEM 10B-4 (CONTINUED)

PURCHASES DISCOUNT — ACCOUNT NO. 514

Date	Explanation	Post Ref.	Debit	Credit	Balance	
					Debit	Credit

SALARIES EXPENSE — ACCOUNT NO. 610

Date	Explanation	Post Ref.	Debit	Credit	Balance	
					Debit	Credit

CLEANING EXPENSE — ACCOUNT NO. 612

Date	Explanation	Post Ref.	Debit	Credit	Balance	
					Debit	Credit

Name ______________________ Class ______________ Date ______________

PROBLEM 10B-4 (CONCLUDED)

REQUIREMENT 3

ABBY'S TOY HOUSE
SCHEDULE OF ACCOUNTS RECEIVABLE
MARCH 31, 201X

ABBY'S TOY HOUSE
SCHEDULE OF ACCOUNTS PAYABLE
MARCH 31, 201X

Name ______________ Class ______________ Date ______________

PROBLEM 10B-5

Date		Account Titles and Description	PR	Dr.	Cr.

Name ____________________ Class ____________ Date ____________

PROBLEM 10B-5 (CONCLUDED)

PAGE 4

Date	Account Titles and Description	PR	Dr.	Cr.

Name ______________________ Class ______________ Date ______________

ON THE JOB CONTINUING PROBLEM

ASSIGNMENT 1

SMITH COMPUTER CENTER
GENERAL JOURNAL

PAGE 7

Date		Account Titles and Description	PR	Dr.	Cr.

Name ____________________ Class ____________ Date ____________

ASSIGNMENT 2

PARTIAL GENERAL LEDGER

CASH — **ACCOUNT NO. 1000**

Date		Explanation	Post Ref.	Debit	Credit	Balance Debit	Balance Credit
2/1	1X	Balance forward	✓			19 3 6 3 76	

MERCHANDISE INVENTORY — **ACCOUNT NO. 1021**

Date		Explanation	Post Ref.	Debit	Credit	Balance Debit	Balance Credit

PREPAID RENT — **ACCOUNT NO. 1025**

Date		Explanation	Post Ref.	Debit	Credit	Balance Debit	Balance Credit
2/1	1X	Balance forward	✓			2 0 0 0 00	

Name ______________________ Class ______________ Date ______________

SUPPLIES ACCOUNT NO. 1030

Date		Explanation	Post Ref.	Debit	Credit	Balance Debit	Balance Credit
2/1	1X	Balance forward	✓			192 00	

ACCOUNTS PAYABLE ACCOUNT NO. 2000

Date		Explanation	Post Ref.	Debit	Credit	Balance Debit	Balance Credit
2/1	1X	Balance forward	✓				2 570 00

PURCHASES ACCOUNT NO. 6000

Date		Explanation	Post Ref.	Debit	Credit	Balance Debit	Balance Credit

PURCHASE RETURNS AND ALLOWANCES ACCOUNT NO. 6010

Date		Explanation	Post Ref.	Debit	Credit	Balance Debit	Balance Credit

PURCHASE DISCOUNTS ACCOUNT NO. 6020

Date		Explanation	Post Ref.	Debit	Credit	Balance Debit	Balance Credit

Name ______________ Class ______________ Date ______________

ACCOUNTS PAYABLE SUBSIDIARY LEDGER

NAME **THE STAPLE STORE** **# 6A3**

ADDRESS **1919 MORAN ST., ANAHEIM, CA 92606**

Date		Explanation	Post Ref.	Debit	Credit	Cr. Balance
2/1	1X	Balance forward	✓			50 00

NAME **QUALITY OFFICE FURNITURE** **# 6A4**

ADDRESS **460 ESCONDIDO BLVD., ESCONDIDO, CA 92025**

Date		Explanation	Post Ref.	Debit	Credit	Cr. Balance
2/1	1X	Balance forward	✓			1 800 00

NAME **PACIFIC BELL** **# 6A5**

ADDRESS **606 INDUSTRIAL ST., SAN DIEGO, CA 92121**

Date		Explanation	Post Ref.	Debit	Credit	Cr. Balance
2/1	1X	Balance forward	✓			170 00

Name ______________________ Class ______________ Date ______________

NAME A-TECH, INC. # 6A6

ADDRESS 101 BELL AVE., SAN DIEGO, CA 92101

Date		Explanation	Post Ref.	Debit	Credit	Cr. Balance
2/1	1X	Balance forward	✓			5 5 0 00

NAME COMPUTERS R US # 6A7

ADDRESS 1020 WIL LANE, LOS ANGELES, CA 92405

Date		Explanation	Post Ref.	Debit	Credit	Cr. Balance

ASSIGNMENT 4

SMITH COMPUTER CENTER
SCHEDULE OF ACCOUNTS PAYABLE
2/28/1X

Name ____________ Class ____________ Date ____________

APPENDIX 10A
FORMS FOR DEMONSTRATION PROBLEM — SPECIAL JOURNALS

J. LING CO.
SALES JOURNAL

PAGE 1

Date	Account Debited	Terms	Invoice No.	Post Ref.	Dr. Acc. Receivable Cr. Sales

CASH RECEIPTS JOURNAL

PAGE 1

Date	Cash Dr.	Sales Discounts Dr.	Accounts Receivable Cr.	Sales Cr.	Sundry		
					Account Name	PR	Amount Cr.

PURCHASES JOURNAL

PAGE 1

Date	Account Credited	Terms	PR	Accounts Payable Cr.	Purchases Dr.	Sundry Dr.		
						Account	PR	Amount

CASH PAYMENTS JOURNAL

PAGE 1

Date	Check No.	Account Debited	PR	Sundry Account Dr.	Accounts Payable Dr.	Purchases Discounts Cr.	Cash Cr.

Name ________________ Class ________ Date ________

FORMS FOR DEMONSTRATION PROBLEM (CONTINUED)

GENERAL JOURNAL

PAGE 1

Date		Account Titles and Description	PR	Dr.	Cr.

ACCOUNTS RECEIVABLE SUBSIDIARY LEDGER

NAME BALDER CO.

ADDRESS 1 ROCK RD., DENVER, CO 66083

Date		Explanation	Post Ref.	Debit	Credit	Dr. Balance

NAME LEWIS CO.

ADDRESS 15 SMITH AVE., REVERE, MA 01545

Date		Explanation	Post Ref.	Debit	Credit	Dr. Balance

Name ______________________ Class ______________ Date ______________

FORMS FOR DEMONSTRATION PROBLEM (CONCLUDED)

ACCOUNTS PAYABLE SUBSIDIARY LEDGER

NAME CASE CO.

ADDRESS 1 LONG RD., MARLBOROUGH, MA 01545

Date		Explanation	Post Ref.	Debit	Credit	Cr. Balance

NAME NOONE CO.

ADDRESS 11 MILL RD., MALDEN, OK 01143

Date		Explanation	Post Ref.	Debit	Credit	Cr. Balance

PARTIAL GENERAL LEDGER

Cash 111

Accounts Receivable 112

Equipment 116

Accounts Payable 210

J. Ling, Capital 310

Sales 410

Sales Returns & Allowances 420

Sales Discount 430

Purchases 510

Purchases Returns & Allowances 520

Purchases Discounts 530

Salaries Expense 610

Name ______________ Class ______________ Date ______________

CHAPTER 10A APPENDIX FORMS

PROBLEM A-1

(1,2)

YUMMY.COM
SALES JOURNAL

PAGE 1

Date		Account Debited	Invoice No.	PR	Accounts Receivable Dr.	Pizza Sales Cr.	Grocery Sales Cr.

(1,2)

YUMMY.COM
GENERAL JOURNAL

PAGE 1

Date		Account Titles and Description	PR	Dr.	Cr.

Name ______________ Class ______________ Date ______________

PROBLEM A-1 (CONTINUED)

ACCOUNTS RECEIVABLE SUBSIDIARY LEDGER

NAME DABNEY CO.

ADDRESS 942 MOSE ST., REVERE, MA 01938

Date		Explanation	Post Ref.	Debit	Credit	Dr. Balance

NAME LUXURY CO.

ADDRESS 8 JOSS AVE., LYNN, MA 01947

Date		Explanation	Post Ref.	Debit	Credit	Dr. Balance

NAME SALLY DROUGHT CO.

ADDRESS 10 LOST RD., TOPSFIELD, MA 01998

Date		Explanation	Post Ref.	Debit	Credit	Dr. Balance

Name ____________________ Class ____________ Date ____________

PROBLEM A-1 (CONTINUED)

YUMMY.COM
GENERAL LEDGER

ACCOUNTS RECEIVABLE **ACCOUNT NO. 112**

Date		Explanation	Post Ref.	Debit	Credit	Balance	
						Debit	Credit

PIZZA SALES **ACCOUNT NO. 410**

Date		Explanation	Post Ref.	Debit	Credit	Balance	
						Debit	Credit

GROCERY SALES **ACCOUNT NO. 411**

Date		Explanation	Post Ref.	Debit	Credit	Balance	
						Debit	Credit

SALES RETURNS AND ALLOWANCES **ACCOUNT NO. 412**

Date		Explanation	Post Ref.	Debit	Credit	Balance	
						Debit	Credit

Name ______________________ Class ______________ Date ______________

PROBLEM A-1 (CONCLUDED)

(3)

YUMMY.COM
SCHEDULE OF ACCOUNTS RECEIVABLE
APRIL 30, 201X

PROBLEM A-2

(1,2)

DAVID'S AUTO SUPPLY
SALES JOURNAL

PAGE 1

Date		Account Debited	Invoice No.	PR	Accounts Receivable Dr.	Sales Tax Payable Cr.	Auto Parts Sales Cr.

Name ______________________ Class ______________ Date ______________

PROBLEM A-2 (CONTINUED)

(1,2)

DAVID'S AUTO SUPPLY
GENERAL JOURNAL

PAGE 1

Date		Account Titles and Description	PR	Dr.	Cr.

Name ______________________ Class ______________ Date ______________

PROBLEM A-2 (CONTINUED)

ACCOUNTS RECEIVABLE SUBSIDIARY LEDGER

NAME GRAHAM CARTER

ADDRESS 9 ROE ST., BARTLETT, NH 01382

Date 201X		Explanation	Post Ref.	Debit	Credit	Dr. Balance
Jun	1	Balance	✓			6 0 0 00

NAME J. SANDERS

ADDRESS 22 REESE ST., LACONIA, NH 04321

Date 201X		Explanation	Post Ref.	Debit	Credit	Dr. Balance
Jun	1	Balance	✓			5 0 0 00

NAME R. VICTOR

ADDRESS 12 ASTER RD., MERRIMACK, NH 02134

Date 201X		Explanation	Post Ref.	Debit	Credit	Dr. Balance
Jun	1	Balance	✓			8 0 0 00

Name ______________________ Class ______________ Date ______________

PROBLEM A-2 (CONTINUED)

DAVID'S AUTO SUPPLY
GENERAL JOURNAL

ACCOUNTS RECEIVABLE — **ACCOUNT NO. 110**

Date 201X		Explanation	Post Ref.	Debit	Credit	Balance Debit	Balance Credit
Jun	1	Balance	✓			1 9 0 0 00	

SALES TAX PAYABLE — **ACCOUNT NO. 210**

Date 201X		Explanation	Post Ref.	Debit	Credit	Balance Debit	Balance Credit
Jun	1	Balance	✓				1 9 0 0 00

AUTO PARTS SALES — **ACCOUNT NO. 410**

Date		Explanation	Post Ref.	Debit	Credit	Balance Debit	Balance Credit

SALES RETURNS AND ALLOWANCES — **ACCOUNT NO. 420**

Date		Explanation	Post Ref.	Debit	Credit	Balance Debit	Balance Credit

Name ______________________ Class ______________ Date ______________

PROBLEM A-2 (CONCLUDED)

(3)

DAVID'S AUTO SUPPLY
SCHEDULE OF ACCOUNTS RECEIVABLE
JUNE 30, 201X

Name ____________________ Class ____________________ Date ____________________

PROBLEM A-3

TENNIS.COM
PURCHASES JOURNAL

PAGE 1

Date	Account Credited	Date of Invoice	Inv. No.	Terms	PR	Accounts Payable Cr.	Purchases Dr.	Sundry Dr.		
								Account	PR	Amount

Name ______________________ Class ______________ Date ______________

PROBLEM A-3 (CONTINUED)

ACCOUNTS PAYABLE SUBSIDIARY LEDGER

NAME MILLER.COM

ADDRESS 12 SMITH ST., DEARBORN, MI 09113

Date		Explanation	Post Ref.	Debit	Credit	Cr. Balance

NAME NEWBURG CO.

ADDRESS 1 RANTOUL RD., CHARLOTTE, NC 01114

Date		Explanation	Post Ref.	Debit	Credit	Cr. Balance

NAME RAPONE CO.

ADDRESS 2 WEST RD., LYNN, MA 01471

Date		Explanation	Post Ref.	Debit	Credit	Cr. Balance

PARTIAL GENERAL LEDGER

STORE SUPPLIES **ACCOUNT NO. 115**

Date		Explanation	Post Ref.	Debit	Credit	Balance	
						Debit	Credit

Name ______________________ Class ____________ Date ____________

PROBLEM A-3 (CONCLUDED)

STORE EQUIPMENT **ACCOUNT NO. 121**

Date		Explanation	Post Ref.	Debit	Credit	Balance	
						Debit	Credit

ACCOUNTS PAYABLE **ACCOUNT NO. 210**

Date		Explanation	Post Ref.	Debit	Credit	Balance	
						Debit	Credit

PURCHASES **ACCOUNT NO. 510**

Date		Explanation	Post Ref.	Debit	Credit	Balance	
						Debit	Credit

Name ______________________ Class ______________ Date ______________

PROBLEM A-4

(1)

MARION'S NATURAL FOOD STORE
PURCHASES JOURNAL

PAGE 1

Date	Account Credited	Date of Invoice	Inv. No.	Terms	PR	Accounts Payable Cr.	Purchases Dr.	Store Supplies Dr.	Sundry Dr.		
									Account	PR	Amount

Name ______________________ Class ______________ Date ______________

PROBLEM A-4 (CONTINUED)

(2)

ACCOUNTS PAYABLE SUBSIDIARY LEDGER

NAME **ALDEN CO.**

ADDRESS **11 LYNNWAY AVE., NEWPORT, RI 03112**

Date 201X		Explanation	Post Ref.	Debit	Credit	Cr. Balance
Mar.	1	Balance	✓			300 00

NAME **BULLMAN CO.**

ADDRESS **21 RIVER ST., ANAHEIM, CA 43110**

Date 201X		Explanation	Post Ref.	Debit	Credit	Cr. Balance
Mar.	1	Balance	✓			800 00

NAME **MOTT CO.**

ADDRESS **10 ASTER RD., DUBUQUE, IA 80021**

Date 201X		Explanation	Post Ref.	Debit	Credit	Cr. Balance
Mar.	1	Balance	✓			1000 00

NAME **REYNOLD CO.**

ADDRESS **22 GERALD RD., SMITH, CO 43138**

Date 201X		Explanation	Post Ref.	Debit	Credit	Cr. Balance
Mar.	1	Balance	✓			500 00

Name ______________ Class ______________ Date ______________

PROBLEM A-4 (CONTINUED)

PARTIAL GENERAL LEDGER

STORE SUPPLIES ACCOUNT NO. 110

Date		Explanation	Post Ref.	Debit	Credit	Balance Debit	Balance Credit

OFFICE EQUIPMENT ACCOUNT NO. 120

Date		Explanation	Post Ref.	Debit	Credit	Balance Debit	Balance Credit

ACCOUNTS PAYABLE ACCOUNT NO. 210

Date 201X		Explanation	Post Ref.	Debit	Credit	Balance Debit	Balance Credit
Mar.	1	Balance	✓				2 600 00

PURCHASES ACCOUNT NO. 510

Date 201X		Explanation	Post Ref.	Debit	Credit	Balance Debit	Balance Credit
Mar.	1	Balance	✓			18 000 00	

Name ______________________ Class ____________ Date ____________

PROBLEM A-4 (CONCLUDED)

PURCHASES RETURNS AND ALLOWANCES **ACCOUNT NO. 512**

Date		Explanation	Post Ref.	Debit	Credit	Balance Debit	Balance Credit

GENERAL JOURNAL **PAGE 1**

Date		Account Titles and Description	PR	Dr.	Cr.

(3)

MARION'S NATURAL FOOD STORE
SCHEDULE OF ACCOUNTS PAYABLE
MARCH 31, 201X

Name ______________________ Class ______________ Date ______________

PROBLEM A-5

(1,3)

ANDREA'S TOY HOUSE
PURCHASES JOURNAL

PAGE 1

Date	Account Credited	Date of Inv.	Inv. No.	Terms	PR	Accounts Payable Cr.	Toy Purchases Dr.	Sundry Dr.		
								Accounts	PR	Amount

Name ______________________ Class ______________ Date ______________

PROBLEM A-5 (CONTINUED)

PAGE 1

ANDREA'S TOY HOUSE
CASH RECEIPTS JOURNAL

Date	Cash Dr.	Sales Discounts Dr.	Accounts Receivable Cr.	Toy Sales Cr.	Sundry		
					Account	PR	Amount Cr.

Name ______________________ Class ______________ Date ______________

PROBLEM A-5 (CONTINUED)

ANDREA'S TOY HOUSE
CASH PAYMENTS JOURNAL

PAGE 1

Date	Check No.	Account Debited	PR	Sundry Dr.	Accounts Payable Dr.	Purchases Discount Cr.	Cash Cr.

Name ________________ Class ________________ Date ________________

PROBLEM A-5 (CONTINUED)

ANDREA'S TOY HOUSE
SALES JOURNAL

PAGE 1

Date		Account Debited	Invoice No.	Terms	PR	Accounts Rec. – Dr. Toy Sales – Cr.

ANDREA'S TOY HOUSE
GENERAL JOURNAL

PAGE 1

Date		Account Titles and Description	PR	Dr.	Cr.

Name ____________ Class ____________ Date ____________

PROBLEM A-5 (CONTINUED)

(2)

ACCOUNTS PAYABLE SUBSIDIARY LEDGER

NAME ROSE KAUFMAN

ADDRESS 87 GARFIELD AVE., REVERE, MA 01245

Date		Explanation	Post Ref.	Debit	Credit	Cr. Balance

NAME SAM KATZ GARAGE

ADDRESS 22 REGIS RD., BOSTON, MA 01950

Date		Explanation	Post Ref.	Debit	Credit	Cr. Balance

NAME MORRIS CURTIS CO.

ADDRESS 22 RETTER ST., SAN DIEGO, CA 01211

Date		Explanation	Post Ref.	Debit	Credit	Cr. Balance

NAME ADAM GRAVES

ADDRESS 2 SPRING ST., WEERS, ND 02118

Date		Explanation	Post Ref.	Debit	Credit	Cr. Balance

Name ____________________ Class ____________ Date ____________

PROBLEM A-5 (CONTINUED)

ACCOUNTS RECEIVABLE SUBSIDIARY LEDGER

NAME **BILL BURTON**

ADDRESS **24 RYAN RD., BUIKE, OH 02183**

Date		Explanation	Post Ref.	Debit	Credit	Dr. Balance

NAME **BELLA FALCO CO.**

ADDRESS **2 SMITH RD., DALLAS, TX 22210**

Date		Explanation	Post Ref.	Debit	Credit	Dr. Balance

NAME **DAVID MULDROW BEASLEY**

ADDRESS **1 SCHOOL ST., CLEVELAND, OH 22441**

Date		Explanation	Post Ref.	Debit	Credit	Dr. Balance

Name ______________________ Class ____________ Date ____________

PROBLEM A-5 (CONTINUED)

NAME ANDREA REAGAN

ADDRESS 18 VEEK RD., CHESTER, CT 80111

Date		Explanation	Post Ref.	Debit	Credit	Dr. Balance

GENERAL LEDGER

CASH **ACCOUNT NO. 110**

Date		Explanation	Post Ref.	Debit	Credit	Balance	
						Debit	Credit

ACCOUNTS RECEIVABLE **ACCOUNT NO. 112**

Date		Explanation	Post Ref.	Debit	Credit	Balance	
						Debit	Credit

PREPAID RENT **ACCOUNT NO. 114**

Date		Explanation	Post Ref.	Debit	Credit	Balance	
						Debit	Credit

Name ______________________ Class ______________ Date ______________

PROBLEM A-5 (CONTINUED)

DELIVERY TRUCK — **ACCOUNT NO. 121**

Date	Explanation	Post Ref.	Debit	Credit	Balance Debit	Balance Credit

ACCOUNTS PAYABLE — **ACCOUNT NO. 210**

Date	Explanation	Post Ref.	Debit	Credit	Balance Debit	Balance Credit

A. RICHARDSON, CAPITAL — **ACCOUNT NO. 310**

Date	Explanation	Post Ref.	Debit	Credit	Balance Debit	Balance Credit

TOY SALES — **ACCOUNT NO. 410**

Date	Explanation	Post Ref.	Debit	Credit	Balance Debit	Balance Credit

Name ______________________ Class ______________ Date ______________

PROBLEM A-5 (CONTINUED)

SALES RETURNS AND ALLOWANCES — ACCOUNT NO. 412

Date		Explanation	Post Ref.	Debit	Credit	Balance	
						Debit	Credit

SALES DISCOUNTS — ACCOUNT NO. 414

Date		Explanation	Post Ref.	Debit	Credit	Balance	
						Debit	Credit

TOY PURCHASES — ACCOUNT NO. 510

Date		Explanation	Post Ref.	Debit	Credit	Balance	
						Debit	Credit

PURCHASES RETURNS AND ALLOWANCES — ACCOUNT NO. 512

Date		Explanation	Post Ref.	Debit	Credit	Balance	
						Debit	Credit

Name ______________ Class ______________ Date ______________

PROBLEM A-5 (CONTINUED)

PURCHASES DISCOUNT **ACCOUNT NO. 514**

Date	Explanation	Post Ref.	Debit	Credit	Balance Debit	Balance Credit

SALARIES EXPENSE **ACCOUNT NO. 610**

Date	Explanation	Post Ref.	Debit	Credit	Balance Debit	Balance Credit

CLEANING EXPENSE **ACCOUNT NO. 612**

Date	Explanation	Post Ref.	Debit	Credit	Balance Debit	Balance Credit

Name ______________________ Class ______________ Date ______________

PROBLEM A-5 (CONCLUDED)

(4)

ANDREA'S TOY HOUSE
SCHEDULE OF ACCOUNTS RECEIVABLE
DECEMBER 31, 201X

(4)

ANDREA'S TOY HOUSE
SCHEDULE OF ACCOUNTS PAYABLE
DECEMBER 31, 201X

Name ______________________ Class ______________ Date ______________

CHAPTER 10
SUMMARY PRACTICE TEST
PURCHASES AND CASH PAYMENTS

Part I

Fill in the blank(s) to complete the statement.

1. The trend in accounting is more to ______________ inventory rather than ______________ inventory.

2. Purchase discounts are categorized as a(n) ______________ ______________ account.

3. The Purchases account has a ______________ balance.

4. Purchases are defined as merchandise for ______________ to customers.

5. The accounts payable subsidiary ledger represents a potential ______________ of cash.

6. The controlling account in the general ledger for the accounts payable subsidiary ledger is called ______________ ______________.

7. The accounts payable subsidiary ledger would be recorded ______________.

8. The balance in the Accounts Payable controlling account should be equal to the sum of the accounts in the ______________ ______________ ______________ ______________.

9. In perpetual inventory, purchases are recorded as ______________ ______________.

10. Changes in individual accounts payable should be posted ______________.

11. A(n) ______________ ______________ that is issued means the buyer owes less money, as merchandise is being returned or an allowance received.

12. A debit memorandum issued or a credit memorandum received results in a(n) ______________ to Accounts Payable and a credit to Purchases Returns and Allowances.

13. A sales discount is a ______________ ______________ to a buyer.

14. The accounts payable subsidiary ledger is listed in ______________ ______________.

15. Purchases Returns and Allowances is increased by a(n) ______________.

16. Cost of goods sold is classified as a(n) ______________.

17. In a perpetual inventory system, freight is recorded in the ______________ ______________ account.

18. Purchases Discounts is increased by ______________.

19. A(n) ______________ ______________ provides the purchasing department the information to then prepare a purchase order.

20. A(n) ______________ ______________ is made out after a company inspects received shipments.

Name ______________________ Class ____________ Date ______________

Part II

Complete the following table:

	Account Title	Category	↑↓	Financial Statement
1.	Purchases			
2.	Purchase Discount			
3.	Accounts Receivable			
4.	Cost of Goods Sold			
5.	Salary Expenses			
6.	Accounts Payable			
7.	Purchase Returns and Allowances			
8.	Cash			
9.	Supplies			
10.	Sale Discount			

Name ______________________ Class ______________ Date ______________

Part III

Answer true or false to the following statements.

1. F.O.B. shipping point means the seller is responsible to cover shipping costs.
2. The Purchases account is a contra-cost of goods sold account.
3. Purchases discounts are the result of paying for merchandise inventory within the discount period.
4. F.O.B. Destination means the seller is responsible to cover shipping costs.
5. Purchases discounts are taken on freight.
6. Merchandise inventory is an asset.
7. The account Cost of Goods Sold is a cost.
8. The balance in Accounts Payable, the controlling account, will be equal to the sum of the accounts receivable subsidiary ledger at the end of the month.
9. A purchase order is completed after the purchase requisition.
10. On receiving a purchase order, the seller may issue a sales invoice.
11. The normal balance of Purchases Discount is a debit balance.
12. The seller will often issue a debit memorandum to the buyer.
13. The account Cost of Goods Sold is used in a periodic inventory system.
14. Returned merchandise inventory by a buyer results in a change in Purchases Returns and Allowances.
15. Trade discounts do not occur because of early payments of one's bills.
16. A seller's sales discount on sales is the buyer's purchases discount.
17. Buying of equipment on account is only recorded in the general ledger.
18. On receiving a debit memorandum, the seller will issue a credit memorandum.
19. Returns in a perpetual accounting system are recorded in the merchandise inventory account.
20. Purchases are contra costs.

SOLUTIONS

Part I

1. perpetual, periodic
2. contra-cost
3. debit
4. resale
5. outflow or payment
6. accounts payable
7. daily
8. accounts payable subsidiary ledger
9. merchandise inventory
10. daily
11. debit memorandum
12. debit
13. purchase discount
14. alphabetical order
15. credit
16. cost
17. merchandise inventory
18. credits
19. purchase requisition
20. receiving report

Name ____________________ Class ____________ Date ____________

Part II

	Category	Increase	Decrease	Financial Statement
1.	cost	Dr	Cr	Income Statement
2.	contra-cost	Cr	Dr	Income Statement
3.	asset	Dr	Cr	Balance Sheet
4.	cost	Dr	Cr	Income Statement
5.	expense	Dr	Cr	Income Statement
6.	liability	Cr	Dr	Balance Sheet
7.	contra-cost	Cr	Dr	Income Statement
8.	asset	Dr	Cr	Balance Sheet
9.	asset	Dr	Cr	Balance Sheet
10.	contra-revenue	Dr	Cr	Income Statement

Part III

1. false
2. false
3. true
4. true
5. false
6. true
7. true
8. false
9. true
10. true
11. false
12. false
13. false
14. true
15. true
16. true
17. false
18. true
19. true
20. false

Study Guide and Working Papers

Preparing a Worksheet for a Merchandise Company

Name ______________________ Class ______________ Date ______________

FORMS FOR DEMONSTRATION PROBLEM

Use one of the blank fold-out worksheets that accompanied your textbook.

Name ____________ Class ____________ Date ____________

FORMS FOR SET A EXERCISES

11A-1

Account	Category	Normal Balance
a. Unearned Revenue		
b. Merch. Inventory (beg.)		
c. Freight-In		
d. Payroll Tax Expense		
e. Purchases Discount		
f. Sales Discount		
g. FICA—Social Security Payable		
h. Purchases Returns and Allowances		

11A-2

a. Net Sales

b. Cost of Goods Sold

c. Gross Profit

d. Net Income

11A-3

Accounts Affected	Category	↑↓	Rules

11A-4

a.

b.

c.

11A-5

Use one of the blank fold-out worksheets that accompanied your textbook.

Name ______________________ Class ______________ Date ______________

FORMS FOR SET B EXERCISES

11B-1

Account	Category	Normal Balance
a. Salaries Payable		
b. Merch. Inventory (beg.)		
c. Freight-In		
d. Payroll Tax Expense		
e. Purchases Returns and Allowances		
f. Sales Returns and Allowances		
g. FICA—Social Security Payable		
h. Purchases Discounts		

11B-2

a. Net Sales

b. Cost of Goods Sold

c. Gross Profit

d. Net Income

11B-3

Accounts Affected	Category	↑↓	Rules

11B-4

a.

b.

c.

11B-5

Use one of the blank fold-out worksheets that accompanied your textbook.

Name ______________________ Class ______________ Date ______________

FORMS FOR SET A PROBLEMS

PROBLEM 11A-1

a.	Net sales	
b.	Cost of goods sold	
c.	Gross profit	
d.	Net income	

PROBLEM 11A-2;
PROBLEM 11A-3;
PROBLEM 11A-4

Use one of the blank fold-out worksheets that accompanied your textbook.

Name ____________________ Class ____________________ Date ____________________

FORMS FOR SET B PROBLEMS

PROBLEM 11B-1

a.	Net sales	
b.	Cost of goods sold	
c.	Gross profit	
d.	Net income	

PROBLEM 11B-2;
PROBLEM 11B-3;
PROBLEM 11B-4

Use one of the blank fold-out worksheets that accompanied your textbook.

Name ______________________ Class ______________ Date ______________

ON THE JOB CONTINUING PROBLEM

Use the blank fold-out worksheet for this problem that accompanied your textbook.

Name ______________________ Class ______________ Date ______________

CHAPTER 11
SUMMARY PRACTICE TEST: PREPARING A WORKSHEET FOR A MERCHANDISE COMPANY

Part I

Fill in the blank(s) to complete the statement.

1. The ______________ system keeps a continual track of the quantity and cost of the inventory on hand.
2. In the periodic inventory system, new inventories bought is recorded in the ______________ account.
3. A continuous record of inventory is kept in a(n) ______________ ______________ system.
4. When using the periodic system, ______________ ______________ will remain unchanged.
5. ______________ ______________ represents a liability on the balance sheet and records money received for a sale or service not yet performed.
6. Freight-in is ______________ to the cost of goods sold.
7. Net Sales less Cost of Goods Sold equals ______________ ______________.
8. ______________ ______________ equals Gross Sales less Sales Discounts and Sales Returns and Allowances.
9. Net Purchases equals Purchases less ______________ ______________ and ______________ ______________ ______________.
10. A(n) ______________ ______________ helps calculate ending inventory.
11. Ending inventory is ______________ from the cost of goods available for sale.
12. Net purchases are ______________ to Beginning Inventory to get the cost of goods available for sale.
13. Gross Profit less ______________ equals Net Income.
14. Purchase discounts ______________ the total cost of merchandise sold.
15. Beginning inventory at the end of the period is assumed to be ______________, and thus a ______________.
16. The ending inventory of one period becomes the ______________ ______________ next period.
17. Ending inventory represents goods not ______________.
18. Net income is put in the ______________ column of the balance sheet on the worksheet.
19. Purchases are increased by a(n) ______________.
20. Sales returns and allowances are used in calculating ______________ ______________.
21. Net income is put in the ______________ column of the income statement on the worksheet.
22. Beginning Inventory and Ending Inventory are never ______________ on the worksheet.

Name ______________________ Class ______________ Date ______________

Part II

Answer true or false to the following statements.

1. Unearned Revenue is a liability.
2. Perpetual inventory keeps a continuous record of inventory.
3. Purchases increase cost of goods sold.
4. Freight-in is added to Purchases in the schedule of cost of goods sold.
5. Figures for Beginning and Ending Inventory are combined on the worksheet.
6. A periodic system is used by companies with low volume and high unit prices.
7. Merchandise Inventory is an asset.
8. Unearned Revenue is a liability on the income statement.
9. Inventory is always taken 10 times per year.
10. Purchases replace ending inventory in a periodic system.
11. A trial balance may be placed directly on a worksheet.
12. The adjustment process updates the inventory account.
13. A post-closing trial balance has no temporary accounts.
14. Sales Discounts is a permanent account.
15. Gross sales are located on the balance sheet.
16. The Sales Returns and Allowances account has a normal balance of a credit.
17. Ending inventory of one period is the beginning inventory of the following period.
18. Net income always means cash.
19. Ending inventory increases cost of goods sold.
20. Net purchases is always the same as total purchases.
21. Gross profit plus expenses equals net income.
22. Unearned Storage Fees is a liability.
23. Merchandise inventory that is sold is assumed to be a cost.
24. Accumulated Depreciation is increased by a debit.
25. Merchandise Inventory can never be listed on a trial balance.
26. Ending Merchandise Inventory can only be found on a balance sheet.
27. The amount of rent expired is used in the adjustment process.
28. Adjustments help update individual ledger accounts.
29. Purchases Returns and Allowances is found on a balance sheet.
30. Beginning Merchandise Inventory found on the balance sheet from the prior period will also be placed in the cost of goods sold section of the balance sheet.
31. Sales always means cash received.
32. Ending Merchandise Inventory of the current period is found only on the balance sheet.
33. Purchases adds to the cost of goods sold.
34. Purchases discounts reduce the cost of purchases on the balance sheet.
35. Beginning inventory can never be assumed sold by the end of a period.

Name ______________ Class ______________ Date ______________

36. Ending inventory in one period becomes beginning inventory for the next two periods.
37. The ending inventory may be calculated from an inventory sheet.
38. Income Summary is used in the adjustment of merchandise inventory.
39. Ending inventory not sold is only placed in the credit column of the balance sheet section on the worksheet.
40. Purchases Discount is recorded in the credit column of the income statement section on the worksheet.
41. Gross profit and net income mean the same.
42. All companies must give sales discounts.
43. A merchandise company does not need a cost of goods sold section on the income statement.
44. Cost of goods available for sale less ending inventory equals cost of goods sold.

SOLUTIONS

Part I

1. perpetual inventory
2. Purchases
3. perpetual inventory
4. beginning inventory
5. Unearned Revenue
6. added
7. Gross Profit
8. Net sales
9. Purchases Discounts, Purchases Returns and Allowances
10. Inventory sheet (record)
11. subtracted
12. added
13. Expenses
14. reduce
15. sold, cost
16. begining inventory
17. sold
18. credit
19. debit
20. net sales
21. debit
22. combined

Name ____________________ Class ____________ Date ____________

Part II

1. true
2. true
3. true
4. true
5. false
6. false
7. true
8. false
9. false
10. false
11. true
12. true
13. true
14. false
15. false
16. false
17. true
18. false
19. false
20. false
21. false
22. true
23. true
24. false
25. false
26. false
27. true
28. true
29. false
30. false
31. false
32. false
33. true
34. false
35. false
36. false
37. true
38. true
39. false
40. true
41. false
42. false
43. false
44. true

Study Guide and Working Papers

Completion of the Accounting Cycle for a Merchandise Company

Name ______________________ Class ______________ Date ______________

FORMS FOR DEMONSTRATION PROBLEM

REQUIREMENT 1

GENERAL JOURNAL PAGE 9

Date		Account Titles and Description	PR	Dr.	Cr.

Name ______________________ Class ______________ Date ______________

FORMS FOR DEMONSTRATION PROBLEM

REQUIREMENT 1

GENERAL JOURNAL

PAGE 9

Date	Account Titles and Description	PR	Dr.	Cr.

Name ____________ Class ____________ Date ____________

FORMS FOR DEMONSTRATION PROBLEM

GENERAL LEDGER

CASH **ACCOUNT NO. 110**

Date		Explanation	Post Ref.	Debit	Credit	Balance Debit	Balance Credit
3/31	1X	Balance forward	✓			6 000 00	

MERCHANDISE INVENTORY **ACCOUNT NO. 120**

Date		Explanation	Post Ref.	Debit	Credit	Balance Debit	Balance Credit
3/31	1X	Balance forward	✓			2 000 00	

PREPAID RENT **ACCOUNT NO. 130**

Date		Explanation	Post Ref.	Debit	Credit	Balance Debit	Balance Credit
3/31	1X	Balance forward	✓			600 00	

PREPAID INSURANCE **ACCOUNT NO. 140**

Date		Explanation	Post Ref.	Debit	Credit	Balance Debit	Balance Credit
3/31	1X	Balance forward	✓			500 00	

Name ______________________ Class ____________ Date ____________

FORMS FOR DEMONSTRATION PROBLEM

DISPLAY EQUIPMENT — ACCOUNT NO. 150

Date		Explanation	Post Ref.	Debit	Credit	Balance Debit	Balance Credit
3/31	1X	Balance forward	✓			3 0 0 0 00	

ACCUMULATED DEPRECIATION, DISPLAY EQUIPMENT — ACCOUNT NO. 160

Date		Explanation	Post Ref.	Debit	Credit	Balance Debit	Balance Credit
3/31	1X	Balance forward	✓				2 0 0 0 00

UNEARNED TRAINING FEES — ACCOUNT NO. 210

Date		Explanation	Post Ref.	Debit	Credit	Balance Debit	Balance Credit
3/31	1X	Balance forward	✓				3 0 0 0 00

ACCOUNTS PAYABLE — ACCOUNT NO. 220

Date		Explanation	Post Ref.	Debit	Credit	Balance Debit	Balance Credit
3/31	1X	Balance forward	✓				7 0 0 0 00

SALARIES PAYABLE — ACCOUNT NO. 230

Date		Explanation	Post Ref.	Debit	Credit	Balance Debit	Balance Credit

Name ______________________ Class ______________________ Date ______________________

FORMS FOR DEMONSTRATION PROBLEM

J. LOY, CAPITAL — ACCOUNT NO. 310

Date		Explanation	Post Ref.	Debit	Credit	Balance Debit	Balance Credit
3/31	1X	Balance forward	✓				7,000.00

INCOME SUMMARY — ACCOUNT NO. 320

Date		Explanation	Post Ref.	Debit	Credit	Balance Debit	Balance Credit

SALES — ACCOUNT NO. 410

Date		Explanation	Post Ref.	Debit	Credit	Balance Debit	Balance Credit
3/31	1X	Balance forward					9,600.00

SALES RETURNS AND ALLOWANCES — ACCOUNT NO. 412

Date		Explanation	Post Ref.	Debit	Credit	Balance Debit	Balance Credit
3/31	1X	Balance forward				500.00	

SALES DISCOUNTS — ACCOUNT NO. 414

Date		Explanation	Post Ref.	Debit	Credit	Balance Debit	Balance Credit
3/31	1X	Balance forward				300.00	

Name ______________________ Class ______________ Date ______________

FORMS FOR DEMONSTRATION PROBLEM

TRAINING FEES EARNED — **ACCOUNT NO. 420**

Date		Explanation	Post Ref.	Debit	Credit	Balance Debit	Balance Credit

PURCHASES — **ACCOUNT NO. 540**

Date		Explanation	Post Ref.	Debit	Credit	Balance Debit	Balance Credit
3/31	1X	Balance forward				15 0 0 0 00	

PURCHASES RETURNS AND ALLOWANCES — **ACCOUNT NO. 550**

Date		Explanation	Post Ref.	Debit	Credit	Balance Debit	Balance Credit
3/31	1X	Balance forward					4 0 0 00

PURCHASES DISCOUNTS — **ACCOUNT NO. 560**

Date		Explanation	Post Ref.	Debit	Credit	Balance Debit	Balance Credit
3/31	1X	Balance forward					8 0 0 00

SALARY EXPENSE — **ACCOUNT NO. 600**

Date		Explanation	Post Ref.	Debit	Credit	Balance Debit	Balance Credit
3/31	1X	Balance forward	✓			1 4 0 0 00	

Name ______________________ Class ______________ Date ______________

FORMS FOR DEMONSTRATION PROBLEM

PLUMBING EXPENSE — **ACCOUNT NO. 610**

Date		Explanation	Post Ref.	Debit	Credit	Balance Debit	Balance Credit
3/31	1X	Balance forward	✓			2 0 0 00	

UTILITIES EXPENSE — **ACCOUNT NO. 620**

Date		Explanation	Post Ref.	Debit	Credit	Balance Debit	Balance Credit
3/31	1X	Balance forward				3 0 0 00	

INSURANCE EXPENSE — **ACCOUNT NO. 630**

Date		Explanation	Post Ref.	Debit	Credit	Balance Debit	Balance Credit

RENT EXPENSE — **ACCOUNT NO. 640**

Date		Explanation	Post Ref.	Debit	Credit	Balance Debit	Balance Credit

Name ______________________ Class ______________ Date ______________

FORMS FOR DEMONSTRATION PROBLEM

GENERAL LEDGER

DEPRECIATION EXPENSE, DISPLAY EQUIPMENT **ACCOUNT NO. 650**

Date	Explanation	Post Ref.	Debit	Credit	Balance	
					Debit	Credit

Name ______________________ Class ______________ Date ______________

FORMS FOR DEMONSTRATION PROBLEM

REQUIREMENT 2

LEDGER SPORT SHOP
POST-CLOSING TRIAL BALANCE
MARCH 31, 201X

Name ______________ Class ______________ Date ______________

FORMS FOR SET A EXERCISES

12A-1

COST OF GOODS SOLD

Merchandise Inv. 12/01/1X	
Purchases	
Less: Purchases Disc.	
Purch. R. & A.	
Net Purchases	
Add: Freight-in	
Net Cost of Purchases	
Cost of Goods Available for Sale	
Less: Merchandise Inv. 12/31/1X	
Cost of Goods Sold	

12A-2

	Account	Category	Classification	Financial Statement
a.	Salaries Payable			
b.	Accounts Payable			
c.	Mortgage Payable			
d.	Unearned Legal Fees			
e.	SIT Payable			
f.	Office Equipment			
g.	Land			

12A-3

Date	Account	Debit	Credit

Name ______________________ Class ______________ Date ______________

SET A EXERCISES

12A-4

F. HENRY CO.
PARTIAL BALANCE SHEET
DECEMBER 31, 201X

12A-5

(a)

Date	Account	Debit	Credit

Salaries Expense

Salaries Payable

(b)

Date	Account	Debit	Credit

Salaries Expense

Salaries Payable

(c)

Date	Account	Debit	Credit

Salaries Expense

Cash

Name ____________ Class ____________ Date ____________

FORMS FOR SET B EXERCISES

12B-1

COST OF GOODS SOLD

Merchandise Inv. 12/01/1X	
Purchases	
Less: Purchases Disc.	
Purch. R. & A.	
Net Purchases	
Add: Freight-in	
Net Cost of Purchases	
Cost of Goods Available for Sale	
Less: Merchandise Inv. 12/31/1X	
Cost of Goods Sold	

12B-2

	Account	Category	Classification	Financial Statement
a.	Wages Payable			
b.	Accounts Payable			
c.	Notes Payable			
d.	Unearned Revenue			
e.	FIT Payable			
f.	Office Furniture			
g.	Land			

12B-3

Date	Account	Debit	Credit

Name ______________ Class ______________ Date ______________

SET B EXERCISES

12B-4

C. BLOSSOM CO.
PARTIAL BALANCE SHEET
DECEMBER 31, 201X

12B-5

(a)

Date		Account	Debit	Credit

Salaries Expense

Salaries Payable

(b)

Date		Account	Debit	Credit

Salaries Expense

Salaries Payable

(c)

Date		Account	Debit	Credit

Salaries Expense

Cash

Name ______________________ Class ______________ Date ______________

FORMS FOR SET A PROBLEMS

PROBLEM 12A-1

NELSON CO.
INCOME STATEMENT
FOR YEAR ENDED DECEMBER 31, 201X

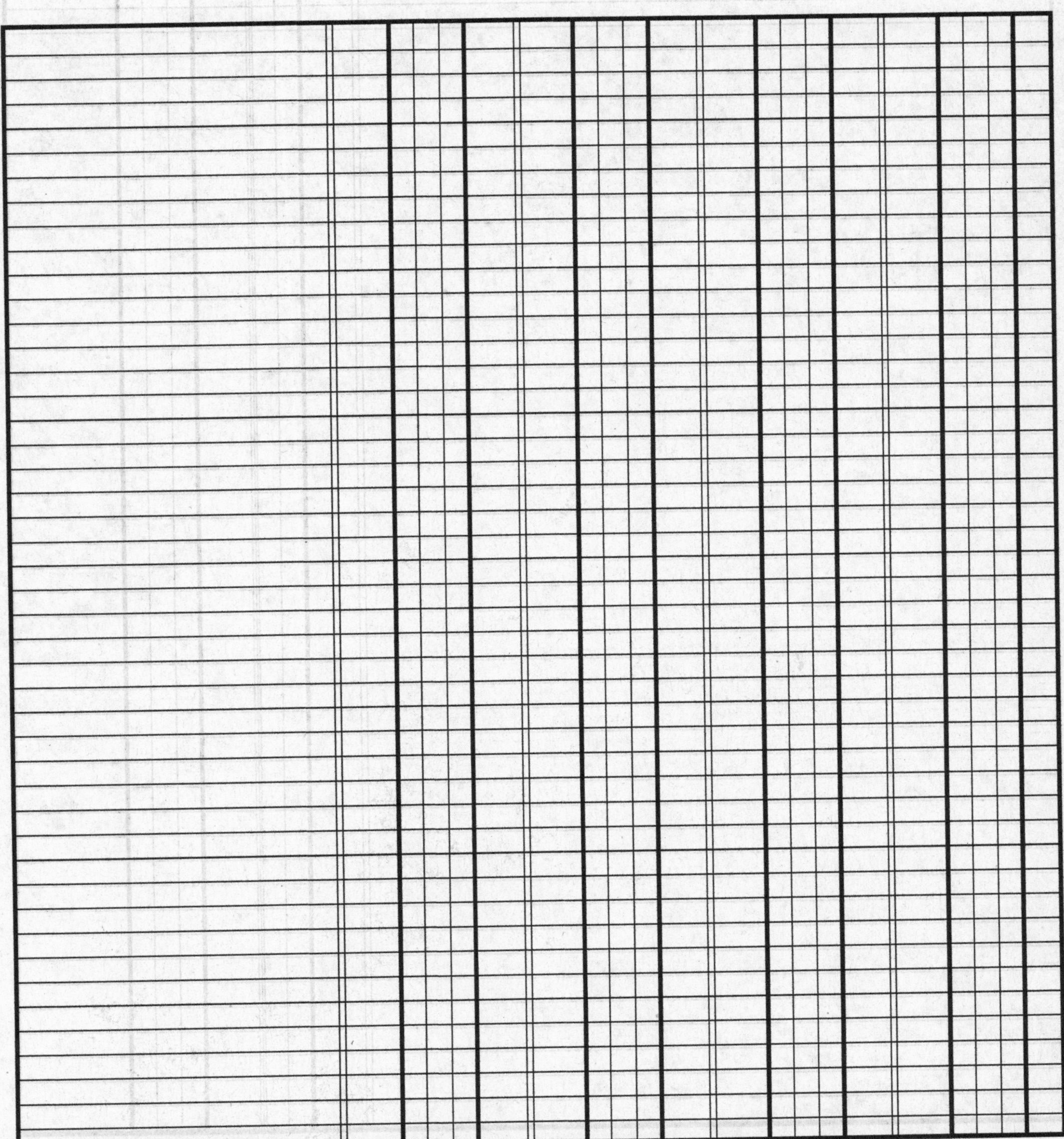

Name ____________________ Class ____________ Date ____________

PROBLEM 12A-2

JAMES CO.
STATEMENT OF OWNER'S EQUITY
FOR YEAR ENDED DECEMBER 31, 201X

Name ______________________ Class ______________ Date ______________

PROBLEM 12A-2 (CONCLUDED)

JAMES CO.
BALANCE SHEET
DECEMBER 31, 201X

Name ______________________ Class ______________ Date ______________

PROBLEM 12A-3

(1) Use one of the blank fold-out worksheets that accompanied your textbook.

(2)

JOSH'S SUPPLIES
INCOME STATEMENT
FOR YEAR ENDED DECEMBER 31, 201X

Name ____________________ Class ____________________ Date ____________________

PROBLEM 12A-3 (CONTINUED)

JOSH'S SUPPLIES
STATEMENT OF OWNER'S EQUITY
FOR YEAR ENDED DECEMBER 31, 201X

Name ____________________ Class ____________ Date ____________

PROBLEM 12A-3 (CONTINUED)

JOSH'S SUPPLIES
BALANCE SHEET
DECEMBER 31, 201X

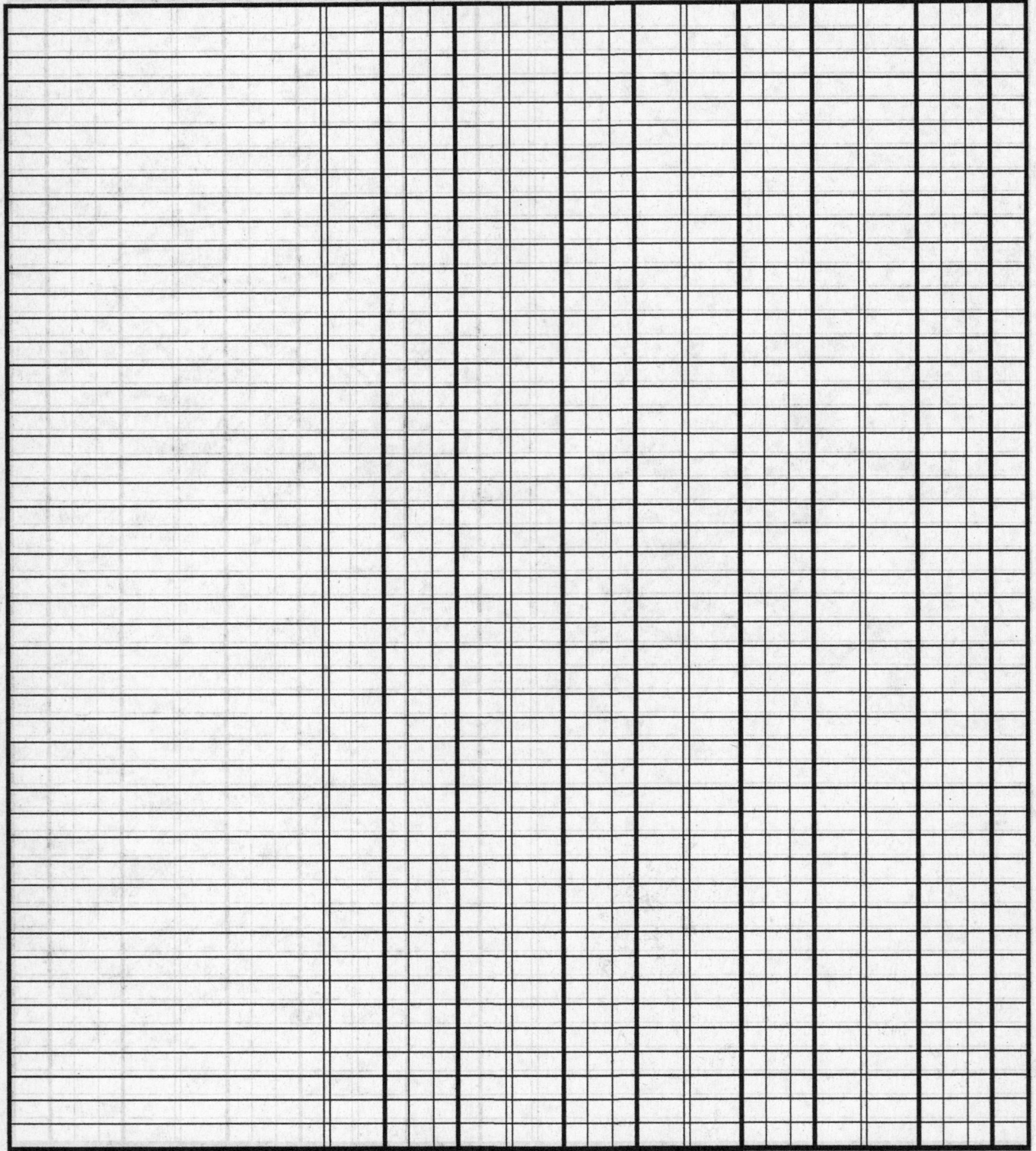

Name ______________________ Class ______________ Date ______________

PROBLEM 12A-3 (CONTINUED)

(3)

GENERAL JOURNAL

PAGE 2

Date		Account Titles and Description	PR	Dr.	Cr.

Name ____________________ Class ____________ Date ____________

PROBLEM 12A-3 (CONCLUDED)

GENERAL JOURNAL

PAGE 3

Date		Account Titles and Description	PR	Dr.	Cr.

Name ______________________ Class ______________ Date ______________

PROBLEM 12A-4

(1) Use one of the blank fold-out worksheets that accompanied your textbook.

(2)

CULLEN LUMBER
INCOME STATEMENT
FOR YEAR ENDED DECEMBER 31, 201X

Name ____________________ Class ____________ Date ____________

PROBLEM 12A-4 (CONTINUED)

CULLEN LUMBER
STATEMENT OF OWNER'S EQUITY
FOR YEAR ENDED DECEMBER 31, 201X

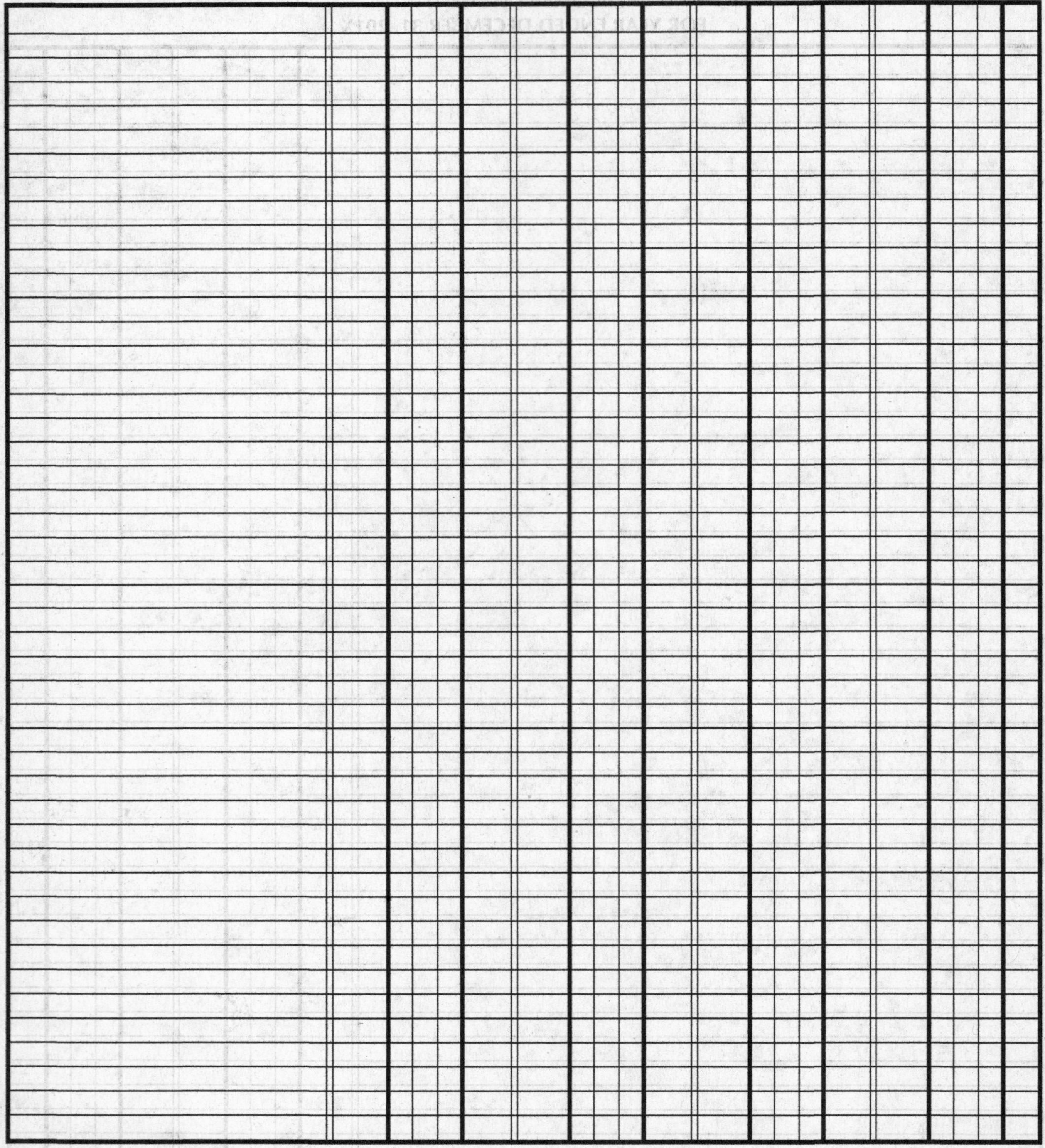

Name ______________________ Class ______________ Date ______________

PROBLEM 12A-4 (CONTINUED)

CULLEN LUMBER
BALANCE SHEET
DECEMBER 31, 201X

Name ____________ Class ____________ Date ____________

PROBLEM 12A-4 (CONTINUED)

(3)

GENERAL JOURNAL

PAGE 2

Date		Account Titles and Description	PR	Dr.	Cr.

Name ______________________ Class ______________ Date ______________

PROBLEM 12A-4 (CONTINUED)

CULLEN LUMBER
GENERAL LEDGER

CASH — **ACCOUNT NO. 110**

Date		Explanation	Post Ref.	Debit	Credit	Balance Debit	Balance Credit

ACCOUNTS RECEIVABLE — **ACCOUNT NO. 111**

Date		Explanation	Post Ref.	Debit	Credit	Balance Debit	Balance Credit

MERCHANDISE INVENTORY — **ACCOUNT NO. 112**

Date		Explanation	Post Ref.	Debit	Credit	Balance Debit	Balance Credit

LUMBER SUPPLIES — **ACCOUNT NO. 113**

Date		Explanation	Post Ref.	Debit	Credit	Balance Debit	Balance Credit

Name ______________________ Class ______________ Date ______________

PROBLEM 12A-4 (CONTINUED)

PREPAID INSURANCE ACCOUNT NO. 114

Date		Explanation	Post Ref.	Debit	Credit	Balance Debit	Balance Credit

LUMBER EQUIPMENT ACCOUNT NO. 121

Date		Explanation	Post Ref.	Debit	Credit	Balance Debit	Balance Credit

ACCUMULATED DEPRECIATION, LUMBER EQUIPMENT ACCOUNT NO. 122

Date		Explanation	Post Ref.	Debit	Credit	Balance Debit	Balance Credit

ACCOUNTS PAYABLE ACCOUNT NO. 220

Date		Explanation	Post Ref.	Debit	Credit	Balance Debit	Balance Credit

WAGES PAYABLE ACCOUNT NO. 221

Date		Explanation	Post Ref.	Debit	Credit	Balance Debit	Balance Credit

Name ______________________ Class ____________ Date ____________

PROBLEM 12A-4 (CONTINUED)

J. CULLEN, CAPITAL — **ACCOUNT NO. 330**

Date		Explanation	Post Ref.	Debit	Credit	Balance	
						Debit	Credit

J. CULLEN, WITHDRAWALS — **ACCOUNT NO. 331**

Date		Explanation	Post Ref.	Debit	Credit	Balance	
						Debit	Credit

INCOME SUMMARY — **ACCOUNT NO. 332**

Date		Explanation	Post Ref.	Debit	Credit	Balance	
						Debit	Credit

SALES — **ACCOUNT NO. 440**

Date		Explanation	Post Ref.	Debit	Credit	Balance	
						Debit	Credit

SALES RETURNS AND ALLOWANCES — **ACCOUNT NO. 441**

Date		Explanation	Post Ref.	Debit	Credit	Balance	
						Debit	Credit

Name ____________________ Class ____________________ Date ____________________

PROBLEM 12A-4 (CONTINUED)

PURCHASES **ACCOUNT NO. 550**

Date	Explanation	Post Ref.	Debit	Credit	Balance Debit	Balance Credit

PURCHASES DISCOUNT **ACCOUNT NO. 551**

Date	Explanation	Post Ref.	Debit	Credit	Balance Debit	Balance Credit

PURCHASES RETURNS AND ALLOWANCES **ACCOUNT NO. 552**

Date	Explanation	Post Ref.	Debit	Credit	Balance Debit	Balance Credit

WAGES EXPENSE **ACCOUNT NO. 660**

Date	Explanation	Post Ref.	Debit	Credit	Balance Debit	Balance Credit

ADVERTISING EXPENSE **ACCOUNT NO. 661**

Date	Explanation	Post Ref.	Debit	Credit	Balance Debit	Balance Credit

Name ______________________ Class ______________ Date ______________

PROBLEM 12A-4 (CONTINUED)

RENT EXPENSE — ACCOUNT NO. 662

Date	Explanation	Post Ref.	Debit	Credit	Balance Debit	Balance Credit

DEPRECIATION EXPENSE, LUMBER EQUIPMENT — ACCOUNT NO. 663

Date	Explanation	Post Ref.	Debit	Credit	Balance Debit	Balance Credit

LUMBER SUPPLIES EXPENSE — ACCOUNT NO. 664

Date	Explanation	Post Ref.	Debit	Credit	Balance Debit	Balance Credit

INSURANCE EXPENSE — ACCOUNT NO. 665

Date	Explanation	Post Ref.	Debit	Credit	Balance Debit	Balance Credit

Name ____________________ Class ____________ Date ____________

PROBLEM 12A-4 (CONCLUDED)

(4)

CULLEN LUMBER
POST-CLOSING TRIAL BALANCE
DECEMBER 31, 201X

	Dr.	Cr.

(5)

GENERAL JOURNAL

Date	Account	Debit	Credit

Name ______________________ Class ______________ Date ______________

FORMS FOR SET B PROBLEMS

PROBLEM 12B-1

WRIGHT CO.
INCOME STATEMENT
FOR YEAR ENDED DECEMBER 31, 201X

Name ______________________ Class ______________ Date ______________

PROBLEM 12B-2

JAGER CO.
STATEMENT OF OWNER'S EQUITY
FOR YEAR ENDED DECEMBER 31, 201X

Name ______________________ Class ______________ Date ______________

PROBLEM 12B-2 (CONCLUDED)

JAGER CO.
BALANCE SHEET
DECEMBER 31, 201X

Name ______________________ Class ______________ Date ______________

PROBLEM 12B-3

(1) Use one of the blank fold-out worksheets that accompanied your textbook.

(2)

JUSTIN'S SUPPLIES
INCOME STATEMENT
FOR YEAR ENDED DECEMBER 31, 201X

Name ______________________ Class ______________ Date ______________

PROBLEM 12B-3 (CONTINUED)

JUSTIN'S SUPPLIES
STATEMENT OF OWNER'S EQUITY
FOR YEAR ENDED DECEMBER 31, 201X

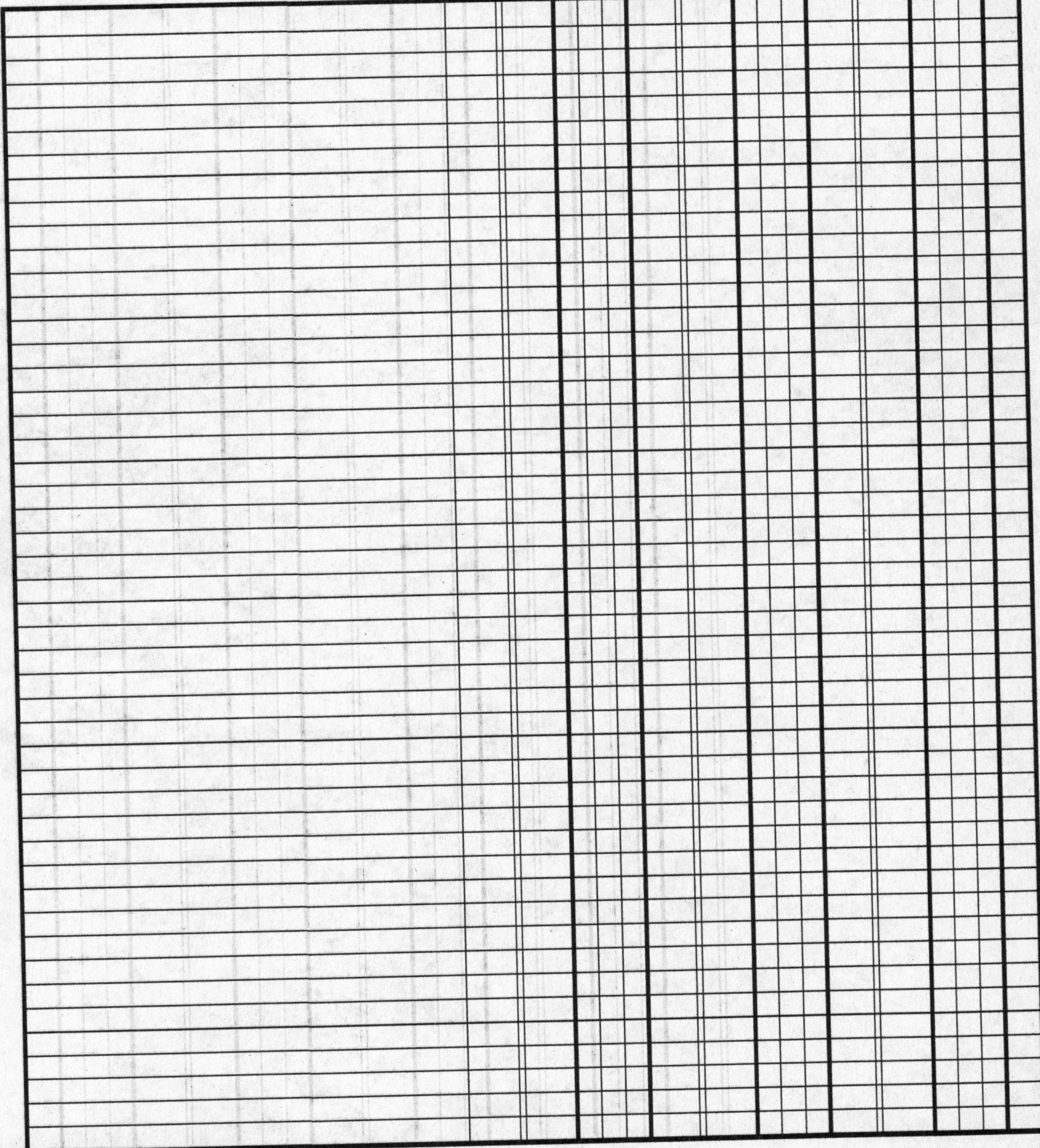

Name ______________________ Class ______________ Date ______________

PROBLEM 12B-3 (CONTINUED)

JUSTIN'S SUPPLIES
BALANCE SHEET
DECEMBER 31, 201X

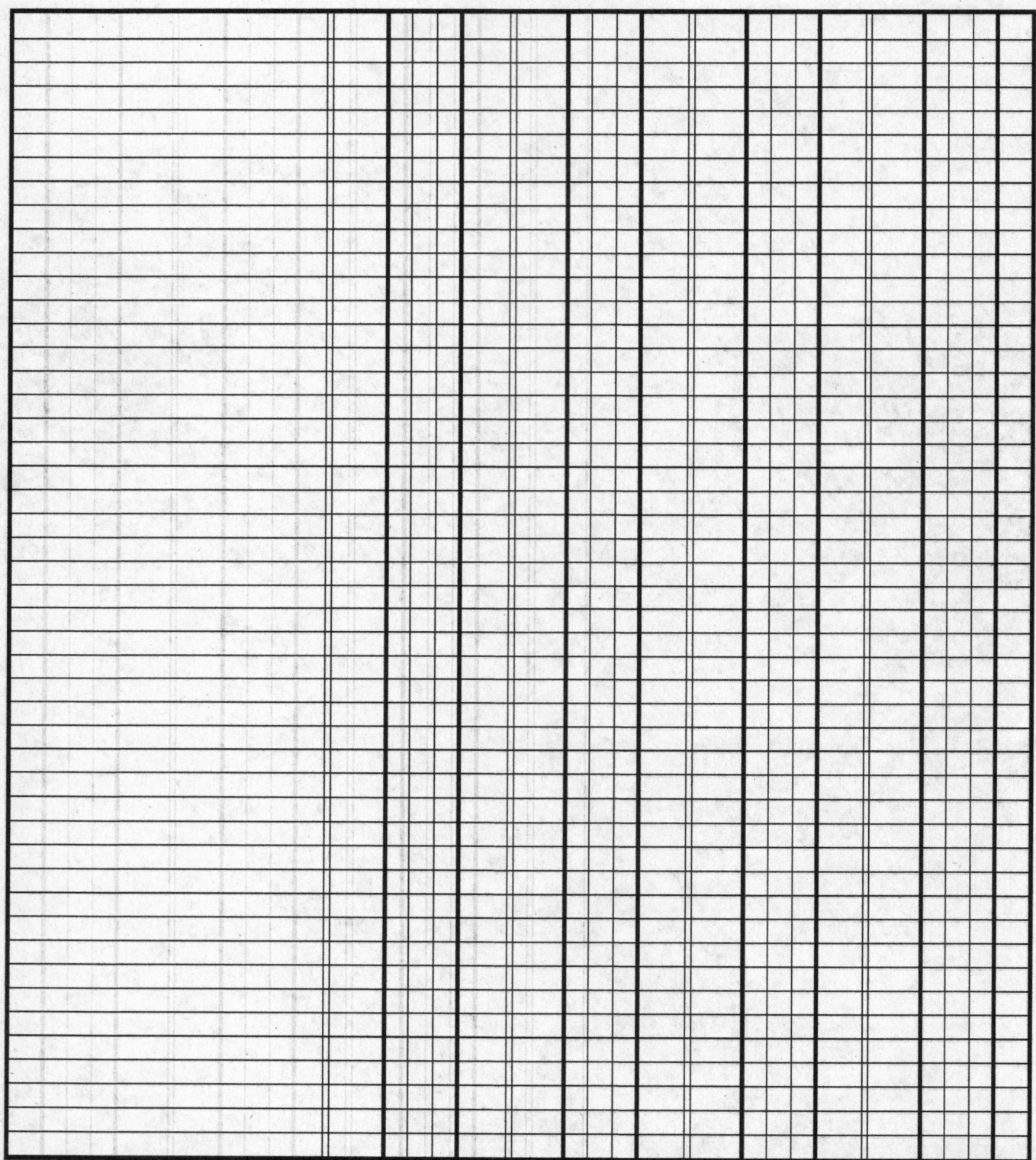

Name ____________________ Class ____________ Date ____________

PROBLEM 12B-3 (CONTINUED)

(3)

GENERAL JOURNAL

PAGE 2

Date		Account Titles and Description	PR	Dr.	Cr.

Name ____________________ Class ____________ Date ____________

PROBLEM 12B-3 (CONCLUDED)

GENERAL JOURNAL

PAGE 3

Date		Account Titles and Description	PR	Dr.	Cr.

Name ____________________ Class ____________ Date ____________

PROBLEM 12B-4

(1) Use one of the blank fold-out worksheets that accompanied your textbook.

(2)

CREW LUMBER
INCOME STATEMENT
FOR YEAR ENDED DECEMBER 31, 201X

Name ______________________ Class ______________ Date ______________

PROBLEM 12B-4 (CONTINUED)

CREW LUMBER
STATEMENT OF OWNER'S EQUITY
FOR YEAR ENDED DECEMBER 31, 201X

Name ______________________ Class ________________ Date ________________

PROBLEM 12B-4 (CONTINUED)

CREW LUMBER
BALANCE SHEET
DECEMBER 31, 201X

Name ______________________ Class ______________ Date ______________

PROBLEM 12B-4 (CONTINUED)

(3)

GENERAL JOURNAL

PAGE 2

Date	Account Titles and Description	PR	Dr.	Cr.

Name ______________________ Class ______________ Date ______________

PROBLEM 12B-4 (CONTINUED)

CREW LUMBER
GENERAL LEDGER

CASH — ACCOUNT NO. 110

Date		Explanation	Post Ref.	Debit	Credit	Balance Debit	Balance Credit

ACCOUNTS RECEIVABLE — ACCOUNT NO. 111

Date		Explanation	Post Ref.	Debit	Credit	Balance Debit	Balance Credit

MERCHANDISE INVENTORY — ACCOUNT NO. 112

Date		Explanation	Post Ref.	Debit	Credit	Balance Debit	Balance Credit

LUMBER SUPPLIES — ACCOUNT NO. 113

Date		Explanation	Post Ref.	Debit	Credit	Balance Debit	Balance Credit

Name ____________ Class ____________ Date ____________

PROBLEM 12B-4 (CONTINUED)

PREPAID INSURANCE — ACCOUNT NO. 114

Date		Explanation	Post Ref.	Debit	Credit	Balance	
						Debit	Credit

LUMBER EQUIPMENT — ACCOUNT NO. 121

Date		Explanation	Post Ref.	Debit	Credit	Balance	
						Debit	Credit

ACCUMULATED DEPRECIATION, LUMBER EQUIPMENT — ACCOUNT NO. 122

Date		Explanation	Post Ref.	Debit	Credit	Balance	
						Debit	Credit

ACCOUNTS PAYABLE — ACCOUNT NO. 220

Date		Explanation	Post Ref.	Debit	Credit	Balance	
						Debit	Credit

WAGES PAYABLE — ACCOUNT NO. 221

Date		Explanation	Post Ref.	Debit	Credit	Balance	
						Debit	Credit

Name ______________________ Class ______________ Date ______________

PROBLEM 12B-4 (CONTINUED)

J. CREW, CAPITAL — **ACCOUNT NO. 330**

Date		Explanation	Post Ref.	Debit	Credit	Balance	
						Debit	Credit

J. CREW, WITHDRAWALS — **ACCOUNT NO. 331**

Date		Explanation	Post Ref.	Debit	Credit	Balance	
						Debit	Credit

INCOME SUMMARY — **ACCOUNT NO. 332**

Date		Explanation	Post Ref.	Debit	Credit	Balance	
						Debit	Credit

SALES — **ACCOUNT NO. 440**

Date		Explanation	Post Ref.	Debit	Credit	Balance	
						Debit	Credit

SALES RETURNS AND ALLOWANCES — **ACCOUNT NO. 441**

Date		Explanation	Post Ref.	Debit	Credit	Balance	
						Debit	Credit

Name ______________________ Class ______________ Date ______________

PROBLEM 12B-4 (CONTINUED)

PURCHASES — **ACCOUNT NO. 550**

Date	Explanation	Post Ref.	Debit	Credit	Balance Debit	Balance Credit

PURCHASES DISCOUNT — **ACCOUNT NO. 551**

Date	Explanation	Post Ref.	Debit	Credit	Balance Debit	Balance Credit

PURCHASES RETURNS AND ALLOWANCES — **ACCOUNT NO. 552**

Date	Explanation	Post Ref.	Debit	Credit	Balance Debit	Balance Credit

WAGES EXPENSE — **ACCOUNT NO. 660**

Date	Explanation	Post Ref.	Debit	Credit	Balance Debit	Balance Credit

ADVERTISING EXPENSE — **ACCOUNT NO. 661**

Date	Explanation	Post Ref.	Debit	Credit	Balance Debit	Balance Credit

Name ________________ Class ________________ Date ________________

PROBLEM 12B-4 (CONTINUED)

RENT EXPENSE — **ACCOUNT NO. 662**

Date		Explanation	Post Ref.	Debit	Credit	Balance	
						Debit	Credit

DEPRECIATION EXPENSE, LUMBER EQUIPMENT — **ACCOUNT NO. 663**

Date		Explanation	Post Ref.	Debit	Credit	Balance	
						Debit	Credit

LUMBER SUPPLIES EXPENSE — **ACCOUNT NO. 664**

Date		Explanation	Post Ref.	Debit	Credit	Balance	
						Debit	Credit

INSURANCE EXPENSE — **ACCOUNT NO. 665**

Date		Explanation	Post Ref.	Debit	Credit	Balance	
						Debit	Credit

Name ____________________ Class ____________ Date ____________

PROBLEM 12B-4 (CONCLUDED)

(4)

CREW LUMBER
POST-CLOSING TRIAL BALANCE
DECEMBER 31, 201X

	Dr.	Cr.

(5)

GENERAL JOURNAL

Date	Account	Debit	Credit

Name ______________________ Class ______________ Date ______________

ON THE JOB CONTINUING PROBLEM

SMITH COMPUTER CENTER
GENERAL JOURNAL

PAGE 12

Date		Account Titles and Description	PR	Dr.	Cr.

Name ______________________ Class ______________ Date ______________

SMITH COMPUTER CENTER
GENERAL LEDGER

CASH — ACCOUNT NO. 1000

Date		Explanation	Post Ref.	Debit	Credit	Balance Debit	Balance Credit
3/31	1X	Balance forward	✓			17 2 6 3 76	

PETTY CASH — ACCOUNT NO. 1010

Date		Explanation	Post Ref.	Debit	Credit	Balance Debit	Balance Credit
3/31	1X	Balance forward	✓			3 0 0 00	

ACCOUNTS RECEIVABLE — ACCOUNT NO. 1020

Date		Explanation	Post Ref.	Debit	Credit	Balance Debit	Balance Credit
3/31	1X	Balance forward	✓			13 0 9 5 00	

MERCHANDISE INVENTORY — ACCOUNT NO. 1021

Date		Explanation	Post Ref.	Debit	Credit	Balance Debit	Balance Credit

Name ______________________ Class ______________ Date ______________

PREPAID RENT ACCOUNT NO. 1025

Date		Explanation	Post Ref.	Debit	Credit	Balance Debit	Balance Credit
3/31	1X	Balance forward	✓			3 5 0 0 00	

SUPPLIES ACCOUNT NO. 1030

Date		Explanation	Post Ref.	Debit	Credit	Balance Debit	Balance Credit
3/31	1X	Balance forward	✓			6 1 2 00	

COMPUTER SHOP EQUIPMENT ACCOUNT NO. 1080

Date		Explanation	Post Ref.	Debit	Credit	Balance Debit	Balance Credit
3/31	1X	Balance forward	✓			5 7 0 0 00	

ACCUMULATED DEPRECIATION, C.S. EQUIPMENT ACCOUNT NO. 1081

Date		Explanation	Post Ref.	Debit	Credit	Balance Debit	Balance Credit
3/31	1X	Balance forward	✓				1 5 0 00

OFFICE EQUIPMENT ACCOUNT NO. 1090

Date		Explanation	Post Ref.	Debit	Credit	Balance Debit	Balance Credit
3/31	1X	Balance forward	✓			3 8 5 0 00	

Name ______________________ Class ______________ Date ______________

ACCUMULATED DEPRECIATION, OFFICE EQUIPMENT ACCOUNT NO. 1091

Date		Explanation	Post Ref.	Debit	Credit	Balance Debit	Balance Credit
3/31	1X	Balance forward	✓				1 1 0 00

ACCOUNTS PAYABLE ACCOUNT NO. 2000

Date		Explanation	Post Ref.	Debit	Credit	Balance Debit	Balance Credit
3/31	1X	Balance forward	✓				3 1 7 0 00

WAGES PAYABLE ACCOUNT NO. 2010

Date		Explanation	Post Ref.	Debit	Credit	Balance Debit	Balance Credit

FICA OASDI PAYABLE ACCOUNT NO. 2020

Date		Explanation	Post Ref.	Debit	Credit	Balance Debit	Balance Credit

FICA MEDICARE PAYABLE ACCOUNT NO. 2030

Date		Explanation	Post Ref.	Debit	Credit	Balance Debit	Balance Credit

Name ______________ Class ______________ Date ______________

FIT PAYABLE **ACCOUNT NO. 2040**

Date		Explanation	Post Ref.	Debit	Credit	Balance Debit	Balance Credit

SIT PAYABLE **ACCOUNT NO. 2050**

Date		Explanation	Post Ref.	Debit	Credit	Balance Debit	Balance Credit

FUTA PAYABLE **ACCOUNT NO. 2060**

Date		Explanation	Post Ref.	Debit	Credit	Balance Debit	Balance Credit

SUTA PAYABLE **ACCOUNT NO. 2070**

Date		Explanation	Post Ref.	Debit	Credit	Balance Debit	Balance Credit

T. FELDMAN, CAPITAL **ACCOUNT NO. 3000**

Date		Explanation	Post Ref.	Debit	Credit	Balance Debit	Balance Credit
3/31	1X	Balance forward	✓				12 2 8 2 00

Name ______________________ Class ____________ Date ______________

T. FELDMAN, WITHDRAWALS — ACCOUNT NO. 3010

Date		Explanation	Post Ref.	Debit	Credit	Balance Debit	Balance Credit
3/31	1X	Balance forward	✓			9 1 5 00	

INCOME SUMMARY — ACCOUNT NO. 3020

Date		Explanation	Post Ref.	Debit	Credit	Balance Debit	Balance Credit

SERVICE REVENUE — ACCOUNT NO. 4000

Date		Explanation	Post Ref.	Debit	Credit	Balance Debit	Balance Credit
3/31	1X	Balance forward	✓				21 8 0 0 00

SALES — ACCOUNT NO. 4010

Date		Explanation	Post Ref.	Debit	Credit	Balance Debit	Balance Credit
3/31	1X	Balance forward	✓				11 6 8 0 00

Name ______________ Class ______________ Date ______________

GENERAL LEDGER

SALES RETURNS AND ALLOWANCES — ACCOUNT NO. 4020

Date		Explanation	Post Ref.	Debit	Credit	Balance Debit	Balance Credit
3/31	1X	Balance forward	✓			460 00	

SALES DISCOUNTS — ACCOUNT NO. 4030

Date		Explanation	Post Ref.	Debit	Credit	Balance Debit	Balance Credit
3/31	1X	Balance forward	✓			198 00	

ADVERTISING EXPENSE — ACCOUNT NO. 5010

Date		Explanation	Post Ref.	Debit	Credit	Balance Debit	Balance Credit

RENT EXPENSE — ACCOUNT NO. 5020

Date		Explanation	Post Ref.	Debit	Credit	Balance Debit	Balance Credit

UTILITIES EXPENSE — ACCOUNT NO. 5030

Date		Explanation	Post Ref.	Debit	Credit	Balance Debit	Balance Credit

Name ______________________ Class ______________ Date ______________

PHONE EXPENSE **ACCOUNT NO. 5040**

Date		Explanation	Post Ref.	Debit	Credit	Balance Debit	Balance Credit
3/31	1X	Balance forward	✓			170 00	

SUPPLIES EXPENSE **ACCOUNT NO. 5050**

Date		Explanation	Post Ref.	Debit	Credit	Balance Debit	Balance Credit
3/31	1X	Balance forward	✓			45 00	

INSURANCE EXPENSE **ACCOUNT NO. 5060**

Date		Explanation	Post Ref.	Debit	Credit	Balance Debit	Balance Credit

POSTAGE EXPENSE **ACCOUNT NO. 5070**

Date		Explanation	Post Ref.	Debit	Credit	Balance Debit	Balance Credit
3/31	1X	Balance forward	✓			40 00	

DEPRECIATION EXPENSE C.S. EQUIPMENT **ACCOUNT NO. 5080**

Date		Explanation	Post Ref.	Debit	Credit	Balance Debit	Balance Credit

Name ______________________ Class ______________________ Date ______________________

DEPRECIATION EXPENSE OFFICE EQUIPMENT ACCOUNT NO. 5090

Date		Explanation	Post Ref.	Debit	Credit	Balance Debit	Balance Credit

MISCELLANEOUS EXPENSE ACCOUNT NO. 5100

Date		Explanation	Post Ref.	Debit	Credit	Balance Debit	Balance Credit
3/31	1X	Balance forward	✓			1 5 00	

WAGE EXPENSE ACCOUNT NO. 5110

Date		Explanation	Post Ref.	Debit	Credit	Balance Debit	Balance Credit
3/31	1X	Balance forward	✓			2 0 3 0 00	

PAYROLL TAX EXPENSE ACCOUNT NO. 5120

Date		Explanation	Post Ref.	Debit	Credit	Balance Debit	Balance Credit
3/31	1X	Balance forward	✓			2 1 8 24	

INTEREST EXPENSE ACCOUNT NO. 5130

Date		Explanation	Post Ref.	Debit	Credit	Balance Debit	Balance Credit

Name ________________ Class ________________ Date ________________

BAD DEBT EXPENSE **ACCOUNT NO. 5140**

Date		Explanation	Post Ref.	Debit	Credit	Balance Debit	Balance Credit

PURCHASES **ACCOUNT NO. 6000**

Date		Explanation	Post Ref.	Debit	Credit	Balance Debit	Balance Credit
3/31	1X	Balance forward	✓			9 3 0 00	

PURCHASE RETURNS AND ALLOWANCES **ACCOUNT NO. 6010**

Date		Explanation	Post Ref.	Debit	Credit	Balance Debit	Balance Credit
3/31	1X	Balance forward	✓				1 5 0 00

PURCHASE DISCOUNTS **ACCOUNT NO. 6020**

Date		Explanation	Post Ref.	Debit	Credit	Balance Debit	Balance Credit

FREIGHT IN **ACCOUNT NO. 6030**

Date		Explanation	Post Ref.	Debit	Credit	Balance Debit	Balance Credit

Name ______________________ Class ______________ Date ______________

SMITH COMPUTER CENTER
INCOME STATEMENT
FOR THE SIX MONTHS ENDED MARCH 31, 201X

Name ____________________ Class ____________ Date ____________

SMITH COMPUTER CENTER
STATEMENT OF OWNER'S EQUITY
FOR THE SIX MONTHS ENDED MARCH 31, 201X

Name ______________________ Class ______________ Date ______________

SMITH COMPUTER CENTER
BALANCE SHEET
MARCH 31, 201X

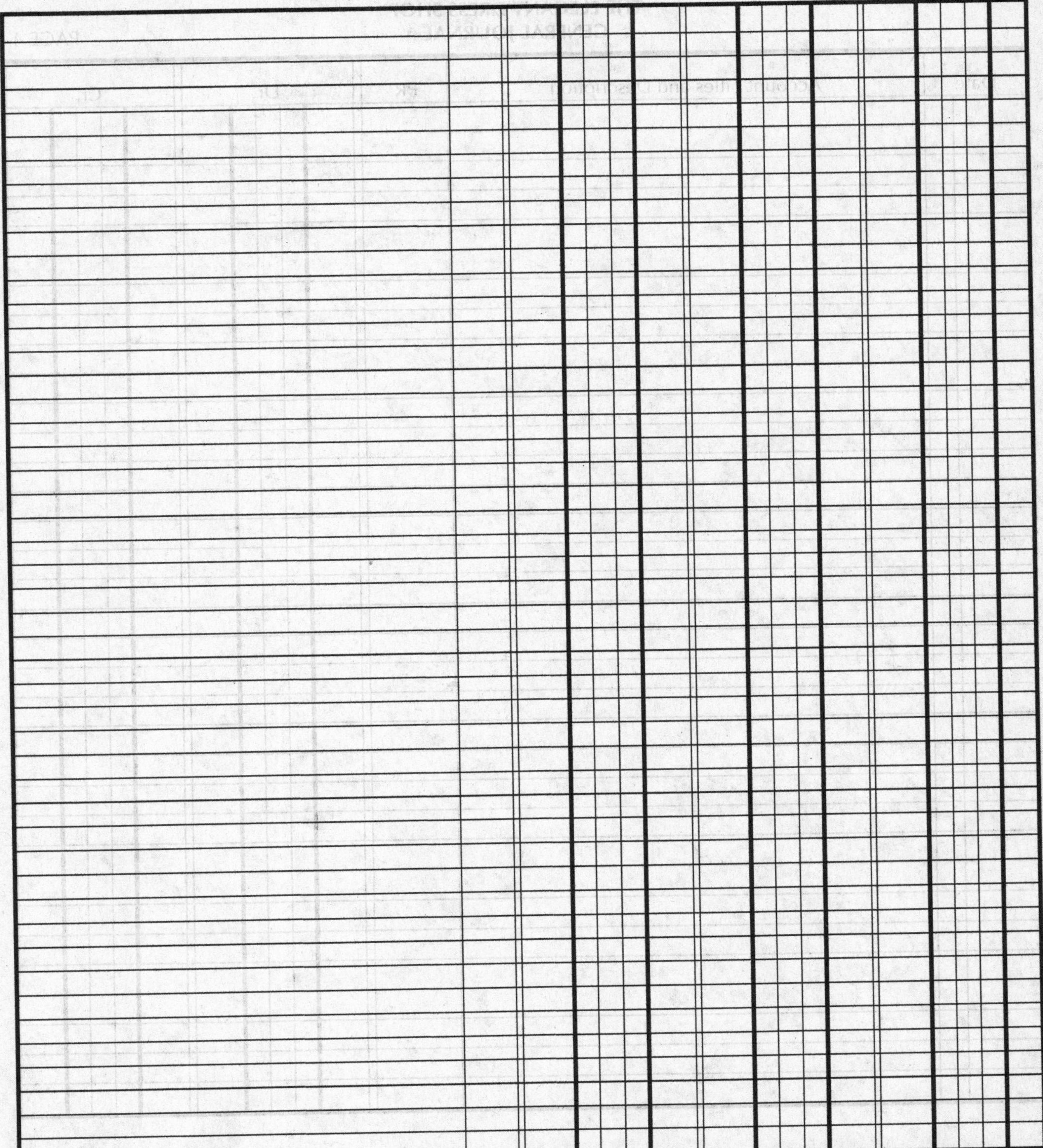

Name ______________________ Class ______________ Date ______________

MINI PRACTICE SET

REQUIREMENTS 2, 7

THE ELEGANT DRESS SHOP
GENERAL JOURNAL

PAGE 4

Date		Account Titles and Description	PR	Dr.	Cr.

THE ELEGANT DRESS SHOP

Use a blank payroll register for this problem that accompanied your textbook.

Name ____________________ Class ____________________ Date ____________________

MINI PRACTICE SET

THE ELEGANT DRESS SHOP
GENERAL JOURNAL

PAGE 5

Date		Account Titles and Description	PR	Dr.	Cr.

Name ______________________ Class ______________ Date ______________

MINI PRACTICE SET

THE ELEGANT DRESS SHOP
GENERAL JOURNAL

PAGE 6

Date		Account Titles and Description	PR	Dr.	Cr.

Name ____________ Class ____________ Date ____________

MINI PRACTICE SET

THE ELEGANT DRESS SHOP
GENERAL JOURNAL

Date	Account Titles and Description	PR	Dr.	Cr.

Name ______________________ Class ______________ Date ______________

MINI PRACTICE SET

THE ELEGANT DRESS SHOP
GENERAL JOURNAL

Date		Account Titles and Description	PR	Dr.	Cr.

Name ________________ Class ________________ Date ________________

MINI PRACTICE SET

THE ELEGANT DRESS SHOP
GENERAL JOURNAL

Date		Account Titles and Description	PR	Dr.	Cr.

Name ______________________ Class ______________ Date ______________

MINI PRACTICE SET

THE ELEGANT DRESS SHOP
AUXILIARY PETTY CASH RECORD

Date	Voucher No.	Description	Receipts	Payment	Category of Payment: Postage Expense	Delivery Expense	Sundry: Account	Sundry: Amount

Name ____________ Class ____________ Date ____________

MINI PRACTICE SET
REQUIREMENT 3

ACCOUNTS PAYABLE SUBSIDIARY LEDGER

NAME **DANMARK CO.**

Date 201X		Explanation	Post Ref.	Debit	Credit	Credit Balance
Mar	1	Balance	✓			2 0 0 0 00

NAME **JOHNSONS CO.**

Date 201X		Explanation	Post Ref.	Debit	Credit	Credit Balance

NAME **MANNY'S GARAGE**

Date 201X		Explanation	Post Ref.	Debit	Credit	Credit Balance

Name ______________________ Class ______________ Date ______________

MINI PRACTICE SET

NAME **THOMAS CO.**

Date 201X		Explanation	Post Ref.	Debit	Credit	Credit Balance

ACCOUNTS RECEIVABLE SUBSIDIARY LEDGER

NAME **BACH CO.**

Date 201X		Explanation	Post Ref.	Debit	Credit	Debit Balance
Mar	1	Balance	✓			1 8 0 0 00

NAME **DANMARK CO.**

Date 201X		Explanation	Post Ref.	Debit	Credit	Debit Balance

Name ____________ Class ____________ Date ____________

MINI PRACTICE SET

NAME **YOUNG CO.**

Date 201X		Explanation	Post Ref.	Debit	Credit	Debit Balance

REQUIREMENT 4

GENERAL LEDGER

CASH **ACCOUNT NO. 110**

Date 201X		Explanation	Post Ref.	Debit	Credit	Balance Debit	Balance Credit
Mar	1	Balance	✓			2 3 6 4 80	

Name ______________________ Class ______________ Date ______________

MINI PRACTICE SET

PETTY CASH — **ACCOUNT NO. 111**

Date 201X		Explanation	Post Ref.	Debit	Credit	Balance Debit	Balance Credit
Mar	1	Balance	✓			55 00	

ACCOUNTS RECEIVABLE — **ACCOUNT NO. 112**

Date 201X		Explanation	Post Ref.	Debit	Credit	Balance Debit	Balance Credit
Mar	1	Balance	✓			18 000 00	

MERCHANDISE INVENTORY — **ACCOUNT NO. 114**

Date 201X		Explanation	Post Ref.	Debit	Credit	Balance Debit	Balance Credit
Mar	1	Balance	✓			49 000 00	

Name ______________ Class ______________ Date ______________

MINI PRACTICE SET

PREPAID RENT — ACCOUNT NO. 116

Date 201X		Explanation	Post Ref.	Debit	Credit	Balance Debit	Balance Credit
Mar	1	Balance	✓			1650.00	

DELIVERY TRUCK — ACCOUNT NO. 120

Date 201X		Explanation	Post Ref.	Debit	Credit	Balance Debit	Balance Credit
Mar	1	Balance	✓			12000.00	

ACCUMULATED DEPRECIATION, TRUCK — ACCOUNT NO. 121

Date 201X		Explanation	Post Ref.	Debit	Credit	Balance Debit	Balance Credit
Mar	1	Balance	✓				3000.00

Name ______________________ Class ______________ Date ______________

MINI PRACTICE SET

ACCOUNTS PAYABLE — ACCOUNT NO. 210

Date 201X		Explanation	Post Ref.	Debit	Credit	Balance Debit	Balance Credit
Mar	1	Balance	✓				2 0 0 0 00

SALARIES PAYABLE — ACCOUNT NO. 212

Date 201X		Explanation	Post Ref.	Debit	Credit	Balance Debit	Balance Credit

FIT PAYABLE — ACCOUNT NO. 214

Date 201X		Explanation	Post Ref.	Debit	Credit	Balance Debit	Balance Credit
Mar	1	Balance	✓				7 4 2 00

Name ______________________ Class ______________ Date ______________

MINI PRACTICE SET

FICA-OASDI PAYABLE
ACCOUNT NO. 216

Date 201X		Explanation	Post Ref.	Debit	Credit	Balance Debit	Balance Credit
Mar	1	Balance	✓				1 153 20

FICA-MEDICARE PAYABLE
ACCOUNT NO. 218

Date 201X		Explanation	Post Ref.	Debit	Credit	Balance Debit	Balance Credit
Mar	1	Balance	✓				269 70

SIT PAYABLE
ACCOUNT NO. 220

Date 201X		Explanation	Post Ref.	Debit	Credit	Balance Debit	Balance Credit
Mar	1	Balance	✓				651 00

SUTA TAX PAYABLE
ACCOUNT NO. 222

Date 201X		Explanation	Post Ref.	Debit	Credit	Balance Debit	Balance Credit
Mar	1	Balance	✓				854 40

FUTA TAX PAYABLE
ACCOUNT NO. 224

Date 201X		Explanation	Post Ref.	Debit	Credit	Balance Debit	Balance Credit
Mar	1	Balance	✓				106 80

UNEARNED RENT
ACCOUNT NO. 226

Date 201X		Explanation	Post Ref.	Debit	Credit	Balance Debit	Balance Credit
Mar	1	Balance	✓				1 000 00

Name ________________ Class ________________ Date ________________

MINI PRACTICE SET

B. DUVAL, CAPITAL — **ACCOUNT NO. 310**

Date 201X		Explanation	Post Ref.	Debit	Credit	Balance Debit	Balance Credit
Mar	1	Balance	✓				12 9 9 2 70

B. DUVAL, WITHDRAWALS — **ACCOUNT NO. 320**

Date 201X		Explanation	Post Ref.	Debit	Credit	Balance Debit	Balance Credit

INCOME SUMMARY — **ACCOUNT NO. 330**

Date 201X		Explanation	Post Ref.	Debit	Credit	Balance Debit	Balance Credit

SALES — **ACCOUNT NO. 410**

Date 201X		Explanation	Post Ref.	Debit	Credit	Balance Debit	Balance Credit

SALES RETURNS AND ALLOWANCES — **ACCOUNT NO. 412**

Date 201X		Explanation	Post Ref.	Debit	Credit	Balance Debit	Balance Credit

Name ______________________ Class ______________ Date ______________

MINI PRACTICE SET

SALES DISCOUINT ACCOUNT NO. 414

Date 201X		Explanation	Post Ref.	Debit	Credit	Balance Debit	Balance Credit

RENTAL INCOME ACCOUNT NO. 416

Date 201X		Explanation	Post Ref.	Debit	Credit	Balance Debit	Balance Credit

PURCHASES ACCOUNT NO. 510

Date 201X		Explanation	Post Ref.	Debit	Credit	Balance Debit	Balance Credit

PURCHASES RETURNS AND ALLOWANCES ACCOUNT NO. 512

Date 201X		Explanation	Post Ref.	Debit	Credit	Balance Debit	Balance Credit

PURCHASES DISCOUNT ACCOUNT NO. 514

Date 201X		Explanation	Post Ref.	Debit	Credit	Balance Debit	Balance Credit

Name ____________________ Class ____________ Date ____________

MINI PRACTICE SET

SALES SALARY EXPENSE — ACCOUNT NO. 610

Date 201X		Explanation	Post Ref.	Debit	Credit	Balance Debit	Balance Credit

OFFICE SALARY EXPENSE — ACCOUNT NO. 611

Date 201X		Explanation	Post Ref.	Debit	Credit	Balance Debit	Balance Credit

PAYROLL TAX EXPENSE — ACCOUNT NO. 612

Date 201X		Explanation	Post Ref.	Debit	Credit	Balance Debit	Balance Credit

CLEANING EXPENSE — ACCOUNT NO. 614

Date 201X		Explanation	Post Ref.	Debit	Credit	Balance Debit	Balance Credit

DEPRECIATION EXPENSE, TRUCK — ACCOUNT NO. 616

Date 201X		Explanation	Post Ref.	Debit	Credit	Balance Debit	Balance Credit

Name ____________________ Class ____________ Date ____________

MINI PRACTICE SET

RENT EXPENSE

ACCOUNT NO. 618

Date 201X		Explanation	Post Ref.	Debit	Credit	Balance Debit	Balance Credit

POSTAGE EXPENSE

ACCOUNT NO. 620

Date 201X		Explanation	Post Ref.	Debit	Credit	Balance Debit	Balance Credit

DELIVERY EXPENSE

ACCOUNT NO. 622

Date 201X		Explanation	Post Ref.	Debit	Credit	Balance Debit	Balance Credit

MISCELLANEOUS EXPENSE

ACCOUNT NO. 624

Date 201X		Explanation	Post Ref.	Debit	Credit	Balance Debit	Balance Credit

Name ______________________________ Class ________________ Date ________________

MINI PRACTICE SET

REQUIREMENT 5

Using one of the blank fold-out worksheets that accompanied your textbook, enter the trial balance and complete the worksheet.

Name ____________________ Class ______________ Date ______________

MINI PRACTICE SET

REQUIREMENT 6

THE ELEGANT DRESS SHOP
INCOME STATEMENT
FOR MONTH ENDED MARCH 31, 201X

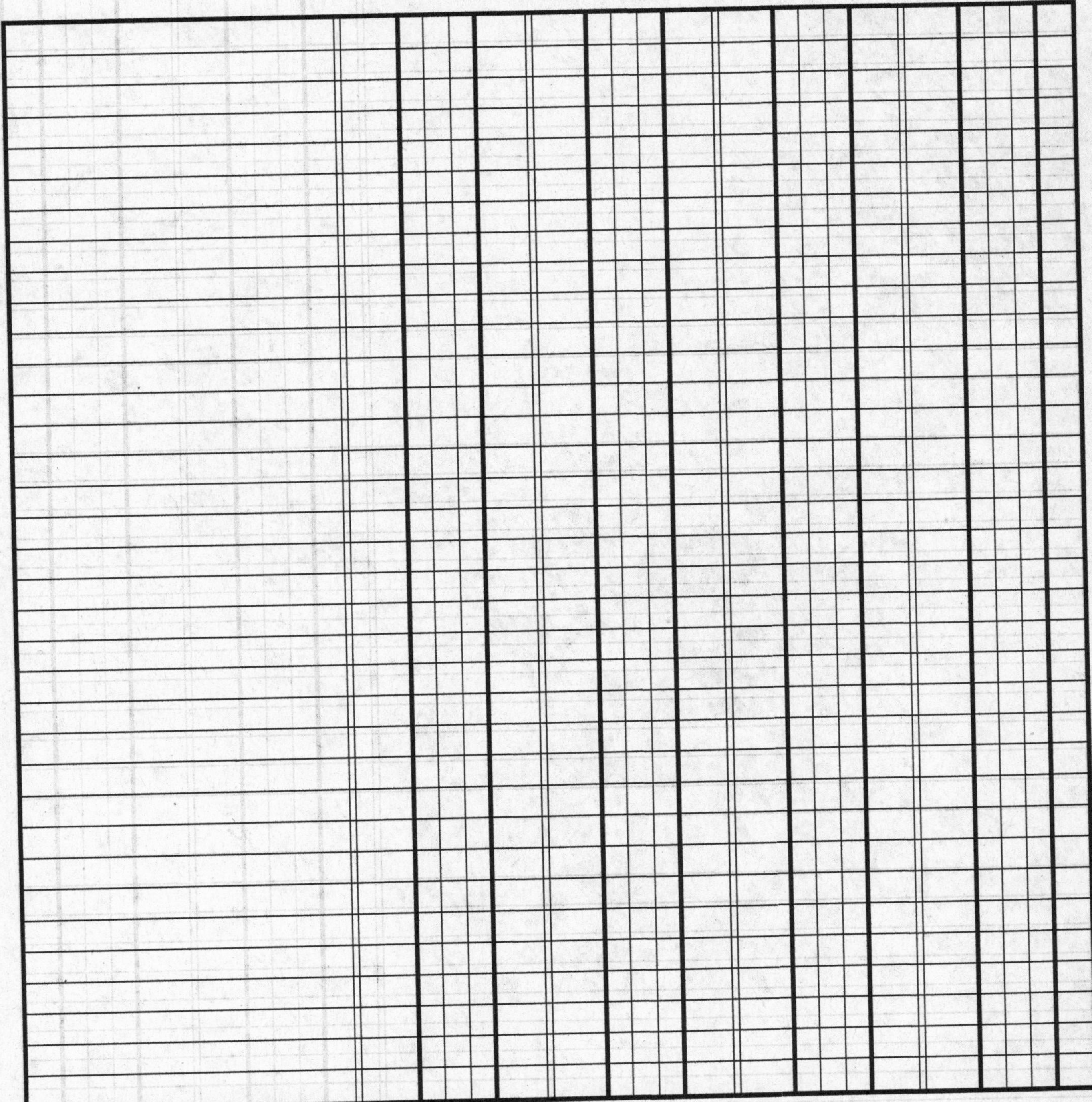

Name ______________________ Class ______________________ Date ______________________

MINI PRACTICE SET

THE ELEGANT DRESS SHOP
STATEMENT OF OWNER'S EQUITY
FOR MONTH ENDED MARCH 31, 201X

Name ____________________ Class ____________________ Date ____________________

MINI PRACTICE SET

THE ELEGANT DRESS SHOP
BALANCE SHEET
MARCH 31, 201X

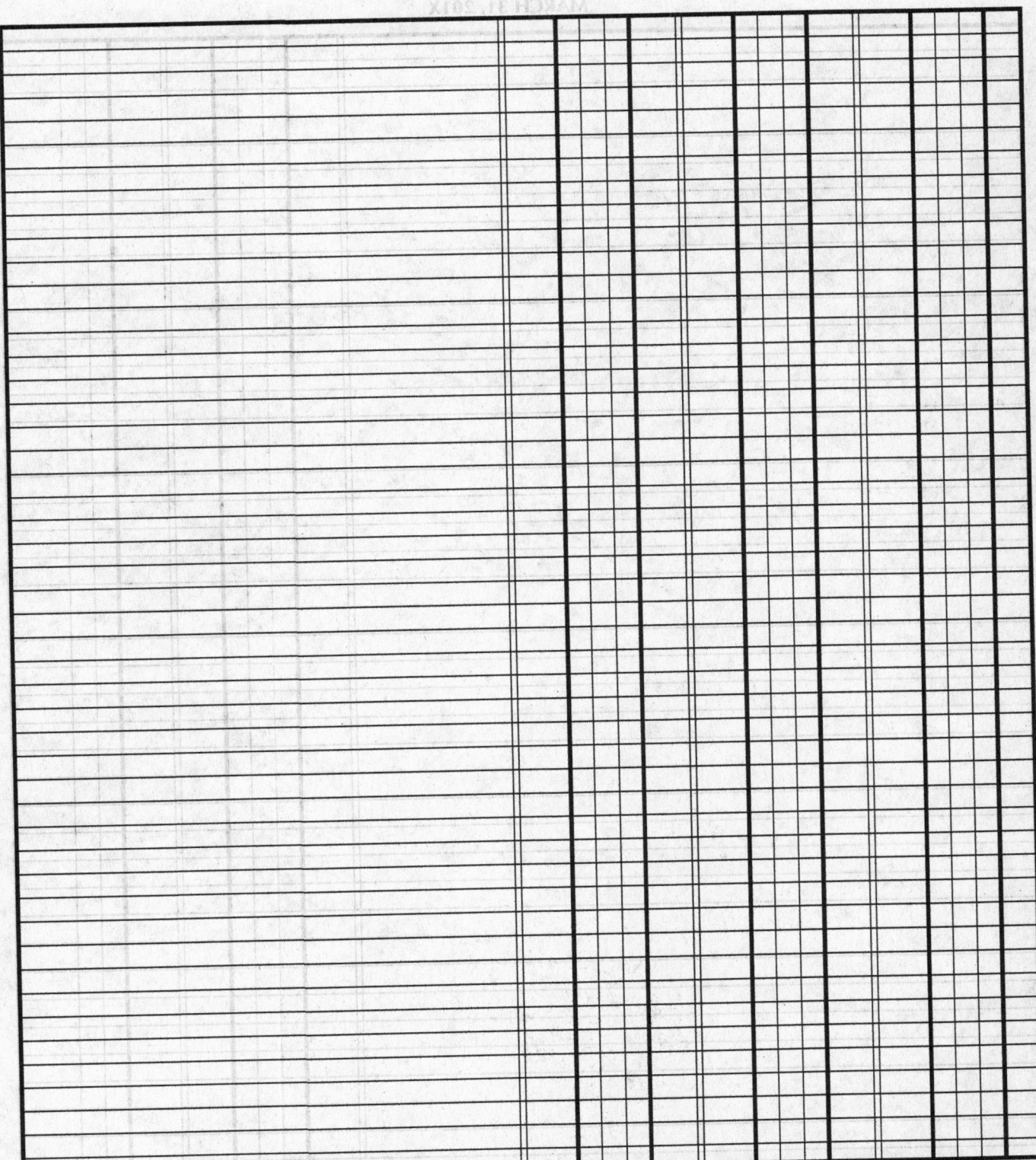

Name ______________________ Class ____________ Date ____________

MINI PRACTICE SET

REQUIREMENT 9

THE ELEGANT DRESS SHOP
POST-CLOSING TRIAL BALANCE
MARCH 31, 201X

Name ______________________ Class ______________ Date ______________

MINI PRACTICE SET

REQUIREMENT 10

950114

Form **941 for 201X: Employer's QUARTERLY Federal Tax Return**
(Rev. January 2014)
Department of the Treasury — Internal Revenue Service
OMB No. 1545-0029

Employer identification number (EIN) [ ][ ] – [ ][ ][ ][ ][ ][ ][ ]

Name *(not your trade name)* ______________________

Trade name *(if any)* ______________________

Address ______________________
Number Street Suite or room number

City State ZIP code

Foreign country name Foreign province/county Foreign postal code

Report for this Quarter of 201X
(Check one.)

- ☐ **1:** January, February, March
- ☐ **2:** April, May, June
- ☐ **3:** July, August, September
- ☐ **4:** October, November, December

Instructions and prior year forms are available at *www.irs.gov/form941.*

Read the separate instructions before you complete Form 941. Type or print within the boxes.

Part 1: Answer these questions for this quarter.

1	**Number of employees who received wages, tips, or other compensation for the pay period including:** *Mar. 12* (Quarter 1), *June 12* (Quarter 2), *Sept. 12* (Quarter 3), or *Dec. 12* (Quarter 4)			1	
2	**Wages, tips, and other compensation**			2	.
3	**Federal income tax withheld from wages, tips, and other compensation**			3	.
4	**If no wages, tips, and other compensation are subject to social security or Medicare tax**			☐	**Check and go to line 6.**
		Column 1		**Column 2**	
5a	**Taxable social security wages**	.	× .124 =	.	
5b	**Taxable social security tips**	.	× .124 =	.	
5c	**Taxable Medicare wages & tips**	.	× .029 =	.	
5d	**Taxable wages & tips subject to Additional Medicare Tax withholding**	.	× .009 =	.	
5e	**Add Column 2 from lines 5a, 5b, 5c, and 5d**			5e	.
5f	**Section 3121(q) Notice and Demand—Tax due on unreported tips** (see instructions)			5f	.
6	**Total taxes before adjustments.** Add lines 3, 5e, and 5f			6	.
7	**Current quarter's adjustment for fractions of cents**			7	.
8	**Current quarter's adjustment for sick pay**			8	.
9	**Current quarter's adjustments for tips and group-term life insurance**			9	.
10	**Total taxes after adjustments.** Combine lines 6 through 9			10	.
11	**Total deposits for this quarter, including overpayment applied from a prior quarter and overpayments applied from Form 941-X, 941-X (PR), 944-X, 944-X (PR), or 944-X (SP) filed in the current quarter**			11	.
12	**Balance due.** If line 10 is more than line 11, enter the difference and see instructions			12	0 .
13	**Overpayment.** If line 11 is more than line 10, enter the difference	.	Check one:	☐ Apply to next return.	☐ Send a refund.

Next ▶

▶ **You MUST complete both pages of Form 941 and SIGN it.**

For Privacy Act and Paperwork Reduction Act Notice, see the back of the Payment Voucher. Cat. No. 17001Z Form **941** (Rev. 1-2014)

Name ______________ Class ______________ Date ______________

MINI PRACTICE SET

950214

Name *(not your trade name)* | Employer identification number (EIN)

Part 2: Tell us about your deposit schedule and tax liability for this quarter.

If you are unsure about whether you are a monthly schedule depositor or a semiweekly schedule depositor, see Pub. 15 (Circular E), section 11.

14 Check one: ☐ **Line 10 on this return is less than $2,500 or line 10 on the return for the prior quarter was less than $2,500, and you did not incur a $100,000 next-day deposit obligation during the current quarter.** If line 10 for the prior quarter was less than $2,500 but line 10 on this return is $100,000 or more, you must provide a record of your federal tax liability. If you are a monthly schedule depositor, complete the deposit schedule below; if you are a semiweekly schedule depositor, attach Schedule B (Form 941). Go to Part 3.

☐ **You were a monthly schedule depositor for the entire quarter.** Enter your tax liability for each month and total liability for the quarter, then go to Part 3.

Tax liability: Month 1 ______ .

Month 2 ______ .

Month 3 ______ .

Total liability for quarter ______ . **Total must equal line 10.**

☐ **You were a semiweekly schedule depositor for any part of this quarter.** Complete Schedule B (Form 941), Report of Tax Liability for Semiweekly Schedule Depositors, and attach it to Form 941.

Part 3: Tell us about your business. If a question does NOT apply to your business, leave it blank.

15 If your business has closed or you stopped paying wages . . . . ☐ Check here, and

enter the final date you paid wages ___ / ___ / ___

16 If you are a seasonal employer and you do not have to file a return for every quarter of the year . . ☐ Check here.

Part 4: May we speak with your third-party designee?

Do you want to allow an employee, a paid tax preparer, or another person to discuss this return with the IRS? See the instructions for details.

☐ Yes. Designee's name and phone number ______________ ______________

Select a 5-digit Personal Identification Number (PIN) to use when talking to the IRS. ☐☐☐☐☐

☐ No.

Part 5: Sign here. You MUST complete both pages of Form 941 and SIGN it.

Under penalties of perjury, I declare that I have examined this return, including accompanying schedules and statements, and to the best of my knowledge and belief, it is true, correct, and complete. Declaration of preparer (other than taxpayer) is based on all information of which preparer has any knowledge.

X **Sign your name here** ______________

Print your name here ______________

Print your title here ______________

Date ___ / ___ / ___

Best daytime phone ______________

Paid Preparer Use Only

Check if you are self-employed ☐

Preparer's name ______________ PTIN ______________

Preparer's signature ______________ Date ___ / ___ / ___

Firm's name (or yours if self-employed) ______________ EIN ______________

Address ______________ Phone ______________

City ______________ State ______ ZIP code ______________

Name ______________________ Class ______________ Date ______________

CHAPTER 12
SUMMARY PRACTICE TEST: COMPLETION OF THE ACCOUNTING CYCLE FOR A MERCHANDISE COMPANY

Part I

Fill in the blank(s) to complete the statement.

1. There are no debits or credits on ______________ ______________.

2. The formal income statement uses ______________ ______________ figures for inventory.

3. The gross profit figure ______________ (is/is not) found on the worksheet.

4. ______________ is a measure of a firm's profitability.

5. ______________ are related to the administrative function.

6. ______________ ______________ could be broken down into selling and administrative expenses.

7. The ______________ figure for capital is not found on the worksheet.

8. ______________ are cash or other assets that will be converted into cash during the normal operating cycle of the company or one year, whichever is longer.

9. ______________ and ______________ are long-lived assets used for the production or sale of other assets or services.

10. Debts or obligations that are to be paid with current assets within one year or one operating cycle are called ______________ ______________.

11. The portion of Mortgage Payable due within one year is an example of a(n) ______________ ______________.

12. Ending merchandise inventory is classified as a(n) ______________ ______________ on the balance sheet.

13. By the adjusting process, the beginning inventory of the period is transferred to ______________ ______________.

14. The ______________ ______________ ______________ contains no temporary accounts.

15. A reversing entry involves certain ______________ entries.

16. Reversing entries are used only if assets are ______________ and have no previous balance and liabilities are ______________ and have no balance.

Name ______________________ Class ______________ Date ______________

Part II

Match the term in the last column to the definition, example, or phrase in the right column. Be sure to use a letter only once.

d	1. EXAMPLE: Computer Equipment	a.	Subtotaling
______	2. Net Sales – Cost of Goods Sold	b.	Unearned Revenue
______	3. Operating Cycle	c.	Current asset
______	4. Inside Columns of Financial Reports	d.	Plant and Equipment
______	5. Gross Profit – Operating Expenses	e.	Reversing Entry
______	6. Operating Expenses	f.	Time Period
______	7. Temporary Account	g.	Net Income
______	8. FICA—OASDI Payable	h.	Current Liability
______	9. Result of an adjusting entry	i.	When earned reduced by a debit
______	10. Petty Cash	j.	Gross Profit
______	11. An asset that is adjusted	k.	Merchandise Inventory
______	12. Ending Capital	l.	Debit Balance
______	13. A Liability showing revenue not earned	m.	Not found on worksheet
______	14. Unearned training fees	n.	Income Summary
		o.	Selling and Administrative

Part III

Answer true or false to the following statements.

1. A balance sheet records all revenue.
2. Cost of goods sold contains only ending inventory.
3. Net sales less cost of goods sold equals gross profit.
4. Operating expenses can only be administrative.
5. Supplies is part of Plant and Equipment.
6. Unearned Rent is an asset.
7. An operating cycle of a business must be one year.
8. Accumulated Depreciation is a current asset.
9. Long-term liabilities are due within one year.
10. Merchandise Inventory is a temporary account.
11. The normal balance of merchandise inventory is a debit.
12. The post-closing trial balance will not contain any unearned revenue accounts.
13. Ending inventory is closed directly to Capital.
14. Reversing entries cannot be applied to all adjustments.
15. Reversing entries are optional at the end of the year.
16. Reversing entries switch closing entries on the first day of the new period.
17. An adjusting entry with an asset decreasing with no previous balance cannot be reversed.
18. Closing entries will update the merchandise inventory account.
19. Beginning merchandise inventory of a period is assumed sold by the end of the period.
20. An adjusting entry for Accrued Wages can be reversed.

Name ______________ Class ______________ Date ______________

SOLUTIONS

Part I

1. financial reports
2. two separate
3. is not
4. Gross profit
5. Administrative expenses
6. Operating expenses
7. ending
8. Current assets
9. Plant, Equipment
10. current liabilities
11. current liability
12. current asset
13. Income Summary
14. post-closing trial balance
15. adjusting
16. increasing, increasing

Part II

1. d
2. j
3. f
4. a
5. g
6. o
7. n
8. h
9. e
10. l
11. k
12. m
13. b
14. i

Part III

1. false
2. false
3. true
4. false
5. false
6. false
7. false
8. false
9. false
10. false
11. true
12. false
13. false
14. true
15. true
16. false
17. true
18. false
19. true
20. true